The Odd Man In

The Odd Man In
Mugabe's White-Hand Man

Denis Norman

WEAVER
PRESS

Published by
Weaver Press, Box A1922, Avondale, Harare. 2018
<www.weaverpresszimbabwe.com>

Typeset by Weaver Press

Cover Design: Danes Design, Harare
Printed by: Directory Publishers, Bulawayo

Photograph on p. viii: Ilo the Pirate
All other photographs from the author's private collection.

ISBN: 978-1-77922-335-7 (p/b)
ISBN: 978-1-77922-336-4 (e-book)

DEDICATION

I dedicate this book to my wonderful wife June, who has supported, encouraged and loved me for over sixty years. Without her sustained back-up and affection, my life would have been very different and this book would never have been written.

This is an important book written by someone who was absolutely central to the events of the early part of the Mugabe government.

It provides a fascinating record by the man who was recommended by my father, Lord Soames, then the Governor, to help steer and serve the newly independent country of Zimbabwe.

The book offers a unique insight into the politics and personality of President Mugabe and his government as they come to grips with power.

Rt Hon Sir Nicholas Soames
Member of Parliament of the United Kingdom

CONTENTS

Denis Norman

ACKNOWLEDGEMENTS

For a number of years, many people have asked me the question, "what was it like serving and working in Mugabe's government?" and they usually followed that query by suggesting I wrote a book detailing those years.

More importantly, my family, having lived through those unusual and absorbing times, have urged me to record my impressions. I am grateful for the confidence and encouragement I have received from June and from all four of our children in finally consenting to put pen to paper. To Kathryn, Diana, Howard and Deborah I owe great gratitude for being so loyally understanding of a father who was frequently absent, and I also thank their respective spouses for their support.

I pay a special tribute to Deborah who has been a tower of strength in deciphering my handwriting, correcting my spelling, and typing and re-typing numerous copies of my scribbles to finally form this book. I also thank her husband Simon, and June for their valuable proof-reading and editing advice.

My sincere thanks go to Irene Staunton and her team at Weaver Press in Harare for their encouragement and enthusiasm in taking on this project. Their expert knowledge and guidance have been invaluable in getting this book to print.

To all those who have wondered, queried and assisted, I hope you will not be disappointed, and that my story satisfies and justifies the confidence you have shown in me.

Denis Norman

With the arrival of 1980 and Independence in Zimbabwe, two events happened almost immediately. The first was a very conciliatory speech by the new Prime Minister, Robert Mugabe, stating that the war was now over and all people both black and white must now get on with their lives, working together in peace.

The second was the appointment of Denis Norman as Minister of Agriculture. Until then Mr Norman had been the President of the Commercial Farmer's Union where he had become extremely well known to farmers and business alike, coolly guiding both through difficult times.

His appointment was inspired as Norman rapidly gained the trust and respect of all sides. He was apolitical and with his agricultural experience he immediately set about the task of building agriculture up to be the leading sector of the country's economy, not only in traditional crops but in areas of diversification too, such as horticulture.

It was an onerous and demanding role which Denis Noman tackled with energy, and the diplomacy often required to steer his portfolio through political needs on one side and agriculture expectations on the other. The result, although not always recognised, was remarkable. How such a sector could move so quickly from bitter conflict to achievement and success must be credited in large to Denis and to those who had the foresight to appoint him.

Finally, mention must also go to his wife June who played a major role behind the scenes in assisting and encouraging him while maintaining an aura of serenity It is now 38 years since Denis Norman took office but the country must remember it was the likes of him who helped steady the ship and prevent turmoil in Zimbabwe immediately post Independence.

John Laurie
Former Senator and former President of the CFU, Zimbabwe

FOREWORD

I first met Denis Norman in early May 1980, after the inauguration of the new government of Zimbabwe. He had just been appointed Minister of Agriculture, and I his deputy. We served together for eight months, until January 1981, when I was moved to become Minister of Industry and Energy Development. However, we remained cabinet colleagues until July 1984, when I left the Government of Zimbabwe, to become Executive Secretary of SADCC. Denis reflects on my passage into that office in this autobiography.

Also, as ministers responsible for key economic ministries, Bernard Chidzero (Economic Planning then Finance), Denis Norman (Agriculture), David Smith (Trade and Commerce) and I (Industry and Energy), spent a lot of time together, co-ordinating economic policies, strategies and programmes. The four of us also travelled together many times in Prime Minister Mugabe's delegations, and when representing the country at regional and international economic fora. In this way, Denis and I developed a strong relationship.

At our first meeting as minister and deputy, Denis asked me what I knew of commercial agriculture. I replied, `Nothing more than picking peas and beans on a commercial farm near my village, to raise money for school fees'. He then told me, `Farmers are never satisfied. There's always either too much or too little of everything.'

The next enduring lesson he taught me about farming, when in the process of preparing proposals to cabinet for agricultural commodity producer price adjustments, was that, `It's always cheaper to pay your own farmers, than those of other countries'.

Denis' autobiography, *Odd Man In*, offers an invaluable contribution to understanding the complex history of Zimbabwe, especially in the early years of independence. He shares candidly, unemotionally and factually the relationships between the 'entrenched' white commercial farming sector, and the fledgling 'socialist' black government. Denis also describes his passion for agriculture, and his yearning to integrate the hitherto racially divided industry, to unite small scale black farmers with their large scale white counterparts.

Odd Man In also narrates how as a farmers' leader, Denis Norman only reluctantly entered the racially polarised and tense political fray, to make an immense contribution, not only to agriculture, but to reconciliation between blacks and whites. He also shares fascinating experiences in bringing the new Zimbabwe into the global agricultural economy. The story of 'Ceausescu's Agreement', aptly demonstrates how you 'swim out of the deep end'.

This memoir shares the hope, promise and opportunities that the new Zimbabwe enjoyed in the first decade of independence. Denis also narrates how quickly corruption was allowed to establish itself, and destroy that promise.

Denis paints a picture of the 'original' Robert Mugabe – accessible, affectionate, compassionate and co-operative; motivated to serve – attributes that few will remember today. The book timeously captures the current mood of the nation, rekindling the hope and promise akin to March 1980, ushered in by November 2017.

This book is an important addition to the as yet small collection of unbiased records of the new Zimbabwe in its formative years.

Simba Makoni
June, 2018

PREFACE

I always believed being born in a chapel was an unusual and fortuitous start. I made my appearance on 26 March 1931 at Chalgrove Manor in the village of the same name in Oxfordshire. The original house was built as a moated manor in the thirteenth century, and despite subsequent additions and alterations as styles of living and comfort changed over the years, it still retains its original appearance and the charm depicted by its name. The room in which I was delivered had been consecrated as a chapel when the Royal Court had left London and relocated to Oxford to avoid the plague in the seventeenth century. This enabled the dons and courtiers of the day, who were accommodated in houses close to Oxford, to have suitable rooms in which to worship. Over time, the need fell away, and although the room was always known as 'the chapel', it was, in effect, just another bedroom.

I was the second of three sons born to my farming parents, and as they were married rather late in life, we three boys were born within 34 months of each other. Village life for a child in those pre-Second World War days was idyllic, at least for a child. It was probably very hard for the adults, though still very self-contained and self-supporting; I recall there was a blacksmith, a carpenter, a miller, a baker and probably other craftsmen living in the village. Most of the work on the farm was either done by manual labour or horse power which entailed employing a relatively large number of workers. As my father operated a mixed farm that included both dairy and beef cattle, a flock of breeding ewes, and arable crops, there was always activity, even during the winter months, when apart from milking cows, there were cattle and sheep to be fed on a daily basis. It was also the time for threshing the corn which had been built into ricks during the summer months. In addition, winter was the time of year to cut and lay the farm hedges that divided the fields; clean out the water ditches to ensure they did not become clogged up and cause flooding, and repair gates and fences. To us as small boys, these operations were always interesting and formed part of our early education. We did possess one early model tractor which was only driven by my father, but as he also milked the cows, it was used rather infrequently. When it was in use, my mother would take tea out to the fields, and we would accompany her with much excitement to see this machine in action. I found it hot and dusty with a strong smell of fuel fumes, but it served its purpose.

My first schooling took place in the village school, which basically consisted of one large L-shaped schoolroom, with a black, cast-iron, pot-bellied stove in the centre, which was lit in the winter to provide warmth. Pupils were divided into groups, relating approximately to their ages, and consigned to one area of the room in which to study. The school was located at the opposite end of the village to our house. In order to reach it, we had to walk most of the way along the main road, which was flanked by a ditch on one side and a brook on the other, with most of the houses and cottages built just beyond these waterways. The brook always seemed to flow quite strongly and was a source of fresh water to many of the residents who lived adjacent to it. In times of heavy rains, it was not uncommon for both the brook and the ditch to overflow their banks, thus flooding the road. On those occasions, my father would send a horse and wagon to collect the children from school and deliver them dry and safe to their respective homes. As we lived the furthest away, I always had the longest ride, which I still remember gave me great pleasure. Despite the many changes which have taken place since I first went there in 1935, the school still functions, and although the number of pupils has increased and more buildings have been added, I am delighted that the original school house still exists and is used for the purpose for which it was built.

Opposite the farm was the corn mill, and in the summer if the weather was warm, we used to go with Bertha, our maid, to paddle up and down in the water and try to catch minnows; all innocent fun which cost nothing. During the festivities to celebrate firstly the Silver Jubilee of King George V and later the coronation of King George VI, our village, like most others, excelled; the houses being bedecked with flags and bunting and, on both occasions, there were parades which were led by the village band, with all the villagers following in fancy dress. For the coronation, my two brothers and I were dressed as toy soldiers and we thought we were terribly smart. Later, there were sports and games, followed in the evening by feasting and fireworks, but unfortunately, we were too young to participate in those activities.

Every Christmas Eve the same band would parade through the village and at predetermined stops would play carols and invite those around it to join in the singing. At some stage, they would arrive at our house and give us a couple of carols which we children would watch from our open upstairs bedroom windows, and this always signified the advent of Christmas. After performing for us, my father would invite them into our large kitchen for jugs of beer which he had drawn from the barrel he kept in the cellar, whilst my mother and Bertha served snacks, which always included mince pies. After partaking of their refreshments, they re-formed their ranks outside, and marched off playing 'Good King Wenceslas' slightly unsteadily and certainly out of tune.

In 1937, we moved to Middleton Stoney, also in Oxfordshire, where my father rented a farm from the Earl of Jersey. This farm was larger than the previous one in Chalgrove, but farming patterns remained approximately the same, except my father now ventured into sugar beet production. In order to include this crop in his annual farming programme he had to hire seasonal workers. Initially they came from Ireland; three men from the same family. They would arrive at the beginning of May and their first task was to hoe the 25 acres of beet by hand. This operation was done twice. Whilst the crop was then left to grow and develop, they assisted on the farm with hay-making and later the corn harvest. In the autumn, they would return to the beet fields, where they would lift the beet and chop off the leaves, again by hand, after the beet had been loosened from the ground by a horse-drawn plough. Unfortunately, in late August 1939, in anticipation of a war coming, the men returned to Ireland permanently. Re-adjustments had to be made and that included using prisoners of war as casual labour – that is until 1942, when workers from the same Irish family returned and continued to come annually until sugar beet was dropped from the cropping cycle in the 1960s. Another labour-intensive crop which was introduced during the war was potatoes, but we usually managed to work that without too much external assistance.

In 1941, my older brother, John, and I were sent as boarders to All Saints School, Bloxham, where we were joined by Jim the following year. These were very happy years for me, despite the obvious shortages and difficulties brought on by a war situation. All of us who were educated during that period suffered from a lack of capable teachers both in the classroom and on the playing fields. But we were well served by those masters who came out of retirement, or because of age or infirmities were unsuitable for military service. However, we undoubtedly took an unfair advantage of the situation, and took liberties which would have been unthinkable if we had been overseen by younger, more dynamic men who would have been less tolerant of any nonsense. Not that we were allowed to become totally ill-disciplined as there were strict codes of punishment; the most common one being corporal. It was a system which was understood and accepted – if you transgressed and got caught you were beaten, no argument and no appeal – and a system against which no-one complained.

A prominent part of our school life was centred on the chapel in which Holy Communion was celebrated every morning. This was for boys who had been confirmed and although voluntary, was usually well attended. At the end of each day, there was compulsory Evensong as well as a sung Eucharist every Sunday morning. We were fortunate to have a dynamic chaplain, the Rev. Sholto Douglas, who inspired religious interest through his general enthusiasm, lively sermons and love of church music. There were always a number of choral scholarships on offer which led to the school having a good, strong choir.

Another important part of our weekly curriculum was military training. Initially, Officers Training Corps when I first joined, it changed to Junior Training Corps in time. It was compulsory and we trained for a morning and an afternoon every week. We were fortunate to have a retired Sergeant Major from the Royal Marines to train us and S. M. Turner was an exemplary British fighting veteran; knowledgeable, smart, understanding and strict, and he certainly earned the respect of the hundreds of boys who he drilled into shape at Bloxham. We also had a very competent military band, which comprised drums and bugles. They were much in demand for performances at local functions such as fund-raising events for the war effort and Remembrance Day parades. A solo bugler would play the Last Post at school every evening at 8 p.m., and no matter what you were doing at the time, all the staff and pupils would pause for two minutes to reflect and remember.

Among the many shortages and difficulties with which the school administrators had to cope was one of the coldest winters ever recorded in the British Isles in 1947. Not only were the playing fields covered in thick snow – we did not see the grass for seven weeks – but we were frozen with severe frost every night for two months. A local farmer kindly provided a unique facility for exercise in the form of a rural ice-skating rink. He had a meadow through which flowed a stream, which flooded and froze and gave us access to a pristine stretch of ice, perfect for hockey matches and skating races, all available with no safety regulations.

But of a more major concern was the fact that the school was unable to get a re-supply of fuel to feed into the antiquated boiler. As pupils, we anticipated the school would have to close and we would be sent home for an extended holiday. The school authorities, however, devised a difficult plan in which all boys had to be in bed by 7 p.m. and were not allowed up until 9 a.m. the following morning. Initially we thought it was a great scheme but soon discovered it was a frustratingly boring regime and were delighted to be released from this routine by a fortuitous big thaw. Not surprisingly this resulted in the next issue of burst water pipes, laid in the dim and distant past with no living person possessing a working knowledge of whence they came or where they went. 'Cometh the hour, cometh the man': and so it was when the insipid school nerd with thick glasses and a spotty face discovered his gift of water-divining and was able to map the underground pipe network with the aid of a forked stick.

Despite these obvious difficulties, under the care and guidance of a very shrewd headmaster Kenneth Dewey, both the school and the pupils survived, and in most instances, flourished. My own school career was very ordinary, as I progressed annually up the school ladder, with more emphasis on the sporting than the academic curriculum. Before I left in 1948, I had managed to obtain a joint Oxford & Cambridge certificate with three passes and three credits. I had also represented the school in a number of sports, but notably athletics – of which I became captain in 1948 – and rugby. During this period, I was also selected to run for Oxfordshire in the school county games and I played rugby for the county schools.

I left school at the end of March 1948, to join my brother John, who was by then working for my father on the Middleton Stoney farm. Apart from general farm work, I also worked in the dairy where we twice daily milked forty cows. Although at times the work was physically hard, life generally was very comfortable; I lived at home, had my meals provided, laundry done, and a farm vehicle to drive. I continued to enjoy sport and played rugby for Northampton, and also represented Bicester in their first ever fixture, plus having a couple of games for Oxfordshire. During the summer, I played cricket for teams called the Oxford Downs, Middleton Stoney, and occasionally the Bicester Hunt; the latter usually when they were short of a player. Socialising and dating were usually undertaken during the winter months when there were a number of dances, balls and theatre performances from which to choose. I always felt the dairy cows could detect when I arrived home in the early hours of the morning and resisted my clumsy attempts to fit the teat cups onto their udders.

During this time, many of my contemporaries were going abroad to seek new opportunities and make new lives for themselves. In 1951, my brother John had gone to work on a tobacco farm in Rhodesia, and two years later the same farm was seeking another assistant, so I offered my services, and within six weeks was on my way.

At that time, I had limited knowledge of the mood which was prevailing after the Second World War, when colonial territories and dependencies in Asia, the Pacific region and Africa began to negotiate and demand the right to self-determination and independence. Some achieved these objectives peacefully; others suffered bitter conflict before obtaining their goals. Regrettably, having achieved their independence, many of the new emerging states then experienced internal disputes as different factions fought for control and supremacy.

Once I arrived in Rhodesia in the early 1950s, I became aware of the changing political movements taking place on the African continent which were creeping ever closer, and it was difficult to avoid the pervading apprehension as to what would be the future of the country. The next fifty years in Africa led me down many paths – a far cry from my sheltered, rural English upbringing. And I was fortunate to be introduced to numerous interesting local and international people who helped, or in some cases hindered, the changing landscape of my adopted home. Without writing a detailed historical account of these events, and whilst trying to avoid an intensely uninteresting autobiography, I have attempted to record some of the actions, decisions and events which I witnessed, or in some instances in which I was involved, during a protracted period of fluctuating public service. During this time, I worked closely with Robert Mugabe, and witnessed his initial pragmatism and inclusiveness deteriorate over time through corruption, bad judgement and ill-advice.

1

Early Life 1931–1955

When I left my home in Oxfordshire, my mother was quietly weeping as she hugged me goodbye; my father's handshake was firm as was his grip on my shoulder, but he seemed incapable of uttering words of farewell. He had given me his blessing and advice the night before, when he had warned me not to leave the hotel during my overnight stop in Nairobi.

His words were, 'Some damn fool will say, "Let's go and see the town." Tell him you're not interested and stay put.' I don't think either of my parents was convinced with my assurances that I would be home in two years, but at that stage I still treated my forthcoming visit to Rhodesia as an exciting adventure and not as a permanent move.

I was driven up to London by my brother Jim, and we spent the journey avoiding the issue of parting and talking about girls and sport. He dropped me at the British Overseas Airways Corporation coach terminal at Victoria, where we formally shook hands, wished each other well, and made assurances to keep in touch and meet soon. I then passed through the doors of the building, and realisation struck home: I was on my own, there was no turning back, and I must honour my commitment to spend the next two years in Rhodesia. However, knowing that I would soon be seeing my brother, John, somewhat lessened my apprehension.

The journey turned out to be long and eventful. I was travelling in a Constellation aircraft belonging to South African Airways as far as Nairobi, with scheduled stops in Rome, Athens, Cairo and Khartoum. When we landed in Rome, tension at the airport was running high as there was a dispute between Italy and Austria over the future ownership of Trieste, and the British were not being viewed with favour by the Italians. We were ushered into a room with a number of nervous menacing armed guards, our passports having been confiscated; there, through the windows, we watched a stream of fighter aircraft taking off and landing. After about a two-hour delay, we re-boarded the aircraft and flew on to Athens, where despite some apprehensions regarding the situation in Cyprus and the role of EOKA – the Greek-Cypriot liberation movement – we experienced no problems. However, our troubles were not yet over, as our arrival in Cairo coincided with a dispute between King Farouk of Egypt and the British government. This, yet again, meant that we were confined in a room with armed guards, who were distinctly more hostile than the Italians. Again, our passports were confiscated, and for reasons which were never explained, the room was sprayed with a mild insecticide. Once more we boarded the aircraft and if I was right that our Egyptian 'hosts' were pleased to see us leave, that feeling was reciprocated. The stop in Khartoum was thankfully uneventful; my only impression was that my thick English clothing was wholly unsuitable for the heat and humidity which I now experienced for the first time.

Somewhere during our flight, the seat next to me became occupied by a man in a brown trilby, who was returning from leave to his job on the Copperbelt in Northern Rhodesia. He quickly discovered that I was a complete rookie regarding travel in Africa and proceeded to give me advice on what to expect at our next destination, Nairobi, Kenya where the Mau Mau uprising had already started. We were due to spend the night there, and he told me in very emphatic terms that buses would take the passengers from the airport to their hotel and return them back to the airport the following morning. He stressed this point and said that on no account was I to take a taxi, as I would probably be robbed or suffer an even worse fate. Having successfully negotiated immigration and customs formalities, I found a large turbaned porter holding my suitcase and enquiring in which hotel I was staying. Having told him the New Stanley, he set off at great speed in his sandaled feet and hailed a taxi. I tried remonstrating, telling him that I wished to go on the bus, but he kept assuring me, assisted by a voluble taxi driver, that this was the correct vehicle for my hotel. Being mindful of the advice I had been given by my unknown companion on the aeroplane, a certain desperation beset me. Glancing around I noticed several of my fellow passengers clambering onto a bus that was parked about fifty yards away. Seizing my suitcase, I ran to the bus, threw it inside and jumped into a vacant seat, with the shouts of the porter and the taxi driver ringing in my ears, as they pursued me across the parking area. We drove off into the night through dimly lit streets. When we eventually stopped, the driver announced that we had arrived at the Norfolk Hotel. All the passengers disembarked and the luggage was unloaded from lockers beneath the bus. My suitcase was dumped on the ground and when everyone had left the bus, I picked it up and put it back on the bus. The driver asked me what I was doing, and I told him I wanted to go to the New Stanley, to which he responded that he was the bus driver for the Norfolk; it was already late and he was returning to the airport. Then with a crashing of gears, and a few violent jolts, we were off again. By this time my spirits were very low. I had been travelling all day. I was weary, hungry, and now seemingly lost in a strange city, with the evening well advanced.

Just as I was questioning my wisdom in leaving Oxfordshire, the bus shuddered to a halt and the driver shouted, 'Out!'

I enquired where we were and he pointed out of his window to a largish building which bore the words New Stanley Hotel. The relief I felt was enormous as I clambered off the bus, once again seizing my suitcase which, like me, was beginning to look a little travel-worn. I tried to express my appreciation to this kindly soul who had safely delivered me to my destination, but he seemed neither interested nor impressed, but drove swiftly away, leaving me covered in diesel fumes.

On presenting myself at the reception desk, I was told they had been very anxious at my non-arrival, and were going to wait another ten minutes before informing the police that I had gone missing between the airport and the hotel. I was given my room number and told that I was sharing it with another chap who had already booked in. On entering the room, I could hear water splashing in the adjoining bathroom, so I called out to announce my presence, and a very welcoming voice replied that he wouldn't be five minutes and that he had ordered me a cold beer which was on the table. When he emerged from the bathroom, I discovered he was a tall, pleasant fellow, a few years older than me, who promptly suggested I had a quick bath, and then accompany him to visit the night spots in Nairobi. At this point my father's warning about some damn fool inviting me to go into town came flooding back, so I thanked him politely, but pleaded tiredness, and after dinner in the hotel dining room, went to bed. I was woken in the early hours of the morning by my room-mate who attempted to tell me what an exciting evening I had missed. I felt, however, that I had already experienced enough excitement on one journey without seeking more.

Later that morning, we returned to the airport to begin the last leg of the trip, and fly south to Salisbury, the capital city of Rhodesia. We boarded a Central African Airways twin-engine Viking for a journey that today would be accomplished in a few hours, but in 1953 took all day. We made frequent stops at what appeared to be remote landing strips, where occasionally some passengers left and others joined the flight. Mail bags were exchanged by ground staff. And usually fuel was pumped aboard, in some instances from 44-gallon drums, strapped into two-wheeled pushcarts, by hand-operated wing pumps. In the meantime, the passengers would wait in the shade and sip warm fruit drinks. My recollection of the entire flight was one of extreme discomfort. It was early November and the tropical thunderstorms were beginning to gather off Central Africa, and at a cruising altitude of 12–14,000 feet, there was no hope of flying above them, so the only alternative was to try and go around them, or in many instances, through them. Having been subject to travel sickness since a child, my stomach soon rebelled against the constant bucking and weaving, and eventually I was violently sick, which was only compensated for by the remaining passengers seeking seats as far away from me as possible.

At last, in the late afternoon, we touched down safely at Salisbury Belvedere airport on 11 November 1953. I had finally arrived, and I was delighted to see my brother waving enthusiastically from the outside of the terminal building. As I was the only immigrant on the flight, I was somewhat delayed while my papers were checked and I apparently gave satisfactory replies to numerous verbal questions. Once outside the building, I was welcomed by John who, after he had finished telling me how good it was to see me, announced he was leaving for England the next morning. Again, not for the first time since I had left home, I felt completely deflated. He drove me into town to Meikles Hotel, where we were to share a room for the night. After a quick bath and change we met up with a friend of his named Paul Scotcher and the three of us dined in the hotel's large, magnificent dining room, to the accompaniment of their resident orchestra. Neither of us went to bed that night; we just sat up swapping stories. John was anxious to catch up with all the home news and in return he tried to brief me on life in Rhodesia and what I could expect from the morrow onwards. At about 5 a.m., he left for the airport, saying he would see me in about a month.

My new employer, Stuart McDonald, arrived at about 8 a.m., and after a hearty breakfast, took me on a bewildering tour of Salisbury, mainly in the industrial sites, where he made numerous purchases of goods for the farm, which were all carefully loaded onto a GMC half-ton truck. By late afternoon, with his business completed, we set off to the farm, Bourton Vale, which was situated north of Bindura in the Matepatepa district.

Shortly after leaving Salisbury, we were driving on a strip road through the fertile Mazoe valley. The strip roads in Rhodesia were a unique road system, constructed during the depression years in the 1930s, as a means of providing employment, and also upgrading the existing dirt and gravel roads. The strips consisted of two lines of tarmac, each approximately eighteen inches wide, which ran parallel with each other in order to accommodate the wheels of vehicles and were constructed on the central ridge of the gravel road. When one met an on-coming vehicle you each surrendered one strip and passed one another with your nearside wheels on dirt and your offside ones on the tarmac. It was a simple and effective system that survived for years. After approximately an hour, the strips ended and we completed the hour-long journey on fairly rough gravel roads, crossing over many low-level bridges that spanned a number of streams and rivers. These waterways were all dry, as the rains had not yet arrived.

It was well after dark when we reached the farm, and I was cheered by a very warm welcome from Stuart's wife, Geraldine, who although younger than me, was already the mother of two children, Peter and Clare. Having exchanged greetings, I was shown my accommodation with the aid of a hurricane lamp. It consisted of one small brick hut, with a thatched roof, situated about fifty yards from the farm house in the middle of a citrus orchard. I was a little astonished to discover that there were no ablution facilities attached to the hut, but I did have access to a bathroom through an external door at the back of the farm house, which I had to share with the McDonald family.

After a week of being shown around the farm, which was some 8,000 acres, I was given specific tasks, which I found far from easy at the beginning. The cropping programme consisted of 250 acres of tobacco, 800 acres of maize, plus certain areas of green crops, and the establishment of improved pastures. In addition, there were approximately 700 head of Africander cattle, which were produced for both meat and draft power. All the land operations were done by these magnificent beasts: ploughing, cultivating, and transportation. The farm had recently purchased a new Fordson tractor, but it was considered too precious to be used and spent most of its time standing in gleaming splendour in the tobacco tying shed. It was a difficult year in which to start my Rhodesian farming career as just prior to my arrival a bush fire had swept through the farm and had completely burnt all the cord wood which had been cut and carefully stacked adjacent to the tobacco barns in preparation for the forthcoming curing season. This set-back led to a frenzy of activity because in addition to preparing all the lands for planting both tobacco and maize, timber had to be cut and carried to replace that which had been lost. All the lands were prepared by hand. In the case of tobacco, small mounds were made using a unique type of hoe called a *badza*, into which a tobacco plant would be placed when the rain came. The maize lands were marked out for planting on a system known as check rows, where long, low measuring wires were dragged across the field at right angles to each other and when in place a team of workers – again using the *badza* – would make small holes about nine inches apart into which two mealie pips would later be placed. It may sound primitive, but if done correctly the resulting pattern of young germinating maize was quite stunning, and cultivating was made reasonably easy due to the straight lines of the check row system. Fortunately, the rains were late that year, which just enabled me to complete most of these tasks before planting.

I soon settled into a daily routine, which meant being in the lands at sunrise, where I usually stayed all day, with breakfast, lunch and tea being brought out to me. Breakfast arrived in a decker, which comprised of three metal compartments held together by a carrying handle; the bottom container was filled with hot water; the second one contained porridge, and the top one usually eggs and bacon. It was a fine concept, if not a great feat of engineering – the main fault with the system was after the bearer, (usually the gardener) had found me, having walked up to three kilometres, the porridge was stiff, the egg and bacon congealed and both were cold. Another difficulty I experienced was language. With little or no time to learn, I found communication extremely frustrating, and I knew the workers were taking advantage of me – I would probably have done the same in their position. In the evenings, after a bath, and dinner with the family, I would thankfully seek my bed, having worked a twelve- to fourteen-hour working day. Sundays were generally considered to be a day of rest – that is once the cattle had been dipped. This was essential for tick control: every beast had to be immersed in a plunge dip, with an arsenic solution, on a weekly basis. Because of the pressure of other farming activities, this operation always took place on a Sunday morning. As the latest recruit, it was my job to supervise the operation. It was not an easy exercise because the fences were few and badly maintained and the cattle had to be found and rounded up – sometimes a slow frustrating (or amusing) process as the workers were often still intoxicated after the Saturday evening beer drink. So it was a task usually only completed by about three o'clock in the afternoon – so much for the day of rest.

A major setback occurred after I had been on the farm about six weeks, when the McDonald's six-month-old daughter, Clare, died of cerebral malaria. As to be expected, both parents took the loss extremely badly; Stuart practically disappeared for several weeks, only making rare appearances on the farm. Where he went, I do not know, and I suspect neither did Geraldine. John was still in England, and I had to keep the farm running with no knowledge whatsoever of tobacco production, and with the reaping and curing about to begin. It was a period of my life that I did not enjoy, as I knew I was floundering and making many bad decisions through lack of knowledge. There was virtually no one I could turn to for advice, as most of the neighbours were well-established farmers in whose eyes a learner tobacco assistant was one of the lowest forms of life, a person to whom they would hardly speak. The notable exception among them was Dennis Sherwood, who owned a large neighbouring farm. He was always pleasant and understanding, but unfortunately did not have a good relationship with McDonald, hence a certain reluctance to assist. During this trying time, the most harrowing moments were the evening meal. Invariably, after a few stilted remarks, Geraldine would flee the table and I would hear her sobbing in the adjoining bedroom.

John had been delayed in England, due to two disastrous crashes by Comet Airlines, when all flights to Africa were suspended, and only later resumed with different aircraft. However, in the middle of February, he eventually returned, and I informed him that I was not enjoying life and was going to go back to England. He persuaded me to change my mind, and with the two of us sharing the orchard accommodation, life became very pleasant.

Not long after his return, I had spent a day in Salisbury shopping for the farm. Driving home in the late afternoon, I found the road completely impassable, with the river flowing several feet above the final bridge. I turned around and drove to the nearest town, Bindura, phoned the McDonalds and explained the situation. Stuart said to stay there the night, then go to the bank in the morning, draw the farm wages and then meet him at the river. Unfortunately, I had no money on me, but I met the owner of the local general store in the hotel. I explained my predicament to him and he agreed to pay for my evening and put the cost on my monthly grocery bill. Next morning having collected the money, I went to the river, which was still in full flood, and met up with Stuart. He had a peculiar quirk about paying, insisting that it was better to pay in coins rather than in notes, as he had a conceived idea that the workers felt they were receiving more. Consequently, I had about a dozen linen money bags of silver which had to be got to the other side of the river. Fortunately, there was a narrow swing footbridge suspended high above the raging waters. He had come with a number of farm workers, so he placed a bag of coins on each of their heads, grabbed one himself, told me to carry one, and we proceeded to cross the swinging, swaying bridge in close formation with him leading and me bringing up the rear, just as the heavens opened with another torrential storm. Another farmer attempting to cross the bridge in front of our procession lost his nerve, dropped to his knees, and grabbing the steel cables by which the bridge was suspended, cried out to be rescued. The response from McDonald was to put his foot into the small of this unfortunate's back and step over him. This procedure was followed by each of the black workers with broad grins on their faces; it had obviously added a little more spice to their lives.

My duties did not end there: Stuart promptly gave me a very wet, fat, and frightened black spaniel, belonging to his mother-in-law, and told me to go back to Salisbury and return it to her. As an afterthought, he produced another shopping list and said, 'Come back tomorrow'. I made the return journey across the swollen river, carrying the spaniel which smelt as only a wet, scared dog can. Back to Salisbury I drove, now feeling scruffy, miserable and wet. As evening was fading, I arrived at Geraldine's parents' home to deliver their dog; but when they opened the door, my life suddenly changed, for there in the entrance hall was the most beautiful girl I had ever seen. I was introduced to her and her mother, but in my confusion, I did not note their names correctly, only remembering that the girl's first name was June. When I related my experience to John, he asked if I knew her name and I said, 'June someone', and he exclaimed, 'That must be June Marshall! God, she's gorgeous! I was thinking of inviting her to the winter cricket ball next month.' This he duly did.

Before John left for the cricket ball, I wrote a letter asking June to join me to celebrate my birthday in ten days' time, which I asked my brother to give to her. Much to my delight she accepted with pleasure. When I collected her for what was our very first date, she said she hoped I didn't mind, but she had invited a special friend, Dorothy Hudson-Beck, to join us. This was not quite what I had expected, but I cheerfully went along with the arrangement; then I had yet another surprise when Dorothy in turn brought along a friend of hers named Tommy Griffiths. In the event, we had a wonderful evening, which seriously depleted my meagre financial resources. Our courtship picked up pace from that point onwards and by August we had officially become engaged. This was not completed without a couple of minor incidents. The first occurred when I asked her mother if I could marry her daughter, to which she replied with an emphatic 'no', stating that no man should marry under the age of thirty; and that June had to complete her contract to the Ministry of Education, with whom she was employed as a teacher. I spluttered that I was nearly thirty (in fact I was twenty-three), and that we did not want to get married for another year.

The second incident involved my own parents, to whom I had written a long letter extolling the virtues and beauty of June, and our desire to get married. Unfortunately, in my attempt to portray all these points, I exceeded the weight restriction for an airmail letter, and the postal services sent my missive by surface mail. Having anxiously waited a month for a reaction – hopefully favourable – and still receiving no reply, I persuaded John to write backing up my claims. This he duly did, but if my letter erred on the side of length, he over-corrected in brevity. His short airmail arrived first, and gave the impression we were already married, which caused a certain amount of consternation in the Norman household. This was corrected the following day when my letter finally arrived and everyone relaxed a little. June's paternal grandfather, who was a medical doctor, had for a number of years been the doctor to my own grandparents, when he was practicing in Lechlade, Oxfordshire, a fact which gave a little more respectability to our forthcoming nuptials.

This romance did wonders to my overall spirits and I began to really enjoy my life in Rhodesia. The farm work and routine became more familiar to me, and at about this time, John and I were joined by another young assistant. This was a most delightful young Irishman named Alec Elliott. Like us, he came from farming stock, and like most Irishmen, possessed a tremendous sense of humour. We were now living in larger accommodation; we had two small round brick buildings, with thatched roofs, known as rondavels, one for sleeping and one for living, with a separate outside kitchen, containing a small Dover wood-burning stove. Furniture was sparse: we each had a bed, a shared wardrobe, and one straight-backed chair in the bedroom. In the living room, we had a table which was for multi-purpose use, one cane armchair with a cushion, and one paraffin-burning fridge that had a tendency to emit black fumes. The straight-back chair was brought through from the sleeping hut in the evenings, and a wooden paraffin box completed the seating arrangements. We had a strict seating rotation, which led you from cushioned chair to wooden box in three nights. Likewise we had a similar scheme for bathing. The galvanised bath was coffin shaped and our domestic worker, Gadzira, brought it into the bedroom, having first pushed the beds aside to make space. He then brought in two four-gallon tins of water: one boiling, which had been heated over an open fire, the other cold. Having decanted these into the bath, we each had our baths, according to strict rotation; therefore every third night you had the luxury of a clean bath. What was common to all three of us was the uneven texture of the bottom of the tub because at some time in its history a careless builder had used it for mixing cement and neglected to clean it out properly.

On a few occasions when June would come and visit me on the farm, she would stay with the McDonalds but would come and dine in our bachelor accommodation. This necessitated an alteration to our seating arrangement, with June having the armchair – minus the cushion – I the straight-backed chair, John the wooden box, and Alec, always gracious and smiling, would sit on the floor, with the added comfort of the cushion from the cane chair. These were great evenings with much laughter and fun, but I must add that no one ever suggested that June should participate in the revolving system of our bathing arrangements.

2

Rhodesia 1955–1965

1955 was a year of change. John left the farm at Bourton Vale to manage another closer to Salisbury at Ruwa. June and I were getting married in August, so it was arranged that Alec would remain on the farm with the McDonalds (and enjoy the pleasure of a clean bath every night) and I would move three miles away and manage a section of the main farm. Our 'married quarters' was actually a burnt-out, large, single, square room, so before we could move in, I put on a thatch roof. I also added an internal cross of four walls, to divide the square into a living room, a kitchen, a bedroom and a bathroom. There was no ceiling and the walls were only nine-foot high so any noise or activity in any of the four rooms could be heard loud and clearly in the other three. We later added the luxury of a verandah to the outside.

In the weeks before our wedding, June went on a visit to Britain, having been selected as one of two young persons to represent Rhodesia on a scheme known as the Princess Elizabeth Birthday Fund. This was established with money collected by the school children of Rhodesia and presented to the then Princess Elizabeth on the occasion of her twenty-first birthday. It was an exchange scheme, where each year two young people from Britain would visit Rhodesia, and two from Rhodesia would visit Britain, one year boys and the next year girls.

It was June's first visit to Britain, and she spent six weeks touring the country, visiting many places and sites of historical interest, but also mixing with people from all walks of life, culminating in a visit to Buckingham Palace for a private audience with the Queen. It also presented a wonderful opportunity for her to meet my family, which must have been a frightening ordeal for her because my father and his brothers *en masse* were a formidable group. However, she quickly captivated them all, and became a firm favourite with both my parents. It was therefore a great delight to both of us when my mother took the unusual, and for her, bold, decision to fly out to Rhodesia to attend our wedding.

We were duly married on 12 August 1955 in the Anglican Cathedral in Salisbury where June, attended by four bridesmaids, was given away by her uncle Huck Rudland. I, in turn, was supported by three ushers, and my brother John as best man. June's mother gave us a splendid reception at the Salisbury Sports Club where our health was proposed by Canon Finch, who had earlier officiated at the ceremony and who had been a friend of June's family for many years.

***

June was born in Salisbury, Rhodesia, where her grandfather Thomas Rudland had arrived in 1890. He was a member of Cecil Rhodes' pioneer column, which had been initially sent to Mashonaland to seek for gold under the Rudd Concession granted by King Lobengula. The large reef which was believed to be there has never been discovered, although many small and profitable deposits were and continue to be worked in the area. June's grandfather, like so many others in that column and the accompanying police force had to quickly find alternative sources of substance and income. Many tried farming, but without herbicides and pesticides, crops were quickly affected by vegetative disease and insect-borne pestilence. In addition, their horses succumbed to African horse sickness and an outbreak of rinderpest all but annihilated their trek oxen. These pioneers were not farmers, and their lack of agricultural, as well as local knowledge, coupled with no mechanical equipment and only some rudimentary handheld tools such as axes and hoes, turned this venture into a major problem.

Rudland who had engineering knowledge joined a company run by a buccaneer called George Pauling who specialised in constructing railway tracks. So, within a few months of arriving in Mashonaland, he left to join Pauling in the small port of Beira, in the then Portuguese East Africa, as the company had been commissioned to construct a railway line from Beira to Umtali in the eastern half of the country, which had become known as Rhodesia. It probably sounded like an exciting assignment – in reality it was anything but. The country through which they pushed their line was swampy; an ideal environment for mosquitoes to flourish, causing all employed, both black and white, to go down with malaria, and indeed many died from blackwater fever. An additional danger came from the large numbers of wild animals, who quite naturally fiercely objected to their territory being invaded. However, despite the many setbacks, logistical as well as medical, the project was successfully completed. Rudland then moved to Natal in South Africa, where in partnership with another engineer, he started his own company. It was whilst he was living there that June's mother Dorothy, her two sisters and brother were born. In the 1920s, he decided to move again, and the family went to Kenya, where coffee production became their main enterprise. It was whilst they were there that Dorothy met Alec Marshall, the eldest of four sons, who had moved to Kenya from England to farm coffee and hopefully make his fortune. They were duly married in Nairobi. Unfortunately, within a few years, the price of coffee beans collapsed so the whole family moved again, this time to Northern Rhodesia and later south to Southern Rhodesia, where Rudland founded another company known as T. W. Rudland & Son; the son being George, also known by his schoolboy nickname of Huck. This company specialised in construction work, and they were awarded many contracts both by the railways and also for road and building projects; in addition, they owned and operated stone quarries.

June's parents went farming in the Marandellas district, where they operated a dairy, and had a milk delivery round. Unfortunately, the thirties were the years of the great depression, and life was hard and unrewarding. At the outbreak of the Second World War in 1939, Alec Marshall joined the army, and after a short while Dorothy gave up the farm, and moved with her two small daughters – June had a younger sister, Diane – into Salisbury. It was also unfortunate that due to the separation caused by the war years, June's parents drifted apart and divorced after the war.

***

When we left the reception, I borrowed a car from June's grandmother to drive to June's mother's house, where I had parked my car for safekeeping. It was an old 1942 Plymouth which I had bought for £200.00. What a mistake! The vehicle was festooned with all kinds of materials and inscribed with many lewd and suggestive messages. With the willing assistance of Jackie, the cook, we restored the exterior to some kind of respectability when suddenly he shouted, 'Fish, fish!' Lifting the bonnet, I discovered a pair of large kippers firmly wired to the manifold. Relating all this to John on my return from honeymoon, I said I gave Jackie 2/6 for helping me clean up everything. He said, 'The blighter, I gave him 2/6 for helping me put it on!' I rather admired Jackie's initiative. He certainly knew how to keep a secret!

As a bride, June did not carry a bouquet, but instead held an ivory coloured prayer book, to which was fixed a simple orchid which had been flown up from Johannesburg on ice. When we left the reception, she wore the orchid on the lapel of her suit, with the intention of wearing it every evening for dinner on our honeymoon. The first night we spent at a small country hotel, which was on the way to the eastern districts and the port of Beira, where we were going to board a ship for Mombasa. She asked the manager if she could place her orchid in the fridge to maintain its freshness. The next day after we had been motoring for about two hours, she cried plaintively, 'My orchid!'

We often speculated about what happened to that flower.

We had one further mishap before we reached our next destination, which was the Leopard Rock Hotel in the Vumba Mountains. A new full tarmac road was in the process of being constructed between Salisbury and Umtali; a distance of approximately 170 miles, which meant we drove for most of the journey over deeply rutted, sandy deviations, where visibility was often reduced to zero because of the billowing dust. Around midday, we reached the small town of Rusape, whose only hotel, the Balfour, fronted on to the main street. We stopped for lunch, which was served on the open verandah next to the main thoroughfare. After a while, I could hear a radio in the background, giving what sounded like a cricket commentary. As I knew England was playing Australia, I excused myself for a minute to go and check on the score. In those days, many hotel bars did not permit women, and as I suspected, the radio was in the bar, with a large contingent of local worthies listening intently to the crackling commentary. To my shame, I must admit I did stay rather a long time, and when I rejoined my wife of one day, she was not the slightest bit interested in knowing either the current score or the state of the game. For the next few miles, I deemed it prudent to journey in silence.

The Leopard Rock Hotel was baronial in style, built largely from local stone, and mainly by Italian workers from a nearby prisoner of war camp. As with most newly married couples, we were allocated a suite which was not named the honeymoon suite, but had a much grander title of the 'Queen Mother Suite'. It had indeed been occupied by that wonderful lady when she visited Rhodesia to open the Rhodes Centenary Exhibition in Bulawayo in 1953. It was magnificent, the only drawback being that confetti had clung to our clothes, and with only hairbrushes to remove it, we left a trail behind us wherever we went, so declaring our newly wedded status. After two days in the mountains, we drove down the steep declining road to Umtali, the only difficulty being that my foot brakes had failed and the gear lever constantly disengaged. We managed the journey by June holding the lever firmly in second gear and me steering with one hand, and operating the handbrake with the other.

Having had a truly wonderful holiday cruising up to Mombasa and then back to Beira, it was time to get down to work again. We moved into our new home. The kitchen was a lean-to on the side of the house with the usual wood-burning stove and a paraffin-burning fridge. The biggest drawback was that there was no water supply. A storage tank had been placed on a kopje behind the house so that the water would gravitate to the kitchen and bathroom. In order to make this system work, I had to fill about ten 44-gallon fuel drums with water from a point three miles away, convey them on a tractor-drawn trailer to the base of the kopje, then push the drums by hand to a point above the storage tank, connect a hosepipe, suck vigorously then quickly place it in the said storage tank. After repeating this exercise ten times, we had our weekly supply of fresh water. However, filling the tank had to be completed on a Sunday, after the cattle had been dipped, because neither the tractor nor trailer could be spared any other day of the week.

Most of the farm work was still done manually which meant that we employed a large labour force; a rule of thumb calculation usually gave a ratio of one worker to one acre of tobacco. Tobacco was the main crop grown on the farm, and entailed about eleven months of concentrated supervision. The season started in August when seedbeds were prepared and sown. To sterilise the soil and try to prevent weed seeds from germinating, and to minimise the effect of root-knot nematodes, broken brushwood was laid to a depth of about two feet on top of the beds, which usually measured four feet wide by one hundred feet long. When the whole site had been covered it was set on fire, and when it had cooled, the ash was removed and the beds were ready for sowing. If this method sounds primitive, it was, and later was replaced firstly by injecting chemicals into the soil, and later still by covering the beds in plastic sheeting and releasing chemical gas from pressurised containers.

Tobacco seed is extremely fine, and the accepted method of sowing was to mix tablespoons full of seed in three-gallon watering cans, with a fine rose outlet, and then walk at a steady pace beside the bed, stirring continuously as you poured the water out. With a little practice the results were surprisingly good. After eight weeks of twice-daily watering, the seedlings were ready for planting out. In the meantime, the lands had been prepared. The soil was ridged to a height of eighteen inches. We had now progressed to mechanical preparation by using tractor-operated soil-ridgers, a huge improvement over the manual system that was in use when I first arrived, and planting-holes were dug on top of the ridges at intervals of a foot. It was at this time that dry planting was first introduced. The expression meant placing the seedlings in dry soil, with added water in order to establish a crop before the onset of the seasonal rains, which usually began to fall between the second and third week of November. As this concept was a new one, there were many forms of experimentation among tobacco farmers, using buckets, cups and hosepipes in order to achieve the best results. One of the most bizarre methods was devised by Stuart MacDonald, who insisted we start work at 4 a.m. to avoid the heat of the day, and thus cause the plants less stress. After much stumbling and fumbling around in the dark, with about fifty workers employed, the results were much as one would have expected: some areas missed entirely, other planting stations having two or more plants in the same hole. Eventually the scheme was abandoned for a more orthodox approach.

As was the custom on those days, all farmers provided basic food for their workers on a weekly basis. This would consist of maize meal (the staple diet for the country), protein in the form of beans and dried fish; salt, cooking oil and vegetables, which varied according to the seasons. These allocations were usually made on Monday afternoons, and were accompanied by much laughter and singing.

Towards the end of that farming season, I felt that with three years of tobacco growing experience, I would look for a new job with greater responsibilities, and hopefully an improved lifestyle. I was spending long hours in the lands, having all my meals except the evening one brought out to me. At the same time I was leaving June all alone in a very remote house with only basic facilities and no telephone (we did not even have a radio). Added to all this, she had become very ill, suffering unbearable stomach pains, which as she had become pregnant, she attributed to the penalties of carrying a child. It was only much later that she discovered the cause of her great discomfort was in fact a rumbling appendix which kept flaring up. Life generally was not an easy one for young wives such as June. Remoteness and distances made socialising difficult and household shopping was not easy as centres were often many miles away, accessible only by narrow dirt roads which were either thick with dust or clogged with mud. Like most farmers in the area we relied on a weekly service supplied by the Rhodesian Railways known as RMS (Road Motor Services) which would deliver a standing order of weekly requirements plus canvas mail bags to designated halts. Our nearest halt was seven miles away and June would drive there and collect our provisions and post once a week. During the rainy season, passing on-coming vehicles was a difficult manoeuvre as either side of the central crest of road was deep with mud. The RMS always carried a dozen strong men in the back of their trucks and if you met one of them, the accepted practice was for you to drive off the road where you were guaranteed to get stuck, and allow them to remain on the central ridge and inch pass you. Once past, the men on the back would jump off and with much shouting, singing and laughter, would push you back onto the road, give a cheery wave goodbye and clamber back on board, only to repeat the whole process again with the next car they met.

Fortunately, I heard of an assistant's position which was becoming vacant on a farm belonging to Jack Quinton in a district called Umvukwes. One Sunday June and I made the three-hour journey each way to his farm. He and his wife Rina gave us an excellent lunch and then Jack drove me around the farm and there and then offered me the post. We could hardly believe our luck; we were to live in a house which had electricity, running water, a daily milk supply and fresh vegetables twice a week, with a starting salary of £60.00 a month; up from the £20.00 a month I was presently earning. Within a short space of time we had made all our arrangements, and on a single day I drove the journey twice, once in Stuart McDonald's lorry with our furniture and the second time in our car with my wife, mother-in-law and our suitcases. Thus we moved to Rumanje Farm to begin a new chapter in our lives. The following week our first child, Kathryn, was born and we really felt our cup runneth over. Jack Quinton was a dynamic character who owned and ran four farms, employing a number of white managers and assistants and a large number of black staff who knew not only how to handle the various farming enterprises, but also how to handle him. He was also very involved in public work and at that time was the Member of Parliament for the area, and later to become a Minister in both Garfield Todd's government and later Edgar Whitehead's. As with most Mashonaland farms, the main emphasis was on tobacco production, but large areas were also planted to maize. In addition, there was a substantial dairy; a commercial beef herd; a pig unit; and he had a thoroughbred stud, breeding race horses.

I was a little taken aback when on the very first morning, I heard knocking and on opening the door I was greeted by a young fresh-faced man who enquired if I was the new assistant. When I replied that I was, Bert Palmer introduced himself and bid me welcome, and said I was the fifty-second member of staff he had seen arrive. I found this information a little disconcerting, but it was correct, and I quickly discovered that many who had worked and learnt their skills under Jack Q (as he was known), moved on and made a success of their own enterprise. Jack also took on seasonal employees, either from the tobacco buying industry, in order that they could acquire an insight into the production side of the crop, or government extension officers who were required to obtain practical farming experience to further their careers.

As with my previous position, the hours one worked were long and arduous. During the tobacco reaping and curing season, it was not uncommon to finish packing barns at 10 p.m. But one's duties did not finish then, as the temperatures had to be checked twice during the night, in order to ensure an even cure. With some thirty tobacco barns to inspect, it was a lengthy procedure.

With so much activity and so many varied interests, life was never dull.

Within the district, there were a large number of young men with new wives, and an ever expanding number of children, which provided a lively and enjoyable social life. This mainly centred on the country club, where there were facilities for cricket, golf, tennis etc. To enjoy these facilities, you had to become a club member, and in order to do so, your employer had to sign a guarantee of £200.00 (which was a considerable sum in those days), to ensure your good behaviour. In the event of unruliness or damage to club property, the employer had to pay up. I did not hear of a single case when this occurred, and I thought at the time, and am still of the opinion, that is was a good scheme, as it did give many young bucks cause to think before they indulged in some stupid or irresponsible prank. To add further spice to our life, there was a new farming area situated just to the north of Rumanje called Centenary that ran to the edge of the Zambezi escarpment, which was being opened up as a resettlement scheme and included the new Centenary Country Club. The area was virgin bush, which had previously been surveyed, and land areas suitable for farming had been pegged. The selection of suitable farmers was decided by a land settlement board who considered all applications, and then made their decisions, based on work experience, available assets (including cash), and in those days, pre-military service was also a requirement; all this culminating in an interview. From that point onwards, you were virtually on your own, and apart from the main access roads, the successful candidate was responsible for most of the remaining structures, which included buildings, fencing, water supplies, etc.

For those who did not qualify under this scheme – and I was one of them – there was another seemingly exciting scheme opening up in Northern Rhodesia, in an area called Mkushi. Many of my contemporaries were going there to start a new life. It sounded attractive as qualifications were lower and government assistance higher; but despite urgings from many friends, June and I decided against moving country. We did, however, feel we had to move after three seasons with Jack Quinton, and three previous ones with Stuart MacDonald. I knew that if I did not want to become a professional farm manager, I had to be bold, take some financial risks and try and establish an enterprise of my own. Despite the hard work – which was common to all of us at that age – we had enjoyed the friendship of a large number of like-minded people. But it was time to leave the comfort zone in which we were living and re-start our lives in another district. I did not have enough money to buy a farm, so I made enquiries with regard to leasing one. Here I was assisted by Peter Gibson, who was married to June's cousin Pat. They were farming in the Karoi district and I went to visit them one weekend, as they had identified a farm which they thought might be suitable. It belonged to George Clift who had been allocated it in 1946 as a soldier settler. The name of the farm was 'Pelele', which means 'finished'. It had gained this unusual name as the area was being surveyed for farms in 1939 and the surveying team were working on the farm when a message arrived telling them to finish and return to Salisbury as the Second World War had broken out. On their return they registered the farm number and someone wrote the word Pelele.

In many circles it is still mistakenly thought that these settlers' farms came absolutely free, which in fact is not true. Before applying for a farm, the candidate had to meet certain criteria, such as practical experience, and be in possession of minimum assets either in cash or kind. Having been allocated a farm, he then had to develop capital structures such as water points, access roads, ring fences, buildings, etc. before he could apply for title. Failure to do so resulted in relinquishing the property. In other words, total development was to the cost of the occupier.

Having met George Clift he asked me what I wanted to do. I replied saying I was looking for a farm to lease. It turned out he wanted to sell, but said he was prepared to lease it to me for one year, and give me the option to buy at the end of that period. I requested a week to think over his offer and returned to Rumanje and June to consider our next move. After three days I phoned him and accepted his proposal, and enquired when we could meet and draw up an agreement. He replied by saying my word was good enough and he did not need an agreement. Six weeks later he phoned me to say he had left the farm and it was all mine. Near panic set in as I had to try and raise some capital with no meaningful collateral, quickly order some essential inputs, pack up the family, move to a farm of which I had only seen the house, and June was expecting our second child. It was certainly the biggest gamble of our lives. We had very little money, but I managed to borrow a small amount from Stuart McDonald, and also a little from my brother. I made application to join the Farmers Co-op, which was a large organisation that could supply nearly all one's farming requirements. They had an agreement with government, which allowed them to take a loan on a farmer's maize crop so that they had first call on all sales until the liability had been met. It was a very good arrangement, and it enabled numerous famers to finance much of their seasonal requirements, while providing the Co-op with some suitable collateral. I duly received a letter from the financial director requesting I call and see him regarding my application. If I was apprehensive when I went into his office, my fears were immediately compounded when he informed me that the General Manager, Mr James Brown, wished to see me. He was a large, genial-looking Scotsman, with a booming voice. He bid me sit down, and then told me the Board of Directors had considered my application, but I had made one mistake. At this point, my heart sank, and I felt I had failed as an independent farmer before I had even started. He then told me I had made no provision for the 'wee wife', and he was sure she would be needing a new dress or a pair of shoes during the coming year, so he had taken the liberty of adding a further £500 to my application, and he was pleased to inform me that the board had approved my application. James Brown was very understanding and a real gentleman, and he probably judged my application as being too low, and therefore increased it, under the pretext of looking after June's wellbeing.

The only assets we possessed were youthful vigour, a little farming experience, and a strong determination to succeed. Soon after our arrival we were blessed by the birth of Diana, which did much to brighten our lives, because as far as comforts went, we had now gone backwards. There was no electricity, and a very poor water supply. We were back to paraffin-burning fridges, a wood-burning stove, and light provided by paraffin-burning lamps. The first year was a near disaster. Instead of the rains arriving in mid-November, the first rain fell on Christmas Day, by which time my small farm dam had dried up, and I had resorted to thatching my tobacco seedbeds in an effort to shade them from the sun, and had to divert my meagre supply of borehole water from the house in order to keep the seedlings alive.

Those first rains were such a welcome blessing, but almost led to tragedy. We had visited the Gibsons, neighbouring farmers, for tea and left at about 5 p.m. to drive the ten miles home to celebrate our first family Christmas in our own home. Halfway there, we came to a small river crossing which was in flood. I got out of the car, walked into the water and decided I could drive through. The water was rising rapidly and in about the middle of the river the car stalled. I went back into the water, June took over the driving seat, and every time I shouted she pressed the starter. We had the car in reverse gear, so with a combination of her starting and me heaving we succeeded in jumping the car out backwards. By now it was getting dark, so I dried out the plugs and manifold, and turned the car round on a muddy slippery road, to start a long circular drive in order to get home. But luck was not with us that night. After journeying for about a mile we came to a river we had previously crossed less than an hour before to find it was now in full spate. This time we tried another plan. First of all, June's sister, Diane, and I carried baby Diana in her carrycot across the swollen waters. I then returned and carried Kathryn (aged three) on my back; returned yet again and formed a small chain with June, her mother and me, and we waded across together, then finally I went back, got in the car and inched it slowly across, and with its rear wheels still in the water it gave one final cough and stopped. By now everybody was thoroughly soaked, but after more drying of spark plugs, we managed to get the car started and off we went, finally to arrive home at 10 p.m., wet, tired, but elated that the rain had finally arrived and I knew that my farming venture had a chance to survive.

I managed to produce a reasonable tobacco crop, but unfortunately the rain was too late for my maize. In April, Stuart McDonald said he wanted his loan repaid, but I had no means of repaying as I had not at that time sold any tobacco. I phoned my bank in Salisbury and asked to speak to the manager. A pleasant-sounding voice came on the phone and asked how could he help? I said I needed a loan of £3,000 and he said, 'Really! How do you intend to pay it back?' I told him from the proceeds of the sale of tobacco. A long pause followed, and then he asked me for my name and account number and to my huge relief said that he would grant me the loan, but would I be kind enough to call and see him when I was next in town. This I did, and it was my first meeting with Alwyn Calder, who went on to become a very successful general manager of the Standard Bank in Rhodesia. He greeted me very courteously and said he never granted loans over the telephone and certainly never to strangers. But he felt my approach was both bold and honest, so he made an exception and thus began a long and happy association with the Standard Bank.

I still find it remarkable that two high profile businessmen like Brown and Calder could be so helpful and considerate to a young aspiring farmer such as me. But I suppose in those days, before computers, calculators or internet banking, all business was done on a face-to-face basis, and you were not reduced to an anonymous reference number, which is sadly how we all now exist.

At the end of that first year, I sold sufficient tobacco, at a reasonable enough price, to enable me to meet my debts, make a down payment against the purchase of the farm and borrow enough money to start another season. The farm cost me £14,000.00, payable in equal instalments over a ten-year period at a fixed rate of interest. On this occasion, George Clift and I did have a signed agreement, and for the next ten years I visited him at his home in Salisbury and gave him a cheque for payment plus interest; again a very workable and gentlemanly arrangement. By 1964, I felt confident enough to purchase a second farm, which was situated a few miles away.

However, the following year, Rhodesia declared its infamous Unilateral Declaration of Independence. This ill-judged action by the Rhodesian Front government led by Ian Smith brought swift condemnation and action by the international community, who quickly imposed United Nations' sanctions on the country. These included both trade and services, but the first major target was the export of tobacco leaf, with the immediate consequence that the tobacco industry went into rapid decline. Tobacco was the country's major foreign exchange earner, and because of its distinct and unique characteristics, it was easily recognisable in the market place. The government's reaction to the embargo on tobacco exports was two-fold; firstly, it created a clandestine tobacco exporting company, which employed some local buccaneering types who relished the challenge of undercover deals with risk-taking characters in unnamed countries. Although the operations were internationally considered to be illegal, and as such did entail a great deal of subterfuge, they achieved their objective of keeping Rhodesian tobacco in some of the established cigarette blends, and also opened up new outlets, which became highly beneficial once sanctions were lifted. Maybe someone who was involved with these activities will one day write an account of their operations which I feel would make interesting reading.

The second measure introduced by the government to protect the tobacco industry was to reduce the size of the crop and thus limit the exposure in the markets. This they did by the simple measure of allocating quotas to all growers, based on previous production levels. For me and many others this was a major setback, which left us with few alternatives, other than to diversify into alternative crops and carry on. I introduced other enterprises into my farming programme, such as beef cattle, cotton and soya bean production and I increased my acreage of maize. In other words, I became a mixed farmer in an endeavour to stay in business. Although this change in farming practice was, in the long term, possibly beneficial to both the individual and the country as a whole, the transition was not as easy as it may appear, mainly as a result of the difficulty in obtaining essential inputs, particularly fuel following the UN embargo on suppliers to the country. However, as time went by, this and other procurement problems were alleviated due mainly to the support and co-operation of South Africa and also of Mozambique, which in those days was still governed from Lisbon.

At that time national politics was very much to the fore, and it was extremely difficult to avoid or fail to notice what was going on around one. African nationalism was becoming stronger and more strident, with demonstrations taking place in the townships, and meetings being banned, which led to many clashes between the police and the protestors. On the other side of the political divide, there was great disillusionment with Britain and a growing number of whites advocating for a complete breakaway to become an independent country in order to maintain their supremacy. Gradually the case and cause for a middle-road approach was disappearing and both individuals and communities were taking up entrenched positions.

The process was certainly hastened by the break-up of the Federation of Rhodesia and Nyasaland. A regional concept which was born in 1953, it engendered much hope and optimism in many quarters, but also fear and pessimism in others. On reflection, despite its economic benefit, it was bound to fail because insufficient notice had been taken of the views and aspirations of the indigenous people. In the two northern territories of Nyasaland and Northern Rhodesia, nationalist leaders and parties were clamouring for their independence, and were gaining growing sympathy in Britain. This, in turn, was causing unease or even fear among the white electorate in Southern Rhodesia; the first noticeable sign of which was the resignation in 1958 of the then Prime Minister Garfield Todd's entire cabinet, which felt he was becoming too liberal in his views and attitudes. He carried on governing for a short while with a handful of supporters. In order to try and stabilise the situation within the party, Sir Edgar Whitehead, who was Rhodesia's representative in the United States, was recalled from Washington and elected leader of the United Federal Party (UFP). But in an arranged by-election in Bulawayo, for a seat in Parliament, he was defeated. This led to Parliament being dissolved and a general election held, which enabled Whitehead to win a seat and continue as premier of the country. The political temperature was now beginning to increase with the two northern territories engaging in talks with the British government on a transfer of power to their own independence. In

1961, Whitehead held a referendum asking for a mandate to widen the franchise in order to give greater representation to the black population. This he succeeded in winning, but the mood of the whites was hardening fast. In the 1962 general election under the leadership of Winston Field, the Rhodesian Front (RF) narrowly defeated the ruling party and became the government.

With both Northern Rhodesia and Nyasaland having obtained agreement for their independence, the new RF government pressed strongly for Southern Rhodesia's own independence. However, the British government were seeking a much broader franchise and were unwilling to accede to their demands. This caused differences within the ruling party, which led to the resignation of Winston Field as Prime Minister. He was replaced by Ian Smith, who was not only a more experienced politician, but was also a more determined advocate of independence. The mood in the country now swung strongly towards unilateral action. However, Ian Smith called a referendum, seeking support for a negotiated independence. It was the first and only time I gave him my vote, on the basis that an agreement with the British government would probably be supported by the majority of black nationalists if it provided sufficient opportunities for them to eventually evolve as the government of the country. My yes vote was cancelled out by June voting no, on the basis that she did not trust him, and if he secured a large yes vote, he would treat it as a mandate to declare independence – how right she was.

On 11 November 1965 came the news for which many were eagerly waiting, and which a few of us were dreading: the announcement by Ian Smith of the Universal Declaration of Independence (UDI). This action, more than any other, I am convinced, brought Robert Mugabe into power fifteen years later. Every political leader or potential leader needs an element of luck, usually influenced by outside events, and that single act I strongly feel was Robert Mugabe's good fortune. For the black nationalists, he quickly emerged as the one man who had the vision, courage and ruthlessness to take on Ian Smith and the RF government. Without UDI, I believe we would have eventually had a black government by 1980, but under different leadership, and without the agony of fifteen years of international sanctions and fourteen years of a debilitating and destructive internal armed struggle.

The government quickly moved to consolidate and strengthen their position within the country and censorship was imposed on the news media. A daily dose of propaganda was put out by the Ministry of Information which left no one in doubt as to what were the government's aims and objectives. All opposition was considered as unpatriotic and was strongly discouraged. The government's endeavours were willingly assisted by large elements in the private sector. Many institutions and organisations, including agriculture, filled their top positions with strong, and in some instances, rabid RF supporters. This in turn gave encouragement to the introduction of increasingly repressive legislation in the name of maintenance of law and order. It also had the unfortunate effect of dividing communities and in some cases even families, particularly where individuals had the temerity to voice an opposing opinion. Our own family was a case in point: June's uncle, Huck Rudland, was elected to Parliament in 1962 as an RF member, and subsequently became a minister and signatory to the UDI declaration; he had the support of the older family members, but June and I and the majority of the younger ones were in complete disagreement.

This single act of bravado and defiance was certainly a defining one for the future of Rhodesia and all its inhabitants. It introduced UN mandatory sanctions on goods and services, travel restrictions on many individuals, and within a few months, the first incident of armed revolt. All these acts and measures were to intensify and increase during that time leading to Zimbabwe becoming what it is today. I felt at the time that UDI was the wrong decision. I still feel it was wrong, and I still maintain that an alternative approach through negotiation could have eventually led to a stable, prosperous and peaceful country, but unfortunately that did not happen.

3

Agro-Politics 1960–1980

It was at this time that my tentative beginnings in agro-politics began. I was elected onto the local intensive conservation area committee in 1960 and became chairman two years later. I was also elected a committee member of the Karoi Farmer's Association becoming vice-chairman in 1968. It was during this period that life changed. I received a telephone call one evening from the association's chairman, David Lazell, to say that the Rhodesian National Farmers' Union (RNFU) in Salisbury was looking for a representative from northern Lomagundi to serve on the grain producers association. This was one of a number of commodity committees of the RNFU whose membership was elected on a regional basis, in order that the views and concerns of all farmer members had the opportunity of being heard. Would I be prepared to serve? I initially declined, to which he responded by saying he would accept the post, and hand over the chairmanship of the farmer's association to me. I then enquired what the grain position would entail and he said a meeting in Salisbury every other month. That did not seem to be too demanding, so I agreed to serve and replaced the telephone receiver.

I quickly discovered that serving on a national committee was much more demanding than a local one, and I soon became involved in related interests, such as becoming a member of the Agriculture Research Council (ARC) and the Grain Marketing Board (GMB). In addition, with input shortages beginning to appear as a result of the implementation of UN trade sanctions, and also with the general shrinkage of farming viability, there was an increased demand to attend farmers' meetings, firstly to listen to their concerns, and secondly to report on measures being recommended and taken to try and alleviate the situation.

The structure of the RNFU was unique, in as much that every registered farmer automatically became a member. Under the legislation of the day, you were not allowed to practice farming operations unless you were licensed, and on payment of your annual licence fee, you thus became registered. The financing of the RNFU was a combination of revenues collected from the annual licence and levies imposed on commodities by the member associations, which were collected by the statutory marketing boards, and passed on to the RNFU. A large percentage of the levy was then channelled into crop research. It was a very good system, which ensured a strong viable RNFU, which was fully represented by registered commercial farmers, and was self-financing.

During this period, two other factors were having an impact on my life. Firstly, we now had two more children, Howard who was born in 1961 and Deborah who arrived in 1964. It is difficult to imagine a better environment in which to bring up four rumbustious children than a remote farm in Zimbabwe. In many respects you had to provide your own entertainment, and in this regard, we constructed a tennis court and built a swimming pool. Diana and Deborah both did their initial schooling through a correspondence scheme, where material would arrive on a weekly basis and June would take them through their learning process and return the results the following week. We would normally journey the fourteen miles to Karoi once a week, for household and farm shopping. Invariably this would turn into a social occasion, by having tea in the local café with neighbouring friends. There was also the opportunity to play tennis at the country club. Normally I would spend most of the day supervising the farm work, with June managing the household, the children and the garden. In addition, she made most of her own clothes, plus dresses for the girls. In the evening, we always set time aside to play with the children and bedtime was always a riotous routine.

After we had been on the farm for several years, we had the pleasurable prospect of mains electricity coming to the area. I was serving on a small committee who were trying to persuade the power authority – the Electricity Supply Commission (ESC) – that the district needed to be connected to the national grid in order to grow and develop and that in turn would be of benefit to the country. After a number of meetings and written memorandums, the ESC finally agreed to bring in a connecting line from the Mangula mine area, a distance of some forty miles, provided that every farmer along the proposed route would pay a connecting fee in advance and would agree to the monthly tariff. Eventually, everyone signed up, except Alan Bunnet, who was at the very end of the proposed line. He had just arrived on the farm and claimed he was not in a position to afford such a luxury as electricity. At this point the scheme faltered. However, in the end, we got it back on track by persuading the ESC to begin the connecting work against a written undertaking by Alan that he would agree to be connected the following year. There was great excitement in the district when work commenced; within a short space of time the connection had been completed and we were given a switch-on date. In anticipation of this, June and I bought an electric stove and fridge, and had the house wired to receive power. When the day arrived, we invited Alan to come and have dinner with us to share the joyful experience. This he duly did but to our great consternation at about 7.30 that evening, we had a power failure. After waiting an embarrassingly long time, we realised that the power would not return and as it was too late to start up the wood burning stove, we ate sandwiches by candlelight. I am afraid we had to bear Alan's hilarious comments about the advantages of electricity with very little defence. To crown the whole evening, the lights suddenly came on at two in the morning, and lit up the whole house like a fairground, as we had gone to bed and forgotten to turn the switches off.

It was also at this time that the first armed excursions into the community occurred. This had a growing impact on the lives of most people in the country for the next fourteen years. The first official acknowledgement of an armed incident was recorded in 1966 when a small group who styled themselves as the 'Crocodile Group' struck in the east of the country. From then onwards, slowly at first, but increasing in numbers and ferocity, the armed struggle spread to many areas. It began obviously in the border districts, but soon infiltrated right into the centre of the country. I, like many in my age group, was a member of the Police Reserve, whose initial role was as a back-up for the regular police force, and to take on duties such as manning roadblocks. It was not long, however, before our blue uniforms were replaced by camouflage fatigues and our batons and shields exchanged for rifles and field radios. This led to many disruptions of ordinary life; call-ups for duties were taking people from their farms and places of work for periods of two to six weeks at a time. Also, if there was a localised emergency you would be called immediately. Duties were not confined to men only; most farmers' wives also volunteered to serve in the women's section and took on responsibilities as wireless operators and police station orderlies.

These years were particularly hard on the womenfolk, as they were expected to play a positive role in the country's defence. They had little alternative but to accept the responsibilities of keeping the farms operating, and still try and project the sense of a normal life and security to their young children. To their credit, most of them achieved all three goals with great courage and fortitude, but I sometimes wondered whether their efforts and successes received the due recognition and appreciation they deserved from the government and those conducting the war campaign.

Despite many successes, dealing with over border attacks, and assurances from the various commanders that we were winning, the reality on the ground was different. I am convinced that if there had not been a political settlement in December 1979, the armed struggle would have intensified, and eventually the country would have been controlled by the ZANLA and ZIPRA forces.[1] These were the two armed bodies representing the two political parties, the Zimbabwe African National Union (ZANU) and the Zimbabwe African People's Union (ZAPU), the former broadly supported by the Chinese and the latter by the Russians. This in turn would have probably led to inter-party conflict, using their respective armed forces in order to achieve domination.

My involvement with agricultural bodies and affairs was also taking up more of my time, necessitating longer absences from the farm. In 1972, I was elected vice-chairman of the Grain Producers Association (GPA) under the chairmanship of Keith Kirkman. I was extremely fortunate in having him as my chairman as he was one of those gifted individuals who had an analytical brain and was always able to express himself clearly and concisely. He was a Rhodes Scholar and an expert farmer, both as a crop producer and livestock manager. I felt he could have been the greatest of all farming leaders if he had not decided to ease himself out of agricultural politics, and turn his attention more to the commercial support services such as fertiliser companies, seed houses, co-operatives and banking.

In 1974, accompanied by our executive officer, Jack Revolta,

---

1 Zimbabwe African National Liberation Army and Zimbabwe People's Revolutionary Army.

we made a trip to the United States via South America to acquaint ourselves with up-to-date production techniques. It was an interesting, educational tour which took place mainly in the mid-west. Not only did we have the advantage of staying on farms and discussing farming issues with farming groups; we also visited the agricultural faculties at both Ames and Purdue universities. Also of interest were the floors of the commodity exchanges in Chicago, where we acquired a small glimpse of price movements and trading, which was foreign to us living in a country with a controlled marketing system. One impression that amazed us was the lack of knowledge people had regarding Rhodesia. In general, our hosts were well acquainted with events in Europe and the Far East, but Africa was less well known or understood. This meant having to do a great deal of explaining regarding the cultural, economic, political and even the sporting aspects of our country, and sometimes led to humorous exchanges. One such was when we were invited to attend a presentation given by the Kansas state agricultural advisory body to a group of farmers from Oklahoma. As a sign of courtesy, we were introduced to the audience as special guests from Rhodesia and were invited to stand up so that the local farmers could see us. After the presentation, the chairman invited questions from the audience and gave an assurance that the panel would answer any questions. To our amusement the first question asked was, 'Where is Rhodesia?' This occasioned much head shaking and many blank looks from the top table. However, one of the farmers, still wearing his Stetson, stood up and said, 'I know!' to which Keith Kirkman quickly replied, 'Well, you tell them.' So, he said, 'Man, it is south of Ethiopia.' To which Keith, chuckling, responded, 'You've got it dead right.'

On another occasion we were entertained at a baseball game in an enormous stadium in front of a huge crowd. It was a new experience but with a few explanations from our hosts, we soon understood the gist of the game. However, there was a gigantic screen which, apart from updating the audience on the state of play and the current score, flashed messages announcing couples with forthcoming nuptials, special anniversaries, births and other such family news; each item being greeted with rapturous applause. One of our hosts, who was watching the screen with a deepening frown on his forehead, excused himself for a few minutes after the match. When he returned he apologised and said he had previously asked the screen presenters to flash a message welcoming his special guests. However, it had never appeared: the reason was they did not know how to spell Rhodesia.

After we left the USA, we flew to Austria where we joined a larger team of delegates from the RNFU. The team, led by the president, Mike Butler, attended the International Federation of Agricultural Producers (IFAP). We were members of this organisation, though regrettably on past occasions had been banned from attending due to the UN sanctions policy. Many of our delegates had their wives with them and I had the pleasure of June joining me the day after I arrived. The conference gave our team a wonderful opportunity to interact with farmers from many countries. Of particular interest to me was the National Farmers Union from Britain, which was led by Henry Plumb, whom I had not met since I played cricket against him when he represented the Warwickshire Hunt Cricket Team and I occasionally turned out for the Bicester Hunt side in the early 1950s. We also felt at home as the chairman of IFAP was Albert Basson from South Africa, who was also leading a large delegation of farmers. For many of us, it was our first visit to Vienna and I found both the city and the country charming. After the comparative austerity of sanctioned Rhodesia, the shops and restaurants were dazzling harbours of many delights. A visit to the opera house, which was built in the nineteenth century, to watch a performance of Beethoven's *Fidelio* in splendid surroundings, was an unforgettable experience. We also visited the Schönbrunn and Belvedere palaces, went to St Stephens' Cathedral and had a wonderful evening watching an outstanding performance at the Spanish Riding School. The woes and worries of Rhodesia were forgotten for a brief period. When the conference ended, June and I met up with Sheila Roberts, a friend from Karoi who was visiting her German partner Kurt in the little town of Passau on the German/ Austrian border. They kindly took us on a week's tour down the Danube Valley where we visited many charming little towns and drank the new green wine.

In 1974, I succeeded Keith Kirkman as chairman of the Grain Producers Association (GPA) and was fortunate enough to have a superb vice-chairman in the person of Strath Brown, a highly successful farmer, and a large, very straightforward man. (His father, incidentally, was James Brown who had assisted me with credit from the Farmers' Co-op.) Under the RNFU constitution, the commodity chairman had a seat on their council, which was comprised of representatives from both the commodities' and the regional branches. The presidency of the RNFU had been taken over by Paddy Millar, who had previously been chairman of the GPA from 1970 to 1972. Paddy served the farming community in many guises over the years, and also had a brief spell in parliament, representing the Mazoe constituency.

Under the RNFU constitution the president could only serve two one-year terms of office, a decision taken in the 1960s to prevent an individual monopolising the position, which had happened in the past. During Paddy Millar's term, he decided to move the annual conference out of Salisbury to demonstrate that the RNFU was truly national. As a consequence, in 1975, it was held in Bulawayo. There was a minor disruption in the hierarchy at that time because Dougie Lyon, the vice-president, decided he did not want to take on the presidency the following year, and so retired from the post.

As his views only became known just before the conference, a huge amount of lobbying took place to find a suitable candidate. With the concurrence of a few councillors, I suggested that John Strong, who was representing the Rhodesia Tobacco Association, would be an excellent choice. June and I therefore took him and his wife Margaret out to dinner and put the proposition to him. As I expected he rejected it out of hand: firstly, I think, because the proposition came as a big surprise and he had had no time to prepare his thoughts; and secondly, he had set his sights on becoming the president of the Zimbabwe Tobacco Association the following year. After much discussion, John agreed to stand, but was sceptical as to whether he would attract sufficient votes from the council to become elected, especially as he was reluctant to canvas on his own behalf. As it was, the position was for vice-president rather than president. I offered to talk to some of the council members and get their opinions in advance of the forthcoming congress. In the event, John was duly proposed and seconded, and as no other candidates were put forward, he was duly elected. He quickly proved to be a wise choice, as he was an extremely hard-working vice-president.

As a result, at the congress the following year in Umtali, he was unanimously elected to follow Paddy Millar as president, which meant that again the position of vice-president was open. I stood against Jeff Perlman and managed to win by a small margin. So, having served on the RNFU Council for two years as the chairman of the GPA, I was elected as vice-president of the RNFU in 1976. This was not only a great honour, but also an enormous challenge, as apart from the declining viability in the farming sector, there was an escalation in the armed struggle within the country. The RNFU had to balance the needs of the farming industry against a growing demand for financial resources to circumvent economic sanctions, and also to meet the requirements of the military. RNFU representatives had to interact with the farmers on a more regular basis, in order to ensure we were kept aware of the severity of the security situation, and thus able to accurately report back to the decision makers in government. This meant much travelling around the country, and leaving one's own farm for extended periods.

In order to meet this requirement, we started to use light aircraft which enabled us to travel greater distances, often to meet small groups of farmers in remote areas, and also provided us with a greater feeling of safety – or so we thought! This safety issue was something of an illusion. I recall a group of us left Salisbury to fly to an area in the lowveld called Mkwasine to meet a group of cotton farmers who were not only having a tough time on the security side but were suffering from unusually heavy rain. We flew down to the area in a Dakota aircraft, in fairly reasonable weather. Unfortunately, the local grass landing field had received continuous rain for twenty-nine days, and towards the end of our landing run, there was a sudden severe lurch and one wheel disappeared into the ground, resulting in the other wheel pointing towards the sky. However, help soon arrived in the form of farm tractors – some of which shared the same fate as the Dakota – and pick-up trucks, and we were all transported to the local community centre where the business of my visit commenced. Flying during the rainy season in Zimbabwe is always an exciting experience as there is usually a great deal of turbulence, so it is not recommended for those who suffer from travel sickness.

Another difficulty can be navigational. On one occasion, June and I were invited again to the Lowveld area, this time to meet cattle ranchers, who were also under severe pressure. When we arrived at Charles Prince airport, the cloud cover was very low, but our pilot assured us it would soon lift and we would be fine. Halfway through our journey, it had intensified and visibility as far as I could assess was almost nil. However, the pilot, as cheerful as ever, told us not to worry, as he estimated our position as approximately overhead a place called Katenga which had large railway marshalling yards. He said if he reduced altitude, he would probably be able to pick up the railway line to Beitbridge, and he would be able to follow it as our landing strip was adjacent to the line. He duly followed this procedure and gave a whoop of joy when he pointed out of the window to a railway line below. June and I smiled, relaxed and thought our problems were over. After quite a long time, our pilot began to show some anxiety, and kept craning his head out of the side window. He suddenly threw the aircraft into a sharp turn and announced we were well into Mozambique, which was at that time a very hostile country. He had mistakenly identified the wrong railway line and was following the one to Maputo. Again, we finally made it to our correct destination.

Another incident was when I had been invited to speak at Fort Victoria Senior School prize-giving and June had been asked to present the prizes. As this was an evening function, we left late in the afternoon. Unfortunately, before we arrived, darkness had fallen and the small airport had no landing lights. The resourceful community quickly resolved the problem by getting a large number of toilet rolls, soaking them in paraffin, putting them in tins and placing them alight along the landing strip; they worked perfectly.

I mentioned the unpleasantness caused by turbulence. On one occasion John Strong and I had been to a rural area, accompanied by Mark Partridge, the Minister of Agriculture, and Ted Osborn, the Permanent Secretary. During our flight, we went through some very stormy weather, which had a bad effect on poor Ted, who desperately looked around for a sick bag but without success. However, he did hold the Ministers' briefcase on his lap, so he quickly opened it and deposited what was worrying him into it, before closing it again. When we landed there was a government car to meet Minister Partridge, who climbed in and asked Ted if he had his briefcase? Ted solemnly handed it over and the car drove off; I never did hear the aftermath of that incident.

During this difficult period there was a steady escalation of the armed struggle which made farming increasingly precarious and placed a greater strain on the RNFU to placate worried farmers and ensure that their essential livelihood could continue unabated. I was extremely fortunate at that time in having alongside me such a fine character as John Strong. He was always cool and calm and had the ability to quickly quell potentially flammable situations and recommend solutions. Moreover, over all the years we worked together in many spheres of agricultural activity, we never had a single major disagreement. I could say the same about my successor David Spain, also an excellent man, who soon after independence in 1980 was tragically killed in a car crash along with his wife and daughter. Former presidents of the RNFU, plus many commodity and provincial chairmen, all made significant contributions towards the viability of the agricultural sector, while simultaneously endeavouring to ensure the security of the rural areas. Their efforts often impacted adversely on their own farming enterprises, and placed a great pressure on their individual finances, as usually their time and effort were given on a voluntary basis, with little or no financial recompense.

Within the country, the political debate on the future was now beginning to boil over. From the early 1970s, meetings and discussions were taking place both inside and outside Rhodesia and the views of the private sector organisations were being sought. The Rhodesian National Farmers Union, in an attempt to look forward and stabilise the agricultural industry, drew up its own land reform proposals. Here, it was conceded that land would have to be made available for emerging black farmers. The proposition was launched at a press briefing in the Monomatapa Hotel in 1977 and written up in *The Farmer*.[2] We also sent copies of the paper to overseas governments; and John Strong, Jeff Perlman and myself were given time on Rhodesian television to explain our thoughts. On reflection, the proposals were short on detail and long on intent, and, as we had expected, were not well received by the Rhodesian Front (RF) government, who at best viewed our suggestions as gross interference, and at worst, treachery. However, we had, as a national body, clearly stated our views.

Soon afterwards, John Strong, accompanied by Giles Dorward, President of the Rhodesian Tobacco Association (RTA), flew to Switzerland to be on hand during the 1976 Geneva Conference, chaired by Ivor Richards, the UK Permanent Representative to the UN. This was quickly followed by me taking a small delegation comprising David Hamilton and Gordon Herrington, a very competent staff member of the RNFU, to Kenya to study the land transfer scheme which had taken place there. Our visit was facilitated by the Foreign Office in London, who not only provided a senior staff member in the High Commission to take care of us, but also made all the internal arrangements regarding travel and accommodation. Because of the sanctions situation, we had to fly first to Johannesburg in order to get a flight to Nairobi. We had a major setback before we left Salisbury as David Hamilton had his briefcase stolen, within which he had his passport. After a few telephone calls to the British High Commission in Pretoria, it was arranged that all three of us would fly to South Africa, where David would be issued with a new passport, though it would not be available until the following day. So, Gordon and I left him overnight in Johannesburg to follow us the next day.

On our arrival, we were met by a representative of the British High Commission, who said he had a car waiting to take us to our hotel. However, on presentation of our passports at the immigration

2   10 June 1977.

counter, we were asked to stand aside. When the immigration official had finished processing all the other passengers, he informed us that we were under detention, as Rhodesian citizens were not permitted to enter Kenya, so we would be put on a south-bound aircraft which was leaving in three hours' time. Naturally, we protested loudly, but he was adamant and would not budge. Our newfound friend from the British High Commission attempted to intercede on our behalf, but also without success. He then informed the official that he would telephone the chief immigration officer in Nairobi, and was told to go ahead but, in the meantime, Gordon and I would be placed in a secure room. Fortunately for us, the only room available with strong locks was apparently the bar, to which we were escorted and duly locked inside. Again, fortune favoured us, as he also left behind the barman – an oversight which I am sure was not intended. We spent the next six hours incarcerated in our bar room prison, while the High Commission tried to sort out the confusion. The barman, despite showing signs of weariness, seemed happy to serve us drinks against our signatures. Eventually, the problem was resolved by the personal intervention of the Minister of Home Affairs, Daniel Arap Moi – later to become president of Kenya – who had authorised our entry in the first place, but no one in the immigration department had thought to inform the airport, so the officer on duty was not prepared to take a risk.

Although the whole episode was both frustrating and wearying, it finished on an amicable note, as the poor representative from the High Commission, who had spent a very considerable time contacting various heads of departments, had finally spoken to the minister just after midnight when the order for our release had come through. That having been done, the High Commissioner's representative told the immigration official that if he had used his common sense and called the minister earlier, we could all have left the airport hours before. This prompted the quick response that if the British representative had been duty immigration officer at Heathrow airport, would he have phoned Jim Callaghan late on a Sunday evening, saying, 'I have two IRA members trying to sneak into England'? This reply brought much laughter and the barman was immediately pressed into duty again, while we all toasted each other's health, and wished our respective countries the greatest of success.

Entry apart, our visit was successful, and we had the land reform scheme explained to us. This was the scheme in which a million acres of formally white-owned farms were acquired for black resettlement. We also had discussions with both black and white farmers and we were given an insight into the horticultural industry, which, although still in its infancy, was rapidly developing markets in Europe for both fruit and flowers. This form of farming production was later to become a major and valuable addition to Zimbabwe's export portfolio of commodities. We also met a number of government ministers, officials, industrialists, bankers and others. By chance we also met Mr Ivor Richards who was in Nairobi on his way down to Rhodesia to see if he could re-start the stalled Geneva Conference. Our conclusions were that although the two countries, Rhodesia and Kenya, were not exactly the same, and there were many areas of difference, there was enough information available to encourage us to believe there was still room to negotiate with the nationalist parties on the land issue. On our return to Salisbury, I reported our findings to P. K. van der Byl, who was the Minister of Foreign Affairs, and much to my surprise, I was listened to with great interest.

In 1979, I paid a visit to London accompanied by Jack Humphreys who was the RNFU's Chief Executive Officer, and George Foot who was our Public Relations Officer. I could not have wished for two better people to support me in an attempt to convince external decision-makers that there were options worth considering on the Rhodesian land issue; it did not necessarily have to remain with no concessions, neither did it have to be totally conceded. But more importantly, post settlement – and we were convinced there had to be a settlement – the best chance of resurrecting the country's economy would be through an expanding and viable agricultural industry. Again, we met many people and on the whole were courteously received. David Owen was the Secretary of State for Foreign Affairs, who I felt initially viewed us with a certain amount of suspicion. During a lengthy discussion on the land issue, I obviously made a remark which caused him great annoyance, as he jumped to his feet, and in no uncertain language, ordered me to leave his office. There were a number of Foreign Office officials present who also rose, and I could feel their embarrassment and noticed their awkwardness. Poor Jack Humphreys and I left with as much dignity as we could muster, and wondered what I had said to trigger such a reaction. Later in the day, David Owen phoned me at my hotel, and told me he was leaving that evening for America, to hold discussions with Andy Young, the United States Ambassador to the United Nations. He went on to say he would be returning the following day and would I be so kind as to go and see him. In way of response, I asked if there was any point in a further meeting. He replied by saying there was something I ought to know. He asked if I could come alone, and assured me that there would be no one else present. The following afternoon, I duly retraced my steps to the Foreign and Commonwealth Office, and was quickly ushered into his presence. He was absolutely charming and showed none of the traces of anger which he had displayed the previous day. He began the meeting by asking if I was aware that the leader of the opposition, Mrs Thatcher, had moved a motion of no confidence in the government. When I assured him that I was indeed aware of this motion, he went on to say that there would be a debate in the House, which the government would win – which they did not. In the event of the motion being carried, Parliament would be dissolved and a general election called, which the Labour Party would win – which they did not. But whatever the outcome of these political manoeuvres, it was unlikely that we would meet again as he was leaving his position as Secretary of State. He said the information he had given me was confidential, and apart from his wife, he had told nobody else, including the prime minister. We parted company on a very friendly and cordial note, with him wishing Rhodesia generally, and me personally, all success in the future. I tried to reciprocate my best wishes to him, but I was totally bemused as to why I should be privy to such a sensitive piece of information. I did meet him subsequently in other capacities, and again I always found him polite, courteous and charming, and that strange conversation was never referred to again.

In the meantime, there were many domestic issues which needed attention. The armed struggle had spread and intensified, and this was placing an enormous strain on the social communities, as it was not only the armed forces who were suffering casualties, but many civilians were also being wounded or killed, some in the most horrifying circumstances. This in turn was also showing signs of reducing public and farming morale. It was against this background that I succeeded John Strong as the RNFU's president. John had been a very bold and imaginative leader of the farming community, and for two very tempestuous years had guided the industry through a worsening security situation exacerbated by increasing time spent on call-up duties, severe shortages of vital imports and the denial of open overseas markets for our agricultural products. With the knowledge that Rhodesia would have to change in the near future, we had changed our name during the course of 1979 to the Commercial Farmers Union (CFU). There were a few isolated protests, but we opted to create a new identity of our own choice, rather than delay the decision, and then have to quickly devise a name to fit the future circumstances. My vice-president was David Spain – a former president of the Cotton Association – and we had joined the Council on the same day. Not only had we worked closely together but we shared the same views on politics and our faith in the country. The Union had now become the symbol of hope for many farmers which meant that David and I virtually became engaged full time in Union matters, in between our lengthening periods on call-up duties. We were ably supported by Jack Humphreys and his assistant Stan Ball, plus a very dedicated team of councillors.

The RF government had long realised that in order to win the conflict they had to win over the hearts and minds of the local people. In this regard, despite determined efforts by the Ministry of Information, the whole programme can only be described as a miserable failure. A concept was then taken up of power sharing between the races, in which both whites and blacks would serve in the government. In order to bring this about an election was held which brought together the United African National Council (UANC) under the leadership of Bishop Muzorewa, and the Rhodesian Front still led by Ian Smith. The election in February 1979 was boycotted by both the ZANU and ZAPU parties who considered the scheme to be a sham and one that did not address the major problem of universal adult suffrage. The new government that was formed was called the Government of Zimbabwe Rhodesia and all major portfolios were allocated two ministers – one white and one black. Structurally, this was an unworkable arrangement and it had no chance of success. In addition, the international community did not recognise the new government, so in effect, as a country we were treading water and slowly sinking.

With the expansion of the armed struggle, which primarily took place in the farming districts, the financial demands on the government continued to grow. This in turn meant that in order to survive, cuts had to be made in the supply of essential goods, and savings had to be sought in national expenditure. These twin programmes severely hampered the ability of many farmers to remain in business, which only added to the deteriorating security situation, and presented a very bleak picture for most farming families. These pressures placed an enormous burden on the CFU, whose main task was to represent the needs of its members, and this essentially meant trying to ensure there was a sufficient supply of basic farm inputs, i.e. fuel, fertilizer, seed and crop chemicals to be available at the right time and at an affordable price. And then to negotiate a price with the statutory marketing boards for a fair return on the commodities to be sold. Most of the major commodities, with the exception of tobacco, were marketed through government appointed marketing boards. The process of arriving at a price was often protracted, usually painful, and always disappointing. The various commodity committees would prepare their case for a seasonal price, based on cost of production, market indications, and other variable considerations. After due reflection, tripartite meetings would take place between the heads of the marketing boards, the commodity chairman accompanied by the president and vice-president of the CFU, and the minister and senior officials from the Ministry of Agriculture. In conclusion, a price for the current intake of crops and livestock would be announced, and usually a pre-planting price for the coming season: this was a guaranteed minimum level that farmers could expect to receive for the coming year. Basically, the system was sound and provided all parties equal opportunities to participate, but the final say always lay with the minister who had to gain approval at cabinet level. As the security situation in the country worsened, and the various diplomatic initiatives stalled, the harder it became to persuade government to make adequate provision for farming produce, when there was a growing demand for military support services and hardware. At times, we in the farming community began to feel we were being taken for granted on the assumption that we would always be there, because, for many of us, there was no alternative. Faced with this dilemma, I and other council members spent much of our time either trying to persuade those in government to be more considerate of the farmer's plight, or attending and addressing farmer association meetings, trying to assure them that their concerns were being addressed, and give them as much support as we could to continue with their farming programmes. Experience had shown that no matter how tough the negotiations were, an agreement was always reached which was moderately acceptable to both parties, and ensured that farming continued for another season.

However, in March 1979, the situation dramatically changed when the prices offered to the farming community were at such a low level as to be rejected. This situation had never arisen before, and it led to an open confrontation between the farming unions and government, with many farmers openly threatening to stop producing altogether, and others advocating abandoning their land and moving into the towns. Obviously, this situation had to be avoided at all costs and I, as president of the CFU, found myself as spokesman and leader of the country's farmers. Mark Partridge, a professional accountant, was the Minister of Agriculture, and along with his co-Minister Joel Mandaza, produced a set of prices and pre-planting prices based on economic models which proved that the average farmer could make a small profit. The flaw in using the models, as I perceived them, was that they may have been economically sound, but they did not take into account extraneous issues, such as security and weather – that year we were suffering one of our periodical droughts – which were severely hampering farmers' attempts to maximise performance. The other factor which we used to counter the governments' proposal was that in all our models only a third of farmers could be classified as average; in other words, two-thirds were considered below average. Could they, we argued, be expected to accept an offer below, or well below, their production and labour costs? The two ministers, however, countered by saying that given the country's severe financial constraints, it was unreasonable to expect the government to subsidise the farmers. I challenged this by stating that we were not looking for subsidies, but that we did expect to get a fair return for our produce. I argued that it would be cheaper for the government to pay the farmer a realistic price for his produce, a move which would keep him on the land and subsidise the consumer, thus avoiding expensive food imports. The latter, I argued, would in effect mean that we would be subsidising farmers in countries other than our own, which made no logical sense. Unfortunately, these arguments did not find favour and for the first time ever, there was a stand-off between government and the farming community.

Once the official announcement was made, I issued a press statement rejecting all the government's suggested prices and asked them to reconsider their offer. As expected, this request was rejected. My next move was to organise an open farmers' meeting in Salisbury and explain my reaction to the government's offer. I invited the ministers and their officials to attend in order for them to explain their position to a larger audience, but this invitation was declined. The meeting was scheduled to take place at 9.30 a.m. at Meikles Hotel on Tuesday 22 May. In the meantime, my staff were inundated with advice from all quarters, some of it encouraging, some of it very unhelpful, and some outright hostile. A number of well-meaning, influential citizens contacted me saying I had made my point and now was the time to gracefully accept the government's offer. They reasoned that finally no one can take on the government and win, and as I would emerge as the loser, my ability to lead in the future would be seriously damaged and my position in society would be permanently destroyed.

I realised the risks I was taking, both to my own reputation and to the status of the CFU as a credible national organisation, but at the time I felt very strongly about the pricing issue, and knew that if I did not attempt to improve the offer, I would have failed the farming community. I had also received a flood of supportive messages from individuals and farming communities urging me to stand my ground, which strengthened my resolve. We estimated that maybe between 200 and 250 farmers would attend, but much to our surprise, and to the dismay of hotel staff, nearly 500 irate farmers arrived. Allowing reasoned debate, while at the same time trying to control the emotions of some of the more vocal members of the audience, posed a challenging task. I began the meeting by inviting each of the commodity chairmen to explain the case they had presented to the ministry, and then give their assessment of what the government offer would mean to their members. Once the explanations had been made, I opened the debate to the floor to give an opportunity to the farmers to state their views, and to put it politely, they were not shy in doing so, with many of them receiving thunderous applause for their remarks. To bring the meeting to a close, we on the Council had prepared a resolution, calling on government to meet with us again, and renegotiate the prices. This resolution was proposed by my vice-president David Spain, who spoke calmly, eloquently and with deep feeling, and much to the relief of all of us on the platform, it was passed unanimously. Having got our mandate to renegotiate, the next step was to get the ministry to agree to meet us on the issue. Unfortunately, Mark Partridge was not prepared to do so, but the deadlock was solved by the Prime Minister, Ian Smith, who made a senior cabinet re-shuffle, moving Mark Partridge to another portfolio and making Bill Irvine the Minister of Agriculture. The latter was a tough, tricky character, who had a reputation as a no-nonsense man. I bumped into Ian Smith the day after these ministerial changes had taken place, and he chuckled when he saw me, and wondered how I would get on with the new minister. The answer to that question was not long in coming as Bill Irvine immediately asked me to see him on his own, with no staff from either side present. During that initial meeting, he was extremely blunt, and said he was prepared to look at our proposals again, but once he had made his decision, that would be final; there would be no more discussion, and no more high-profile meetings. I thanked him sincerely for this offer to re-present our case and said that was all I, or the farmers, were requesting. Meetings duly took place and the outcome was a small increase in the price for the current crops, and an enlarged increase in the pre-planting price for the coming crop, which was at a sufficient level to encourage farmers to continue farming. These new prices were accepted and what had become a very tense stand-off came to an end, which was a great relief both to me and the farming community. I believe that relief was also shared by other sectors of the country, who had been watching what had become a high-profile dispute with a certain amount of alarm and trepidation.

In the meantime, the war continued to escalate with the insurgents greatly assisted by the territorial aid they were receiving from Mozambique and Zambia. This enabled them to construct sophisticated military bases ever closer to the Zimbabwe Rhodesian border. Although these bases did suffer from heavy air and ground attacks, they were not totally eliminated and continued to be used for strike raids into the country, causing major disruptions in certain areas. Further to that problem, the Zimbabwe Rhodesian forces were severely hampered and constrained by the virtual total withdrawal of South Africa's material, financial and moral assistance. To all intents and purposes, the country was on its own.

In August 1979, the Commonwealth Heads of Government Meeting was held in Lusaka, where once again the question of Rhodesia and its future was debated. It was proposed that yet another attempt should be made to try and construct an acceptable, workable constitution for the country. Although many people felt that the newly elected British Prime Minister, Margaret Thatcher, was only lukewarm, she agreed to support the idea of a constitutional conference that would be held in September at Lancaster House in London, to which all major political parties would be invited. This included the UANC led by Bishop Abel Muzorewa; the RF led by Ian Smith; ZANU led by Robert Mugabe and ZAPU led by Joshua Nkomo. On the surface this looked like a volatile and toxic mix, with little hope of success. But to many observers, it was considered to be the last chance to obtain a reasonable agreement which would satisfy or pacify all political shades of opinion, despite in many quarters hopes not being very high. However, no one had reckoned on the calibre and determination of the conference chairman, the British Secretary of State for Foreign and Commonwealth Affairs, Lord Carrington. He was a person who did not suffer fools and who assembled a very capable team of both politicians and officials in order to make a serious attempt at ensuring a successful conclusion to the conference.

The private sector in Zimbabwe Rhodesia felt that a presence in London, through which views could be advanced, could be of use to the negotiating parties. As a result, Jim van Heerden, representing commerce and industry, and I, representing farming and agriculture, were invited to go. There was excitement and apprehension in the air. We were given many opportunities to express our points of view, both separately and together. My closest contact at the time was with David Smith, who was the Zimbabwe Rhodesia Minister of Finance, and deputy to Ian Smith in the RF delegation. Jim van Heerden and I had many meetings with businessmen and organisations, who were all showing great interest in the security of future investments in the country. Although we did not hold any official position, we did have discussions with a number of quasi-political organisations, NGOs and other groups interested in health and education, such as the Red Cross, who were all trying to assess what the potential was likely to be, in the event of a constitutional agreement being reached. We also held talks with UANC delegates, but not with those of ZANU or ZAPU for the simple reason that we were not invited to do so. Due to the delicate nature of the main talks, we felt it would be unwise, and probably misinterpreted, if we were seen to be holding discussions without instructions or a clear mandate to do so. We later learned that a few individuals did try and make contact with representatives from the two nationalist parties, only to be severely rebuffed by both parties for their efforts. Unofficially and always socially, I did see a little of George Smith, who was a senior civil servant, when we used to meet for a drink and a chat at a pub called The Turks Head. Here, we would discuss the home scene and enjoy talking about matters of mutual interest such as sport, but never once did he ever pass on confidential information. He went on to become Secretary to the Cabinet, and then later a prominent and respected judge.

After two weeks with no sign of a resolution in sight, I saw no point in remaining in London, and flew home. The talks dragged on, with rumours alternating between possible success and complete breakdown. I was kept fully updated by Bill Irvine, who was not only Minister of Agriculture but also one of the most senior RF members in Salisbury during the period of the talks and who was in daily contact with London, and gave me his views on the progress or lack thereof, as he interpreted the information. Soon after my return, I was invited to address the South Africa Farmers Union at their annual conference in Natal. It was while I was there with June that I read press reports to the effect that I was in London, as the talks were now focusing on the land issue. Jack Humphreys, director of the CFU, phoned from Salisbury to say that the views of the Union were being sought and could I get over there as quickly as possible. I left my wife to fly back to Salisbury and I took the overnight flight to London.

The reason for my return visit to the Lancaster House talks was to try and present a favourable case for land reform. Most issues concerning a new constitution for the country had appeared to have reached a workable consensus, but land ownership was still being debated in a fairly hostile manner. Opinions between the negotiating parties moved between two extremes, from, 'all land belonged to the State', to 'maintaining the status quo'. On arriving I was met by Rowan Cronje, one of the RF ministers in Ian Smith's team who was very concerned that if a solution could not be quickly found then the talks could well fail and lead to a rapid escalation of the bush war. The CFU had produced a position paper, endorsed by its members, suggesting that an option for land transfer could be based on willing seller, willing buyer. We were convinced that if such a scheme were written into the new independence agreement, and sufficient funds were made available by international donors, then many white farmers would avail themselves of the scheme and a sizeable portion of land would quickly become released for resettlement purposes on whatever basis an incoming government were to decide. The difficulty was that time was running out, and acceptance of a land reform scheme, which was both feasible and affordable, was urgently being sought.

During the next two weeks, I held numerous meetings with delegates from both the RF and the UANC delegates, plus I met with a number of individuals and organisations within the British government who were keen to see an agreement reached. These included the deputy Prime Minister William Whitelaw; the PM's private secretary Charles Powell and Sir Ian Gilmore, a senior member of the British negotiating team, who all undertook to convey my views and thoughts to the prime minister herself. I also addressed The Tory Reform Group and The Monday Club, a conservative pressure group, and in addition gave a number of press interviews. I returned home after two hectic weeks, having been given ample opportunity to present the views of the CFU and with a feeling that the talks were now nearing an agreement; one that hopefully gave confidence to all sectors of society.

On my departure, I noticed among certain delegates a feeling of quiet optimism. Certainly no one was openly talking of a breakthrough, but some of the British delegates were looking less harassed. Within the Rhodesian team there seemed to be a little more spark. It was certainly evident with the likes of David Smith, Rowan Cronje and Chris Andersen, although Ian Smith's expression remained as inscrutable as ever. I was, therefore, delighted when I later learned of the establishment of a fund, which would be funded jointly by the governments of Britain, the United States, Canada and the Nordic states amongst others. The aims and objectives of the fund were to assist the new Zimbabwe to balance economic and social development within the country. Part of that re-balancing exercise was the acquisition of under-utilised land for settlement for further agricultural purposes. It went on to state that acquisition would only be lawful if adequate compensation was promptly paid. In the cases of dispute, the person(s) whose property was so acquired would be guaranteed the right of access to the High Court to determine the amounts of compensation to be paid. These proposals and conditions were then applied to the willing seller willing buyer scheme, which would enable the new government to acquire land coming on to the market. Additionally, it was envisaged that from the fund, monies would also be made available to assist the incoming farmers to establish themselves on a viable basis.

When a constitutional agreement was finally reached in December, after many weeks of negotiations, it took many people by surprise. The talks had gone on for so long that it looked as if an agreement would be impossible. Again, those twin feelings of excitement and apprehension were being felt, but I think the overall view of the white community was one of wait and see. However, after that, events moved very quickly: a general election was scheduled for 14 February; there were to be twenty seats reserved for white voters out of a total of 100 assembly seats; likewise, there would be ten reserved seats for whites out of a total of forty in the Senate. Assembly points were to be established throughout the country where freedom fighters from both liberation armies were expected to register, but they would be allowed to retain their weapons. Certain elements of the British army and Commonwealth forces were to be deployed to assist with this operation. The whole election and de-commissioning exercise was to be overseen by a British Governor General, to be appointed by Great Britain. The choice of Lord Soames, although not initially welcomed by everyone, turned out to be inspirational. He was polite and courteous to everyone, but he was also tough and firm and he pursued his duties with great energy and enthusiasm. In addition, he was a big man who had an impressive bearing, which quickly earned him the respect of many people and communities with which he had to deal. He was more than adequately supported by his charming wife Mary, who quickly endeared herself to all those with whom she came into contact. They made a great team and much of the credit for what followed in the next few months was entirely due to them.

The mechanism for holding the election was quickly put into place, and electioneering and canvassing got underway. All the nationalist leaders returned to the country with varying degrees of popular support. The last to arrive was Robert Mugabe, who was greeted by a crowd which was estimated by some to be a million strong; whatever the correct number, it was certainly impressive and certainly outnumbered all others. Despite reports of violent incidents in certain areas, on the whole the campaign seemed to take place fairly smoothly. The Governor General had the right to proscribe any individual or party if in his opinion he or it was in danger of derailing or seriously disrupting the election. From recollection, Enos Nkala was the only person so punished. He was barred from standing because of his antagonistic and extreme views and his disregard for protocol which was deemed to be detrimental to the whole election process. Although he had delayed his arrival, Robert Mugabe quickly got his campaign into top gear. One of the measures he took was to seek meetings with leaders of the private sector. He began these discussions with the CFU. So, at his invitation, I went to meet him in February 1980 accompanied by the ever-supportive Jack Humphreys. He greeted us by introducing a team of five of his senior supporters, with the opening remark: 'Has just come from...' and concluded with Dar es Salaam, or Maputo or somewhere. The last person in the line was Maurice Nyagumbo, but having shaken his hand, there was silence. I then asked him where he had come from and he replied, 'Salisbury prison,' to which I stammered, 'Oh, never mind, where were you before that?' And to my embarrassment, he said, 'Pretoria prison'. At this point I felt it prudent to ask no more questions.

Nyagumbo was an old-fashioned nationalist who had become an activist at a very early age. He spent part of his early working life in the hotel industry in Cape Town, where he was constantly in trouble with the authorities for openly expressing his views, which were diametrically opposed to those of the South African government. However, I never found him hostile; in fact, he was a gentle person, with a warm sense of humour and a great liking for Scotch whisky. He went on to hold a number of ministerial portfolios, but was always out of his depth, and in my opinion, could have served the country better by remaining a top official within the party, or just possibly by serving in some diplomatic post where his warm personality and outstanding friendliness could have been used to great advantage. Jack Humphreys and I were naturally apprehensive about going to meet with a person whom the Rhodesian government had portrayed as being an evil communist who was dedicated to the removal of white power in the country, and the destruction of western civilisation as we knew it. However, our initial fears were quickly dispelled by the warm and courteous reception we received from Mugabe and his team.

Soon after the election that brought Mugabe to power, he sent for me one day and said he wanted me to help Maurice Nyagumbo to get a farm. He explained that because of his rather chequered career, he had not had the opportunities of getting a good education or any position of influence, but he did want to become a farmer. Mugabe said he had heard of a white farmer who was willing to sell Maurice his farm at an agreed price, but, unfortunately, the latter had no money, so could I please help? I was somewhat surprised by this request, but promised to see what I could do. I contacted the chairman of the Agricultural Finance Corporation (AFC), Jeremy Field, and explained the situation to him. Jeremy, in turn said, that although the request was extremely unorthodox, he would talk to Maurice. The result was that the farm was bought and Maurice moved onto the property and started farming. The following year he came to see me and said the whole experience had been a huge mistake and he could no longer live there and could I relieve him of his burden? Following a brief discussion with him, I discovered that many members of his extended family had also gone to live on the farm and expected him to support them, which he was unable to do and he just wanted to shed the whole problem. Again, I returned to Jeremy Field and asked him if he could repossess the farm, and with a chuckle he said he would do the best he could. A few weeks later he phoned me and said the repossession had taken place and he had also succeeded in selling the farm to someone else at an enhanced price, so at the end of the exercise, Maurice was happy to get out of farming, someone else was happy to get in and the AFC had made a profit out of the whole protracted saga. Sadly, however, events finally overcame Maurice and he took his own life in April, 1989 by drinking insecticide. He certainly did not deserve such an ending.

Another case of rescuing a failed agricultural scheme had a very different conclusion. This concerned the first State President of Zimbabwe, Reverend Canaan Banana who also acquired a farm outside Marondera – how I do not know – on which he established Kushinga Phikelela, an agricultural training centre to teach young aspiring Zimbabweans how to farm. I had heard of this venture but knew little of its workings until the president contacted me and suggested that the Ministry of Agriculture should take it over as he was in danger of going broke. I was not keen on taking on an institution which was obviously underfunded and was advised by my officials to reject the offer. However, as it was at the president's request, I felt I had better seek further advice. So, I went to the Prime Minister, Robert Mugabe and related the story to him. Much to my surprise, his reply was short and to the point: 'Let him go broke,' he said. When I queried this suggestion, he smiled and said, 'Then you will get the project for nothing.' So, I duly informed the president that I had no funds in my budget for new acquisitions and in due course the liquidators were called in and the assets of the company sold off, including the company football team called the State House Rangers.

At that initial meeting in early February, Mugabe told us that he understood that agriculture was the key industry in the country and that as his party was going to win the forthcoming election – a point on which he was extremely confident – he would like to send some of his top aides to our offices to get a better understanding of the implications. Similar discussions also took place with the other private sector organisations. Significantly, ZANU was the only party to meet and have such talks with the private sector.

Once the political candidates started electioneering, the process, apart from a few isolated incidents, proceeded smoothly, albeit with a certain amount of tension, mainly because of the uncertainty, though the state media fed the country a diet of propaganda suggesting that Muzorewa's UANC would win the largest number of seats. Polling took place over three days, and on the first day, along with many fellow farmers, I was on duty at a rural polling station. It was an extraordinary experience for not only did the queue never seem to grow any shorter but everyone was in very good humour. I was ably assisted by my fellow duty officer, a splendid sergeant from the British police force, who stood well over six feet in height in his distinctive blue uniform and helmet. This seemed to greatly amuse the voters as I was all of five foot nine, wearing my Police Reserve fatigues and carrying my FN rifle. Periodically the policeman rocked backwards and forwards on his heels barking in a stentorian voice, 'Step up now, step up, or we shall be here all day!'

At one stage we thought we may have to halt the voting as we were uncertain as to whether the ballot boxes would be large enough to hold all the ballot papers, but we did manage to ensure that they were correctly thrust through the slit. Very early in the day, it became very evident that the voters were overwhelmingly in favour of ZANU. That evening I received a number of phone calls from people who had also been guarding polling stations, giving me the same information; the overall consensus was that Mugabe was heading for a runaway victory. Many of my callers urged me to try and establish what the likely position was, and if at all possible, to try and judge how the government would deal with it. I phoned General Walls, Chief of Combined Services and suggested a meeting with him. He readily agreed, but said he would prefer to see me at 6 p.m. as there would be fewer people around at that time.

I had always had a high regard for Peter, whom I considered to be a very professional soldier, and who always appeared calm under pressure. When we met that evening, we discussed the likely outcome of the election, and I gave it as my opinion that it was developing into a one-horse race in favour of Mugabe. He was interested to know on what my thinking was based. I could only reply that it was from my own observations and reports I was receiving from people in similar positions to myself. He said he felt he had to disagree with me as military intelligence was telling him the complete opposite, and that the Bishop would emerge as a clear winner. He then asked me what my reaction would be if after the results were known, the army moved in and took control of the country. This question took me by complete surprise and I answered it by saying that if there was no clear winner and fighting between the various parties broke out and there was strong possibility of a complete breakdown of law and order and anarchy ensued, then I would strongly support such action. However, if troops were used to try and remove a lawfully elected party, I would certainly oppose it. He then questioned whether I was speaking on behalf of the farming community, and if I could carry them with me? I obviously was not, as the question of military intervention had never been considered in our circles, but I said I would go to the farmers, present my views and strongly urge them to support me, as I felt it would be morally wrong to try and overthrow a properly elected government, on the basis that you did not approve of them. He thanked me for my views and indicated he was being pressurised by other people and groups to take such draconian action. After an hour I left him, and I never knew whether my views were helpful or otherwise in assisting him come to a decision. All I do know is that he looked a very lonely and worried man as I left, and I felt extremely sorry for him. When the votes were all counted, the result was certainly clear enough. Ian Smith, as was predicted, won all the twenty seats reserved for whites. Joshua Nkomo took the twenty constituencies in Matabeleland, and of the remaining 60 seats, Mugabe won 57, and Muzorewa managed only a pitiful three. So, Mugabe had a clear majority over all other parties, and did not need to form a coalition to govern. However, his government was one of the Patriotic Front,[3] which comprised both ZANU and ZAPU, and that has technically remained the position right up to the present, despite the departure from cabinet of some key ZAPU figures after the arrests in the early 1980s of prominent ZIPRA leaders such as Lookout Masuku and Dumiso Dabengwa, the expulsion of Joshua Nkomo and the subsequent horror of the Gukurahundi massacres.

During this election period, I came into contact with many members of the press corps, both regional and international. They were never in any doubt as to the electoral results, many of them predicting the result to within one or two seats. The only noticeable exception to this generally held consensus was the Rhodesian Broadcasting Corporation, which became confused by its own propaganda, and got their forecasts hopelessly wrong.

---

3 At the urging of the Frontline States prior to the 1976 Geneva Conference, ZANU and ZAPU formed an alliance, the Patriotic Front, which was represented by Robert Mugabe and Joshua Nkomo.

4

National Politics 1980-97

On Tuesday, 11 March 1980, I was presiding over the first of our two-day monthly CFU council meetings, when I received a message to say that the Governor General Lord Soames wished to see me at 6 p.m. that evening. I phoned June to say I would be late in getting home, and she urged me not to stay long as we were due to go to a reception for a couple who had been married in England, and were being given a second celebration for close friends and relatives who had been unable to attend the first one. When I arrived at Government House, Lord Soames greeted me as cordially as ever, and inviting me to sit down, he poured me the largest whisky I had ever seen, and announced that I was the new Minister of Agriculture.

He was right, I needed that whisky. His pronouncement was a shock and all I could do was protest vigorously, saying that I didn't want the job and was totally ill-equipped for such an important post. Meantime, Lord Soames strode about the room, gesticulating while he repeated, 'No one better! An ideal fit! Poacher turned gamekeeper – it always works!'

I was not convinced the metaphor was appropriate, as I did not consider I had the skills to be a successful poacher and I had no ambition to become a gamekeeper. Eventually he said, 'Go away and think about it and come and see me at nine tomorrow morning, and you can give me any answer you like, providing it is yes.'

He then added a rider to the effect that if I mentioned it to anybody else, he would have to deny that our conversation had ever taken place. I told him I would tell June, to which he smilingly agreed, and then added that Tony Duff was waiting to see me on my way out. Sir Anthony Duff was a senior official in the Foreign Office, and at that time was number two in Government House. He was tall, distinguished, and a beautifully mannered gentleman, who warmly shook my hand, congratulated me, and said he understood my fears, but all would be well, and they needed someone who could act as a stabiliser in the potentially turbulent times that lay ahead. He said I had been chosen as that person, and that he was confident I could fulfil such a role. At that point I drove away with my thoughts in a complete turmoil.

In less than ten minutes I had arrived at the wedding reception which was already developing into a lively party. As I walked into the lights, I was greeted by my eldest daughter Kathryn, who said somebody wished to speak to me on the phone. I enquired where it was and she responded by waving her arm and saying, 'Through there'. I walked into a hall and saw the handset lying on the floor. I picked it up, saying 'Hullo', and a voice enquired if I was Mr Norman. After I replied in the affirmative, he then told me his name, but in my confused state, and with the celebratory noises around me, I missed it completely. He did, however, add that he was calling on behalf of the BBC. He then asked if he could congratulate me on being made Minister of Agriculture. I was a little annoyed, as I had only just left Government House, with a warning from Lord Soames not to mention our conversation to anyone, and here was a member of the media, apparently in possession of the facts. I told him that no, he could not congratulate me. He then asked why I had been to see Lord Soames, to which I replied that we had been discussing the drought. Peals of laughter followed my response, and more irritated than ever, I asked him what was so funny. He said that mine was the silliest reply he had ever heard, to which I told him it was the only one he would get and hung up. I rejoined the party, got myself a drink and went and found June. After a few minutes she asked me what Lord Soames had wanted, and I said I had something I needed to discuss with her, and we went out into the deep shadows of the garden, where I relayed what had taken place. She was very distressed and dissolved into tears, pleading with me not to accept. I understood her apprehension as it came as a complete shock, and she quickly assessed it would be a life-changer for both of us, one for which we were unprepared and had not sought. So I assured her I would try and extract myself, but I felt the decision had already been taken without me having been consulted. After much agonising, we decided to return to the party, to be met by the agitated mother of the bride, who said she had been searching for me, as the man who was to propose the health of the bride and groom had gone home. I gave a very emphatic no, which seemed to surprise her, so she asked why, and I replied that I had a lot on my mind. She then laughed, saying, 'Oh balls!' Little did she know.

Her husband, now standing at the top of the stairs, called for order, and announced that I was about to propose a toast. I quickly asked for the bridegroom's name and slowly moved forward trying to formulate some appropriate words while muttering, 'Andrew, not Anthony, don't get it wrong'.

After my speech, which passed in a blur, June and I felt the need to escape and consider what to do next, so we drove to David Smith's house, which was close by, to get some advice from him. Soames had already told me that David had agreed to serve in Mugabe's cabinet, so I would have nothing to fear, as he would be able to assist and advise me. David greeted us by saying that he'd been expecting us, as he had agreed to serve in Mugabe's government providing I also did so. I told him I did not think I could accept, first because I had no desire to become a politician; and second, because I felt I was not competent to become one. David argued that Zimbabwe was about to embark on a ground-breaking exercise, one vital to its future prosperity and the well-being of all its people, concluding that I should consider it my duty to accept. After about an hour, we left with neither June nor I convinced that I was obligated to serve.

By this time, the enormity of the prospect began to sink in, so feeling the need to lessen the tension, we went back to the party. Eventually, we returned home drained and exhausted, particularly as we felt we could not confide in anyone other than David Smith. It was one of the few nights of my life when I did not sleep at all. We sat and drank tea and talked over the issues facing us, from every conceivable angle. We finally concluded that as president of the CFU, I had a duty to my council members to inform them, in secrecy, of the possibility.

The following morning, I went to my office and asked my vice-president, David Spain, if I could have a few words with him. He immediately asked if Lord Soames had any startling news. So I told him the outcome of my discussions of the previous evening. He walked around my office in a dazed state, asking me if I intended to accept, and what would happen to him. After five minutes we both sat down and planned the next move. It was decided he would go into the council chamber and ask all members of staff to leave, as I wanted to address the Council in committee. As I arrived, the staff were leaving, and I heard one member speculating on the possibility of me asking the Council to give them a substantial pay increase. But even more disconcerting, I heard another wondering aloud if

I was the new Minister of Agriculture. I then told them that I had been offered the post, and I was due to meet Mugabe within the next half an hour. The information was received in shocked silence and disbelief. I told them I needed their endorsement to take on the position, because if they were opposed to it, there was absolutely no point in me trying to run the agricultural portfolio in very changed circumstances without at least their tacit support.

Unanimously, they gave me that endorsement and I handed over the chair to David Spain and drove to Mugabe's house in time for my meeting. Security was tight on the street where he lived, with both government police officers and freedom fighters patrolling the area with automatic weapons. Just before I entered his gate, I bumped into C. G. Tracey, a prominent farmer and businessman, who told me that a South African friend of his had phoned him that morning to say that the South African papers were reporting that I was to become the new Minister of Agriculture. Tracey added, 'How stupid can they get?' To which I replied, 'Quite.' He then quickly prompted, 'You haven't been asked, have you?'

To which I answered, 'Yes, I have, but I have not yet decided what to do.' I also said that despite speculation in the media, nothing had been confirmed and the whole matter was classified. He nodded, wished me luck with my decisions, and said he would not breathe a word to a soul.

I went into the house where I was warmly greeted by Mugabe. After the usual exchange of pleasantries, he said he was delighted I was going to join his government, and wanted me to become the Deputy Minister of Mines, under Maurice Nyagumbo. I quickly told him that I thought he wanted me to be the Minister of Agriculture, and I would not accept the post he was offering. He said he had changed his mind and that he thought I would be very happy in the Ministry of Mines. After a few more minutes of mild disagreement over my potential position in government, I left in a fairly angry mood, as I felt I was being used in some sort of political game in which I did not want to be a participant. I went straight to State House and asked to see Lord Soames, but was told he was engaged in an important meeting. I insisted on seeing him, saying that I too had an important message for him. He agreed to see me and, as always, was his usual charming, courteous self. When I told him the result of my meeting with Mugabe, he said there must be some mistake and he would sort it out. I responded by saying that I had had enough and they had better look for another person to fill the role. He asked me not to make hasty decisions, and tried to convince me that my membership of the new government was pivotal to the success of the country. I thanked him for his confidence in me, but reiterated my view that I was becoming some sort of political pawn on a chessboard. On that note, I left him and returned to the CFU council meeting where I told them they could all relax as the offer had been changed and I could not accept the alternative. Later that day, I was attending a meeting with other members of the private sector in the office of the Secretary of Finance, Mr David Young. Just after 5.30 p.m., his phone rang. Having answered it, he handed it to me. 'It's a call for you.' It was Lord Soames, who began by saying; 'Congratulations, you're the Minister of Agriculture, and Mugabe is broadcasting to the nation, naming his cabinet, at 6 o'clock.'

He suggested I leave my meeting and go home to hear the news. I turned to David Young and asked if he would excuse me as I had something to attend to and he replied asking if it was in order for him to offer me his congratulations. With a wry smile, I said thank you. When I arrived home, I told June what had happened, having previously rung her to tell her that it was all off. At that time, we were sharing a townhouse with her mother, so she suggested that I told her before the news broadcast, in order to lessen the shock. When I did so, she responded, 'I knew that. It was obvious.' So much for lessening the shock!

When the names were read out on the news broadcast, having a name beginning with 'N', I came approximately in the middle of the list, but before they got to Zvobgo the phone rang and it was our daughter Kathryn, who said, 'Listen Dad, we kids always thought you were a bit of a nit, but hell, this time!' At this point there was a loud knocking on the door and our neighbours Dick and Meriel Ternouth were standing there smiling and laughing, hugging a bottle of champagne, saying they wished to be the first to offer their congratulations.

After a night that was a haze of telephone calls and visits by well-wishers, reality had to be faced the following day. It began with a return visit to Government House for a meeting between the leaders of the private sector and Lord Soames in which he spelt out the importance of co-operation between all sectors of the economy and industry and the new government, in order to assist in a smooth transition of power. When the meeting broke up, he asked me to remain behind. He then offered me his thanks for accepting the agricultural portfolio. He said he knew how difficult would be my task, but then added the gratitude and appreciation of the British government which, he said, felt that my presence would not only be of benefit to the agricultural sector, but would lead to political stability in the country.

The following day, I went to my office in the CFU building and started to prepare to depart across the town to my new office. There was an unusual buzz within the building which I suppose was only natural, with everyone expressing their views on the new developments. However, to my surprise, I found my excellent secretary, Shireen Baldwin, in quite a distressed state, and on enquiring what was upsetting her, she said everyone seemed pleased and excited, but no one had asked her for her views, and she did not know what would happen to her. I told her that she had nothing to be concerned about, as she would remain as the secretary to my deputy, David Spain, who would become the new president of the CFU. At that point she burst into tears and said she wanted to come with me. Although this was a great compliment, I had no idea what the protocol of appointing government private secretaries was, but I promised I would try and assist her.

The next day I began my political career by moving offices from the CFU to the Ministry of Agriculture. On arrival, I was greeted by the permanent secretary, Edward (Ted) Osborn, and other senior staff members. They were all very friendly, but I think also bemused by their new minister who had in effect been something of an adversary in recent years. Some ten minutes after my arrival, Ted Osborn entered my office with a letter which he said was addressed to me, and suggested I should read it and in due course give him my answer. It was a letter written to the minister three days previously from myself requesting a meeting to discuss increasing producer prices for all the main farm commodities. Perhaps not the most tactful of starts, but one which both he and I found amusing, and at least I had the advantage of knowing what the CFU's proposals were, and I was also now holding the key position in making a realistic and, hopefully, viable response.

I quickly brought up the question of a private secretary, and was told that I would be able to choose one from those available within a government pool. When I said I wished to bring the one I had had within the CFU, I was told that was very irregular and would not be permitted under the prevailing conditions of employment within the Civil Service Act. I nevertheless stuck to my guns and Ted Osborn said he would see what he could arrange. There were a number of objections raised revolving around security clearance and other bureaucratic difficulties. However, I remained adamant, and Shireen Baldwin followed me across and became my first secretary. Her work and support were invaluable to me, and certainly contributed hugely in helping me to get to grips with my new job. Unfortunately, after a year, she and her husband emigrated to Australia. With her replacement, I was equally fortunate. Shirley Netcher was already in the civil service; not only was she extremely efficient, with one of the best commands of the English language one could hope to find, but she also had the wonderful ability of knowing who to allow into my office, and who to turn away, without causing offence.

Indeed, I was extremely fortunate in all my staff, whether within the ministry or the specialist departments, such as veterinary, research, extension services or indeed the parastatals, who had the responsibility for marketing all the agricultural produce with the notable exception of tobacco, although even with this commodity, the regulations and controls were governed by the ministry. The chairmen and board members of the parastatals were by and large drawn from the private sector and were appointed by the minister in recognition of their expertise and experience – banking, legal, marketing and so on. I was very heartened by the response and attitude of these individuals. All pledged their immediate support, while a number, realising the difficulties and struggles that lay ahead, offered their own resignations in order to create vacancies which I could then use to fill with candidates who would be considered more acceptable to the new government. At the time, I thanked them for their consideration and invited them to continue in their posts.

I had another stroke of good fortune in the appointment of Simba Makoni as my deputy minister. Like all the members of government, he was unknown to me, and I did not meet him for a few weeks, as he was still out of the country. When he did arrive, he was a surprise, to put it mildly: firstly, I was struck by how young he was; secondly, he arrived at the office to start work dressed in casual trousers and what I can only describe as a Hawaiian beach shirt. But what a gem he turned out to be: he was extremely bright, articulate, and a complete human dynamo. From the beginning we forged a relationship based on mutual respect, and over the years this friendship remains intact.

It is interesting to note that this was the first time in the history of the country that all farming and agriculture had come under the jurisdiction of one ministry. Previously there had been one ministry for commercial farmers (mainly white), and another for subsistence farmers (all black) – usually a department within the Ministry of Home Affairs. As a result, farmers who came under the jurisdiction of the Ministry of Agriculture had the advantage of a fully funded ministry whose estimates were annually approved by Parliament, whereas those who lived and farmed in the communal lands only received support from a department within a large ministry looking after the internal affairs of the country. As a consequence, funding for agricultural improvement in this sector was usually woefully lacking. This, in effect, kept the small-scale farmers at a subsistence level at best, and certainly provided no opportunity for growth in this sector. Thus, the amalgamation of the two farming systems under one ministry was a development which I greatly welcomed, for now there would be no 'us' and 'them', and all occupiers and workers of the land would be known as farmers. There still remained a number of administrative difficulties, the greatest being the boundaries and distribution of the various landholders between commercial farmers, communal farmers and state land. All were controlled by separate and sometimes conflicting pieces of legislation. But as I did not hold the portfolio of lands – this was controlled by a separate minister and ministry – I decided to concentrate all my energies into increasing farm production at all levels. I believed from the beginning that if tensions and bitterness were to be avoided in the new Zimbabwe, the level of production in the small-scale sector had to be raised in the shortest possible time. My immediate target was to convert those farms from subsistence to cash economies. This would also have the added advantages of not only improving the way of life for communal farmers, but also making their areas an attractive target for investors, slowing down and perhaps even reversing urban migration. This task presented an enormous challenge, and was one which I relished and looked forward to directing.

Although we had all been appointed to our various portfolios, and had been allocated offices and staff, we were technically unable to start our work as the government was still under the control of Lord Soames, and we had to wait for Independence Day to be officially handed over. One amusing story which occurred during this grey period, concerned Edison Zvobgo, the Minister of Local Government and Housing, who in discussion with Lord Soames expressed his frustrations at not being able to take up his duties, and sought advice as to what he should be doing. Lord Soames suggested he went to his office building, familiarise himself with its layout, and introduce himself to some of the staff, so that when the day arrived for him to assume full control he would find his task much easier. Following this advice, he went to the building in which his office was housed, and took the lift to the appropriate floor. Leaving the lift, he noticed an office door open, so he peeped inside. There was a rather elderly white male working behind the desk, who said, 'Run away boy, we have no work for you here.'

Edison withdrew and immediately met another white member of staff who this time recognised him, greeted him correctly, welcomed him to the ministry and offered to show him where his office was. He told him there was some mail waiting for him and then asked if he would like some tea. Going back down the corridor, he met his colleague and told him he had just greeted the new minister. The former, now realising his mistake, confessed his stupidity and asked what he should do. The advice that he was given was to apologise for his error. This he duly did, and Minister Zvogbo smiled and told him not to give it another thought, saying that we are all new to the changing circumstances and will get to know each other better over time. The relieved official thanked him profusely then compounded his gaffe by saying his problem was that he couldn't tell one boy from another! This exchange was fairly typical of the banter taking place within the different ethnic groups in those early days of independence.

In the weeks between the election and the handover of power by Britain, there was enormous activity taking place throughout the country. Robert Mugabe was beginning to win the confidence of the people, by not only making conciliatory speeches but also retaining key people in existing posts, such as the service chiefs, the Commissioner of Police and senior figures in the judiciary. Restrictions on travel were lifted, trade sanctions were removed, and influential visitors from all over the world began visiting Salisbury.[1] After a prolonged armed struggle, and over fourteen years of sanctions, there was a real feeling of optimism and hope. There was also a huge relaxation of attitudes between the races, as each started to greet the other as equal citizens in the same country. There were a few unpleasant incidents, but these were far outnumbered by the goodwill and genuine friendship developing on all sides. Approximately a hundred countries sent representatives for the celebrations leading up to the independence ceremony. In addition, organisations such as the United Nations and Organisation of African Unity were also represented, and there was a large influx of journalists from the world's leading media houses. This obviously placed a large strain on the hotel and tourist industry, but no one seemed to mind, as the country was beginning to enjoy its newfound freedom and the recognition which accompanied it.

Many countries sent their head of state, but usually it was their head of government. Great Britain was represented by the Prince

---

1 Salisbury changed its name to Harare in 1982. However, from this point, we will refer to the capital city as Harare.

of Wales, who acted on behalf of Queen Elizabeth, while the government was represented by the Secretary of State for Foreign Affairs, Lord Carrington, who had played such an able, crucial and diplomatic role as Chairman of the Lancaster House Conference and was considered by many to be the architect of the independence agreement. Mugabe, through his office, ensured every visiting dignitary was greeted at the airport by at least one cabinet minister, sometimes more. For the arrival of Prince Charles, he took the entire cabinet and had them form a reception line and then escorted the Prince, introducing each one by name. When he arrived at my station, he said this is Mr Norman, my Minister of Agriculture who knows nothing about politics, to which the Prince retorted;

'Ah, but does he know anything about farming?'

I was delegated to meet, greet and look after the delegations from three different countries. First Belgium, which passed off smoothly enough. Then, the delegation of Greek Cypriots representing Cyprus, who arrived on time, but when we arrived at their hotel, we found that their rooms had been occupied by the delegation of Turkish Cypriots. The hotel manager was wringing his hands in despair, while a furious argument ensued between the representatives of Greece and Turkey. I quickly decided I could be of little use in this situation, more especially as I had to return to the airport to meet my final delegation which was arriving from the island of Vanuatu. Unfortunately, they were not on the plane, and after making extensive enquiries, somebody thought they had gone to Lusaka. By this time, it was late in the evening and I felt I could do no more, so I went home. The following day I checked on my charges and found the Belgians happily going about their business, and the Greek Cypriots more or less mollified as alternative accommodation had been found for them. I never did meet the delegation from Vanuatu. So, I marked my performance as one win, one draw and one loss.

The date for the handover of power was fixed for the 18 April, and the venue chosen was Rufaro Stadium, which was normally used for football matches. When June and I arrived at the stadium, it was easy to detect the crowd's jubilation, many of whom had already been there for several hours, enjoying the various bands and dance troupes which were providing the entertainment. Having been shown to our seats our eyes began to water and sting, as we realised tear-gas had been used, presumably to quell over-excited members of the audience, or more likely those outside the stadium who were making strenuous attempts to enter without valid tickets. The gas hung in the air for a long time, and as each VIP arrived, they quickly reached for a handkerchief to cover their nose and mouth like a mask. The actual handover ceremony was conducted with great dignity with all the major participants including Prince Charles, Lord Soames, Prime Minister Robert Mugabe, and the Chief Justice, Justice Hector McDonald all performing their roles with calm distinction. For the large audience, the most symbolic moment was the lowering of the Union Jack and the raising of the new Zimbabwe flag. The brief era of independent white rule – a mere ninety years – had ended, and a new form of multiracial democracy had begun.

The new beginning almost exploded – literally – before it began. The main stand had been heavily wired with high explosives, with the detonating mechanism fixed to a set of traffic lights at about half a kilometre away. Fortunately for all the dignitaries and invited guests, the intelligence agents employed by the previous Rhodesian and Zimbabwe Rhodesian governments had a whistle-blower in their midst who had already pledged his allegiance to the incoming government. This resulted in a massive defusing exercise, averting a national disaster and securing him a decoration for bravery from the new government and continued employment in the intelligence sector.

Prince Charles and all other visiting dignitaries departed after the opening ceremony and welcoming functions had been completed, leaving Lord Soames there for another month to oversee the formation of the incoming government of the independent state of Zimbabwe. This period also saw the opening up of many diplomatic missions, and the arrival of a number of new ambassadors and high commissioners and their attendant staff. Many of those who were appointed were of the highest calibre and made outstanding contributions in assisting the new country during its formative years. Prominent among them was the new British High Commissioner, Robin Byatt, who along with his delightful wife, Jilly, quickly established a rapport with all members of what was still an uneasy society, which in turn led to a lessening of racial tensions. Another area of great success was the arrival of the British Military Advisory Training Team (BMATT), whose task it was to assist in training the newly integrated army. Fortunately, they stayed for many years, bringing stability and professionalism to the force. Indeed, I always thought it was a great mistake when they were finally withdrawn in 2001. They were initially led by Brigadier Patrick Palmer, an outstanding officer who went on to achieve higher rank within the British army and at the time of his death was Constable and Warden of Windsor Castle.

Unsurprisingly, after such a long and bitter struggle, there were many pivotal issues to be addressed in the initial months after independence and tricky situations to be circumvented. An illustration of this came early on in my tenure of office when I attended a fairly hostile and certainly vocal Farmers' Association meeting in the Marondera/Wedza area. The contentious issue was a circulating rumour that the new government was going to acquire the whole district in order to settle small-scale farmers. I told them I had no knowledge of such a scheme, but I would contact my colleague, Minister Moven Mahachi, the Minister of Lands and try and persuade him to go to the area and address a public meeting and explain government's policy. This I duly did and much to my surprise the minister agreed to go. He was, however, very nervous about the prospect of addressing a large gathering of potentially angry farmers. I advised him to stay calm and to begin his address with a joke. He smiled weakly and said he did not know any jokes. In the event he performed extremely well, as he started his speech by sympathising with the farmers because of the severe drought they were experiencing, and said it was creating problems of a different type for government, because as the water levels in the farm dams dropped, the ammunition and weapons which had been hidden there came to the surface. This was a reference to some farmers who after the end of internal hostilities were by law required to hand in their military ordinance, and had decided that hiding it was a better option. His remark was greeted by hoots of laughter and the feedback I received from the meeting was that the minister was a good guy and one with whom they could work. Sadly, many years later, Moven was killed in one of the many unexplained car crashes.

Also during this period, and for some time to come, there were periodic incidents of an explosive nature, designed to destabilise the new Zimbabwe. Buildings were bombed; bridges and private houses were also targeted; even the military ordinance stocks at some barracks were badly damaged. Examples of this were the ZANU-PF offices in Manica Road; ammunition at Nkomo army barracks and a temporary archway proclaiming the new Zimbabwe on the airport road. In most cases the perpetrators were never discovered or convicted, though regrettably a few innocent people were arrested and detained without questioning, but later released because of the lack of credible evidence. These actions were symptomatic of the tensions simmering as the new order settled. The notable exception and most high-profile incident of them all occurred when a large number of military aircraft were destroyed on the ground at Thornhill Air Base in July 1982. This led to the arrest of six senior officers who had transferred from the Rhodesian to the new Zimbabwean air force. They were charged with the destruction of these aircraft, but when their case was heard in court, they were all acquitted. On leaving the courtroom they were promptly re-arrested and held in prison without trial. Furthermore, it was alleged that they were being tortured in order to extract a confession of guilt. This whole episode, obviously, and quite rightly, created much concern and indignation, as it was viewed by many as a failure of justice and human rights. One of those who took great exception to these actions was the British Prime Minister Margaret Thatcher, who threatened to recall the British High Commissioner and to halt all aid to Zimbabwe. This concerned officials in the Foreign and Commonwealth Office, who tried to persuade her to first discuss the situation with someone from Zimbabwe. She reluctantly agreed to this suggestion, but stipulated that it had to be soon otherwise she was going ahead with her own actions. In consequence, I received a message to say I had been chosen to discuss this problem with the British prime minister. My qualifications for such a delicate mission were nil. In addition, I had no direct knowledge of the case, so I felt I was poorly equipped to speak about the whole sordid affair. Before agreeing to the meeting, I specified that I would have to have the consent of Mugabe and consequently I briefed him about the request that I had received. Much to my astonishment, he approved of the arrangement and said that as I was going in an unofficial capacity, he would be very interested in hearing what Mrs Thatcher had to say. However, he did caution me not to commit him or his government to any agreement. With this endorsement I flew to London, where a room had been booked for me at The Royal Horseguards Hotel. The following morning, I was briefed by officials in the Foreign Office prior to going to Number 10 Downing Street to meet the prime minister. I was warned that my forthcoming meeting could be very difficult and would only last for fifteen to twenty minutes. Having by now decided I was on an impossible mission, I duly arrived at Number 10 and was met by a charming man called Mr Colville. He explained the procedure that would follow, including the fact that he would be present at the meeting, but his role would be limited to taking notes and he would not participate in the discussions. He then ushered me into the room where the prime minister was waiting. She was very courteous but I felt slightly perplexed as to what was my role or position. She began by inviting me to explain the situation that had led to the arrest of the air force officers, pointing out that they had been cleared by the courts and had now been re-arrested. Being very conscious of the limited time I had been allocated for the meeting, I launched straight into the explanation of events as I understood them. She listened very intently, then interrupted me to tell me she was totally opposed to detention without trial. I responded by saying, 'What about Northern Ireland?' to which she replied, 'What has that got to do with it?'

I retorted that I thought she was talking about detention without trial. This exchange led to a long pause, during which I thought I had blown my chances of helping to resolve the issue. However, she eventually relented and asked if we could return to the problem in Zimbabwe. After further dialogue, she said she would be prepared to receive the six officers in England if Mugabe would release them without further charges – in other words to draw a line under the whole affair without too much loss of face. I undertook to take that message back to Mugabe and to brief him on our meeting. She concluded by saying that she would be attending the Commonwealth Heads of Government meeting in India in two weeks' time; she suggested that this would provide the opportunity for the two of them to meet to see if they could reach an agreement along the basis that she and I had discussed. The only stipulation she insisted on was she wished to have the discussion with Mr Mugabe in private with no one else in attendance. I said I would relay her suggestions to our prime minister on my return. On that note, I rose to leave and she thanked me very cordially for explaining the situation and said that she hoped her offer would be accepted. When I left, Mr Colville expressed surprise that our meeting had gone on for so long – eighty minutes – (he estimated that I had spoken for seventy-five of them) and that the basis for a resolution had been reached.

On my return to Harare, I immediately briefed Mr Mugabe on my meeting and passed on the proposals made by Mrs Thatcher. He thanked me for my efforts and said he would be delighted to discuss the issue further when he and the British prime minister met in India. The meeting duly took place, but nearly floundered before it began, because despite being told it could only be on a one-to-one basis, Mugabe took his foreign minister, Witness Magwende, with him. However, the end result was achieved and having suffered at the hands of their gaolers, lost their livelihoods and careers, and having had their families endure much stress, the officers were released and flown to England and this whole distressing chapter was concluded.

In my new position I had one big disadvantage, which was offset by an equally large advantage. On the downside, all members of the new cabinet, with the exception of David Smith, were unknown to me, but well known to each other. This naturally raised a certain amount of curiosity; probably even suspicion, but never hostility. The only exception was Herbert Ushewokunze, then Minister of Health, who was a maverick. From the very beginning he tried to undermine my position, not I believe from evil malice, but more to demonstrate what a clever person he was. Knowing very little about farming, he engaged in a small ambush which he thought would discredit me. Without warning, he circulated a minute from the previous government's cabinet, that of Bishop Muzorewa, in which I was quoted on a specific issue, saying that he now believed I was arguing from the opposite position, and thus suggesting I was no more than a man of straw and could not be trusted. I sought permission from Mugabe to delay my reply until the following week. All cabinet minutes are issued to ministers using a numbering system and not their names; furthermore on leaving office, they have to be destroyed. I took one of the photocopied minutes that Herbert had circulated back to my office, and my officials, using a person with special skills, lifted the erasure over the top of the page, and we were thus able to identify who had supplied the information. Armed with this knowledge, I informed cabinet of what I had done, and enquired if they were interested in knowing who had leaked classified material. Mugabe quickly stepped in and said he did not think that would be necessary, and suggested the whole subject be dropped. A few minutes later, a note was passed around the cabinet table to me; it came from Herbert, suggesting that we talk when the meeting was over. This we did. He greeted me with a huge smile and told me he thought I would be a pushover, but realised it was not going to be like that, and suggested a lot more could be achieved if we became friends. From that day onwards, he became very supportive of all I was trying to do, and during the period he served as Home Affairs minister, he released many prisoners or squashed a number of sentences in cases where I considered people had been unfairly treated. These considerations were probably an unusual form of networking, but we were operating in unusual times; many white Zimbabweans and their families benefitted from his response to my requests, but few if any knew who their benefactor was because if it had become common knowledge the system would have had to stop. Unfortunately, he, along with other members of that first cabinet, succumbed to the AIDS pandemic.

On the positive side, my position was strengthened by the fact that none of my newfound colleagues had any detailed knowledge of agriculture production, or the complex subject of commodity marketing, both internal and international. Initially, I saw my task and objectives as being twofold: first, to raise the prices paid to all producers through the single channel marketing system to a viable sustainable level; second, to quickly establish support systems to improve the level of production of the small-scale farmer, in order to give them the opportunity to move from subsistence to being members of the cash economy. The method of fixing agricultural commodity prices was protracted and sometimes acrimonious. The farmers' unions, through their commodity associations, would submit proposals to the Ministry of Agriculture. These proposals would indicate the price required to sustain the viability of farmers, and, in some cases, would also try and prove what level of return would be needed to encourage the expansion of a particular crop. After weeks of correspondence and numerous meetings, the whole process usually culminated in a meeting between the minister and his senior advisors, and the president of the unions supported by their commodity chairman. The final act required the minister to gain approval from the cabinet before an announcement could be made. As producer prices became operative for the delivery season beginning on 1 April each year, I did not have much time in which to hold discussions with the farming bodies, and then prepare my proposals to government. As I had always strongly held the view that food self-sufficiency was the best means of ensuring political stability, I aimed at a level of price increases which I believed would achieve this goal. In addition, it would leave the country with a cushion of carry-over stock, as a hedge against drought. And, finally, it should provide a small exportable surplus.

Maize, being the staple food of the country, was my obvious pivotal commodity in order to set a benchmark for all the other products. Much against the advice of the ministry officials, and to the surprise of the farmers, I proposed a 50 per cent increase in the price per tonne, thus increasing it from a level of $80 per tonne to $120 per tonne. Supported by a certain amount of knowledge, and a few years of experience of price negotiations, I felt this was my best opportunity to raise farm commodity prices to a higher level, where it would be easier to make smaller seasonal adjustments in subsequent years. Taking advantage of my position, I was able to convince cabinet to accept my proposals for all controlled products, with the notable exception of the price for beef. In this instance I had put forward a proposal for an increase of 30 per cent. No amount of arguing could persuade my colleagues to agree with me; in fact, they countered with a suggestion of a 5 per cent increase. In order not to jeopardise my crop prices, to which I had already got agreement, I suggested that I withdraw the beef prices and submit them at a later date, which met with cabinet approval.

Nationally the farmers were delighted with the new prices and I also think it had a positive effect on what I loosely describe as the support industries. These included banks, fertiliser companies, crop chemical suppliers, seed houses, etc. The cattle men were understandably disappointed, but accepted my assurance that I would vigorously plead their case. I presented my proposals again the following week and again failed to get acceptance. I realised I now had a serious battle on my hands, and rather than place myself in a position of having to accept a compromise figure, I withdrew my position paper, and reintroduced it on the following week's agenda. This tactic I followed for fourteen consecutive weeks, during which time the cabinet slowly increased their offer, much to the chagrin of the cattle producers, who were becoming increasingly depressed, and even on one occasion accused me of not trying hard enough. However, on the fourteenth week, the combined cabinet invited me to accept a 29 per cent increase. This I refused to do. At this point, Mugabe, who I sensed was beginning to lose patience with me, asked me to explain myself. He said that they had moved from a 5 per cent to a 29 per cent increase, which was only one per cent less than my request. But I had not budged, and he wanted to know why. I responded by saying my position was simple; I had presented a carefully worked out proposal, supported in great detail by economic facts and marketing data, which illustrated that 30 per cent was indeed the required increase. The cabinet on the other hand had presented no evidence to support their percentage figures, other than they were lower than mine, and I said I was not sitting at the table in order to take part in a reverse auction. Mugabe laughed, slapped the table, and loudly declared that a 30 per cent increase was accepted. This was not quite the end of this little saga, as someone asked when the new price became operative. Mugabe with a dismissive wave of his hand said 'tomorrow'. I then stunned the meeting by saying, 'No, it is back-dated to 1 March.'

This resulted in a chorus of shouts saying I could not make a price retrospective. I replied by saying in the case of beef marketing, the year ran from 1 March to 28 February the following year, and this was clearly stated in my presentation paper, and if they had taken the trouble to read it, they would have seen that it was so. I was told this was completely unacceptable; the new price began the following day and I must inform the farmers accordingly. This I undertook to do, but I said I would tell them that the new government had reneged on the accepted marketing agreement by refusing to recognise the laid down starting and expiry dates. This brought about a shock of disbelief; that someone could talk in such a manner which they interpreted as total impertinence. Mugabe stared across the table straight into my eyes; I in turn stared back and we held this position for about thirty seconds, in total silence, with all the other cabinet members holding their breath. At last in very slow measured words, he said, 'Don't ever do that to me again! The starting date will be backdated to March.'

I am convinced that my first exercise in presenting an agricultural case had worked in my favour as it set a precedent which assisted me in all future proposals and requests I made to cabinet on issues pertaining to my portfolios. The following day, Mugabe asked me to go and see him, and in discussing the previous day, he asked me why I had not fully briefed him in advance, and I told him it was all clearly spelled out in my position paper. He said he did not have time to read every minister's papers, and if I had something contentious to put forward, he would find it easier if I went and explained the subject before it got to be debated. I thought this to be sound advice, and took the opportunity of briefing him in advance of the cabinet meetings on numerous occasions during my time in government. I would not claim that I won every proposal, but it certainly helped, and led to a better understanding of many difficult issues.

Occasionally, these cabinet debates could be very amusing. Once, for example, I wished to get an increase in the price of dressed poultry. In those days the only control within the poultry industry was on dressed birds. There was no control on eggs, day-old chicks or any live birds. But trying to explain that a 'dressed' chicken was one that was dead and had no feathers; and one that was 'undressed' was usually alive and possessed of its feathers was hilarious. And so, they accepted my proposals amid much laughter and no dissent.

My second objective, and one of greater importance, was to increase the viability of the communal farmers. These were farmers who lived in areas designated by previous governments, with oversight largely provided by the traditional leaders, but falling under the overall control of the Ministry of Home Affairs. These areas, which in 1980 comprised just over 40 per cent of the land mass of Zimbabwe, were largely impoverished due to the lack of investment such as roads, communications and adequate water availability, and without any forceful agricultural programmes having been initiated. The lack of a coherent farming policy had led to an over-utilisation of arable land and uncontrolled grazing by livestock – both cattle and goats. This despite some major efforts by a few dedicated and far-sighted civil servants, who recognised the problems but were never granted enough government funding to make meaningful changes, in what after all, was paternalism at its worst. By and large the enormous potential of the communal lands was still undeveloped and unprotected. However, there were a number of successful farming operations run by church missions. Another successful organisation was the African Farmer's Union (AFU), which catered for the needs of the Master Farmers. These were farmers who had attended farming courses and obtained a certificate of competence which entitled them to farm in dedicated areas of tribal trust lands (later known as communal lands). These farmers were proficient, and while they were inhibited by the lack of infrastructure, they still managed to produce crops and livestock over and above subsistence levels. They then sold this surplus to the government statutory boards. Their organisation also had a close relationship with the CFU and its predecessor the RNFU, and held regular joint meetings on mutual subjects such as price negotiations, research programmes and input costs. After independence, they changed their name and became the Zimbabwe Farmer's Union (ZFU) and their first president was the pleasant and articulate Gary Magadzire, with whom I had many dealings when I was president of the CFU and Minister of Agriculture. Unfortunately he died suddenly at quite an early age and upon arriving at his home to pay my respects to his family, I joined a throng doing likewise which indicated the high respect in which he was held. Unexpectedly, I was asked to make an impromptu tribute, in which I spoke of his achievements in the role of agriculture. I told the mourners that he was a good farmer and a good leader, but a poor teacher as he had undertaken to teach me Shona and failed miserably – maybe I was a poor pupil. He was then honoured with a burial at Heroes Acre, the cemetery situated on the outskirts of Harare which was reserved as the final resting place for all those who had served the nation with distinction, mainly military and political. President Mugabe led the mourners in the ceremony and tributes, and I was invited to lay the wreath on behalf of the farming community.

A large misconception at this time, which still persists to this day, is that subsistence farmers were placed on the poorest soil, and in drought-prone districts. This was not necessarily the case. True, not many of these areas were located in regions I or II, where the heavy, more fertile soils were to be found. These heavy soils are difficult to work and even with the introduction of modern sophisticated machinery, they are not easy. In addition, in seasons of low rainfall, crops are liable to heat stress and perish quite quickly. On the other hand, the lighter, sandier soils were much easier to work, and were more suitable to the production of tobacco, cotton and many varieties of beans and other legumes. My task, as I saw it at the time, was to try and increase the production of these areas by introducing a number of simple programmes which would lead to greater volumes by using incentives as the key ingredients.

The overall plan, which I devised with my officials, was uncomplicated and workable and thus potentially effective. The plan had three main prongs: education, availability of inputs, and access to markets. My idea of education was not the formal type which is taught in the classroom or lecture hall, but more practical and 'hands on'. During this time, I was often approached by well-meaning people seeking my support to develop an agricultural syllabus for schools. I always resisted these overtures, by stating that it was not my job to teach children how to farm, but to assist farmers how to farm.

In 1980 the small-scale peasant farming sector was occupying 41.9 per cent of the land mass, but production was little more than subsistence, and in many instances, the hard work was undertaken by women and children. There was obviously great scope for improvement in this area, and my first response to those calling for further education was to educate the farmers already *in situ*. In pursuing this approach, we quickly organised short courses ranging from a day to a week. Many field days, discussion groups and competitions were also quickly put in place. Often these were fairly rudimentary but the intention was to stimulate interest and enthusiasm within this largely neglected sector.

I must point out this part of the programme was not done by government alone. Many support and supply industries such as fertiliser companies, seed houses, machinery franchise holders and banks, among others, quickly recognised the advantages of supporting the communal farming sector. Government made concessionary finance available to the small-scale farmers in the communal lands through the Agricultural Finance Corporation (AFC) at a rate of 2 per cent below that available to commercial farmers. This may look like a discriminatory concession, but repayment conditions were the same for all farmers, and the interest level charged was low enough to attract a considerable number of small-scale farmers to take advantage of the scheme. Having stimulated enormous interest through the awareness programmes, and then devising a system of easier access to essential inputs, the remaining challenge to both the Ministry of Agriculture and the farmer was to reduce the cost of transport of crops to the market place, by amending the existing system, and through new designated depot locations, taking the market place to the production areas.

Prior to 1980, all grain and cotton marketing board depots had been situated along the line of rail, with the obvious advantage of ease of onward movement. There were a few licenced buyers who operated in the communal areas who were permitted to buy the farmers' surplus crops for onward sale to the marketing authorities. However, the quantities were small, no more than just a few bags or buckets of grain from individual growers. In addition, as the majority of these licenced buyers also owned and operated general trading stores, their method of payment tended to be very unscrupulous to say the least. In many instances, instead of cash, the farmer having handed over his grain would leave the trading store with goods, thus enhancing the profit for the store owner. Under such a barter system, it was extremely difficult for the peasant farmer to source money to meet next year's production costs. In addition, barter offered limited scope for paying costs such as school fees or the purchase of school books. The simple solution was to establish delivery depots or collection points in all the major growing areas. In order to achieve this, a plan was drawn up which put no farmer further than sixty kilometres from his nearest depot. This was a huge step forward, whereas previously many farmers were as far as 200 kilometres away from a depot. A final refinement to this scheme was subsidised road transport, from the farm to the depot. In order to make it work, a fixed charge of ten cents per 90-kilo bag was levied on every bag delivered, regardless of distance travelled. Many thought the scheme would not work because of the glaring unfairness resulting from those living on the outer limits of the catchment area paying the same price as those with only a short distance to travel. But work it did and I believe it was a great deal easier and less complicated than having a variable scale of costs, based on distance. This would have only led to dissension, whereas we were trying to harmonise and simplify the whole operation.

The one concept I firmly insisted upon, in formulating these schemes to increase and improve production from the communal lands, was that nothing was going to be free; all costs and operations had to be paid for. Again there was initially much opposition to such thinking, and views were expressed that instead of increasing production, I would in effect reduce it. I argued, however, that if goods and services were instead made available on a grant basis, these would be greatly appreciated in the first year; certainly be expected the following year; and would then become the norm, thus undermining if not destroying any initiative to improve. I also held a view that in all cultures, there is a certain dignity in honouring one's debts and paying one's way. I battled hard to convince opponents of this philosophy, who thought I was being unreasonable, but I always felt this approach was the key to the way forward. I never demanded a full recovery of cost, as I knew that for many, if not most, of the farmers this was impossible. But a contribution on each and every item would be a first step in moving people from subsistence farming into the cash economy.

The livestock industry was not neglected during this transformation period. The problems here were different, and in many aspects, more difficult. Cattle-rearing within the tropics presents its own particular difficulties brought about by heat and disease. To overcome these problems, a high degree of management is required and strict control regimes enforced in practices such as livestock movements, vaccinations and tick control methods. Unfortunately, due to the liberation struggle, many of these essential systems had either collapsed or had been seriously damaged. The containment of tsetse fly is a case in point. The fly spreads trypanosomiasis among cattle and sleeping sickness in humans, if they happen to be bitten. In the years between 1890 and 1970, the fly had practically been eradicated within the borders of Rhodesia. This was achieved by a slow, painstaking method of spraying and trapping the fly which was repeated on an annual basis. However, with the escalation of the armed struggle, the control measures had to be abandoned and the fly regained approximately 20,000 square kilometres below the 1,000 metre contour, above which height it cannot survive. Most of this affected area was in the Zambezi Valley, which is hot, hostile country, containing few domestic cattle or permanent human settlements. It was also a major entry point for the freedom fighters during the armed conflict, but with that problem now removed, it was a top priority to once again eliminate the fly. This was a monumental and often hazardous undertaking, but it is a great credit to the officials and operators concerned that this task was completed within the first five years of independence. It was achieved by a combination of baiting traps (using manufactured odour of ox breath) and night-time aerial spraying. The latter always seemed a hazardous operation to me, where small fixed winged aircraft would fly on fixed beams at treetop height during the hours of darkness. The pilots, who were all experienced young fellows, thought it was an exciting and challenging occupation – which no doubt it was – but it says much to their skills and expertise that during that period we never suffered a single accident. I had the privilege on one occasion to be invited into the Valley to witness the night-time operation. I was impressed with the skills of these pilots and the manner in which they relished the thrill of tree-top flying in the dark – but I suppose we were all young once.

Two other control measures were also severely damaged and adversely affected the cattle industry. Many of the communal cattle dips, situated in the tribal farming areas, were either damaged or destroyed. These acts of deliberate vandalism led to a build-up in the tick population, resulting in the rapid spread of tick-borne diseases. Fortunately, although the effect of tick-related diseases was severe, the problem was one of the easier ones to correct, as it did not take too long to repair and reconstruct the plunge dips and the requisite stock-handling facilities.

The third area of animal disease control which had to be urgently addressed was foot and mouth, which is endemic in parts of the country. Doing so was essential, not only to contain the disease, but also to convince overseas markets that we would not be guilty of exporting infected animal products of any kind, as to do so would jeopardise their own herds. In order to control and contain this disease, the country had been divided into free and non-free zones. Before any beast could journey from one place to another, all cattle owners throughout the country were required by law to obtain a movement permit. Obviously, in a war situation, this was not always easy to enforce, and breaches in the zoning policy occurred. Once the armed conflict had ceased, we were once again able to enforce the regulation controlling cattle movement.

During the initial period when I was in charge of the Ministry of Agriculture, I spent a large part of my time travelling vast distances to the remote areas of the country to meet with subsistence farmers to try and explain to them my views, policies and hope for their future. I was always heartened by the warmth and enthusiasm I received on these visits; it was not because it was me: the reason was that someone was now showing an interest in them and their welfare. Organising small competitions where they could compete with their skills and show off their products always generated great enthusiasm and created an atmosphere for renewed efforts. Fortunately, I had the support of many white commercial farmers, especially those who lived in close proximity to the communal lands, who were willing to provide advice and practical support in the form of assisting communal farmers with planting, cultivation, transport, etc.

The final problem that faced the cattle industry in 1980 was climate. The 1970s had basically been a decade of drought. This had resulted in poor grazing and led to a decline in cattle numbers, either through death or deliberate de-stocking programmes. The challenge facing both the government livestock departments and the cattlemen of the country was simple: restore and enforce veterinary control measures and rebuild the cattle population in the shortest possible time. Fortunately, one of the most valuable legacies inherited by the new government was an extremely professional and dedicated department of veterinary services, located within the Ministry of Agriculture. Their responsibilities were divided into two main areas – control and research. It did not take this team of veterinarians long to re-introduce the necessary measures, bearing in mind that legislation was already in place to gain control of the country's animal disease problems. At the same time, the main marketing agency of beef animals, the Cold Storage Commission, quickly reactivated its support schemes, such as becoming a residual buyer of live animals in communal land cattle sales and increasing the scope of its pen feed schemes, in which large numbers of animals were purchased or in some cases customer operated, and fed a high protein ration, usually for about ninety days, prior to being slaughtered. However, I contend that the main incentive to restoring confidence in the beef industry was a substantial increase in the producer price to which I have previously referred.

At this time, we were granted a temporary quota of 9,500 tonnes of beef, to be marketed into Europe under the Lomé Convention. This was of enormous value to us, as it provided a lucrative outlet for our high value, top quality hindquarter cuts. Although the Zimbabwe population was a large consumer of meat (mainly beef) the majority of the population tended to favour cheaper cuts or joints for obvious reasons. Thus, under the Lomé agreement, we were able to maximise the financial return from the whole carcass, with the more expensive cuts being sold in the EU states, and the cheaper portions finding a ready outlet on the home market. We also had a small but nevertheless valuable market in other non-EU countries, notably Spain.[2] Most of these meat exports were flown on a Zimbabwe air-freight carrier called Affretair. This was an airline which had previously been used as a vehicle for breaking trade sanctions during the UDI period. It was owned and operated by a most delightful character called Jack Malloch.

---

2 Spain joined the EU in 1986.

However, once Zimbabwe became independent, the use to which it had previously been put was no longer required, but a home-owned air-freighter had obvious advantages. However, there existed one major handicap: the airline was seriously under-capitalised and owed a considerable amount of money by the previous government. Much to my alarm, I was presented with a bill for most of the outstanding debts, as at some time in the previous decade, and in order to keep clandestine meat markets supplied with regular product, the Ministry of Agriculture had signed a guarantee in favour of the debtors. After some fancy negotiating between the banks, the government and the airline, a deal was struck whereby the government honoured the debts, took over the airline, and engaged Malloch to operate and fly the aircraft (there was only one). On balance, I think it would be safe to say that this particular arrangement suited all parties concerned. Jack was a very skilled and competent pilot and the ideal person to run such an operation. Sadly, in 1982, he suffered a fatal crash when flying a Second World War Spitfire for a documentary film.

Other markets for livestock products were also quickly developed. Following the expansion of the dairy industry and the growth in milk production, export opportunities for processed dairy products by the Dairy Marketing Board were established. These tended to be more or less on a regional rather than an overseas basis, but again we were able to compete and market on quality.

Additional products which also provided valuable foreign exchange were private sector initiatives, mainly in pig and pork products, plus initiatives in the poultry industry which saw growth in a number of areas. Further sectors of agricultural production quickly began to develop, such as horticulture, ostrich rearing, crocodile farming, hybrid seed production, and they all became significant contributors to both the farming sector and the national economy. The two dominant factors, to which Zimbabwean farmers always adhered in order to achieve success, were quality of product and continuity of supply, without which no long-term marketing strategy can be maintained.

The key industry to kick-start the revival of the Zimbabwe economy was tobacco. Since the end of the Second World War, tobacco had made two significant contributions to the country's economy. First, it was the largest single earner of foreign currency, and second, it was also the largest employer of labour. Despite fourteen years of economic sanctions in which tobacco was a targeted product, it had survived the onslaught. Thanks to a small body of entrepreneurs and a few selected civil servants, Rhodesian tobacco had continued to be bought by many countries under many guises, despite its distinctively identifiable character. As a matter of fact, during this period, a few new markets were explored and developed. Obviously, the crop size had shrunk considerably between 1965 and 1980, but the industry was very much alive and raring to go.

One of the inhibiting factors faced in 1980 was sourcing affordable finance to loan to tobacco merchants to enable them to purchase the leaf on offer. The Zimbabwe Tobacco Association (ZTA) – a body representing tobacco growers – under the leadership of its energetic president, Roy Ashburner, had managed to negotiate a considerable sum of money to be made available by the banking sector, provided the total was guaranteed by government. At a meeting in my office, they requested that I approach the Minister of Finance and try to secure such a guarantee. I thought their request eminently reasonable, and could see the importance of ensuring financial confidence to the tobacco buying companies. I also felt strongly that a rapid return to the open international tobacco market would provide the largest and quickest injection of badly needed foreign currency into our economy. Unfortunately, my senior advisors in the ministry viewed the request differently. They argued, with a certain amount of justification, that it was morally wrong to support what was in essence, a private sector industry with public sector finance, i.e. taxpayers' money. They were very concerned that such an approach would harm the whole of the private sector, as in the eyes of the government it would be perceived as capitalistic greed. After many hours of discussions, I said I was going to make the request. The Permanent Secretary (PS), with the backing of his deputies, said he could not support me, and furthermore, he would contact the PS Finance, inviting him to concur with his view and not to attend any meeting convened to discuss the proposition. From a purely ethical position, their view and action were totally correct. Again, I was faced with a personal challenge, but I believed then, as I do now, that having heard all the arguments, from all sides, at the end of the day you have to do what you honestly believe is right, and in a political context I felt a strong case could be made. So, I phoned the Minister of Finance, requesting a meeting, and as I felt the outcome of such a meeting would impact favourably or adversely on a large sector of the workforce, I asked the Minister of Labour, Kumbirai Kangai, if he could also be present. The reason for my request being that as the tobacco industry was the largest single employer in the country any serious demise in its fortunes would have a serious negative impact on the labour market. Arriving at the Minister of Finance, Enos Nkala's, office, I found Minister Kangai already there, but no officials from either ministry. I was quickly asked to state my case, which I did as briefly and as accurately as I could. Having finished what I had to say, Nkala turned to Kangai, and asked him if he was happy or if he needed further clarification. He replied to the effect that he was satisfied, and at that point Nkala called in his private secretary and dictated a brief instruction, saying that government would guarantee the loans advanced by the banks for one season. I asked him if he would not have to take that decision to cabinet for approval, to which he replied that he was the Minister of Finance, and he was using the authority vested in himself to make a financial decision which he judged to be correct, without reference to or consent from anyone else. I was impressed with his forthright approach and it confirmed a view I already had that he was a dynamic and decisive minister. Of the many ministers who have held the finance portfolio since independence, I would rate him as one of the best, because of his ability to make rapid decisions. I am not suggesting that he was always right, but he certainly left no one in any doubt about his views and policies. This enabled others to quickly respond, because most people can react to a yes or a no, but it is extremely difficult to have a positive reaction to a 'maybe'. Not long after my return to my office, Roy Ashburner phoned to hear if I had been successful. I was pleased to assure him I had, but was a little perplexed to learn from him that they had a small problem. They had forgotten to include an interest factor if the loans were utilised. Not being too pleased, I asked him if he had a figure in mind, and this he gave to me. I quickly phoned Nkala, explained the position, and asked him to increase the guarantee. This he readily agreed to do, but he informed me that the matter was now closed and he did not want me to come back to him again. With the guarantee in place, the buyers started to buy the tobacco leaf with confidence; the whole market became buoyant; established companies and customers increased their purchases; new customers were quickly attracted to a quality product; and much to my relief, the government was never called upon to honour their guarantee and the tobacco industry rapidly re-established its position as the world's third largest exporting nation. This small experience demonstrated to me what can be achieved when public institutions and private sectors agree to work together.

At that time tobacco farmers grew, reaped and cured the leaves of the tobacco plant; graded them according to length, colour and texture to ensure uniformity; pressed the leaves into bales weighing up to 100kgs; wrapped them in specially prepared paper; sewed them into hessian and sent them to the auction floors to be sold. Tobacco sales were always exciting events because it was a walking auction method, unique in the world to Zimbabwe. The bales having been weighed and identified are laid out in rows with enough space for people to walk between them. This was essential as the process of auctioneering can only be described as on the move; on one side of the bales would be the starter who would shout out a starting price; next was the auctioneer who would take the bids; third was an individual known as a ticket marker who would record the selling price and buyer and tag it onto the bale. The buyers walked on the other side of the bales and the whole sale was over in a matter of seconds, before the team moved on to the next bale. Because of the speed with which the sale takes place, it is not possible for the buyer to check the quality of his purchase until after the auction and the buying teams have moved forward. At that time, there is an opportunity for both buyer and seller to quickly view the transaction. If the buyer finds fault with his purchase and he is not satisfied with its presentation, he can reject the bale. Likewise, if the seller feels the price offered is too low, he has the right to decline the price by tearing a corner of the bale ticket, which in effect cancels the sale. To the uninitiated this might sound absurd, but in practice it worked very well, and on balance led to orderly marketing. It was a very professional system and many visitors and tourists would go to the floors just to witness this unusual and fascinating system of selling.

Agriculture was the pivotal industry within Zimbabwe, but within this sector, tobacco was the key product. Most of its support services, although controlled by government legislation, were to a large extent financed by the industry members themselves, the industry being the growers and the buyers, with the former making the major contribution. Their funds were gathered normally through self-imposed levies, which were usually collected at source. That meant a percentage of the sale revenue was deducted from each bale of leaf sold. Using this fairly painless but effective system, they were able to establish and fund possibly the best tobacco research station in the world, catering for the needs and requirements of the grower, buyer, manufacturer and ultimately the consumer. I deliberately mention the consumer, as great care was taken to interact with medical bodies and health organisations, which interested themselves with the known and perceived dangers of smoke and nicotine inhalation. The tobacco research programmes were devised and run by a dedicated team of scientists, who became admired and respected on a global scale, and ensured that Zimbabwe's tobacco maintained its position as the highest quality in the world.

Marketing was another arm of the industry which received participant funding. Government provided the protective legislation, and employed the enforcing staff to ensure hygiene and quality were adhered to. Again, the complicated system of organising and running a huge national industry succeeded because of the close working relationships and understandings between private and public sectors.

Mention must be made of the interest taken by Mugabe in the agricultural sector. By his own admission, neither he nor his ministers had much knowledge on large-scale farming. In a serious attempt to acquaint himself with the complexities of the industry, many visits were arranged for him to go to farming districts and to also go to institutions such as research stations, marketing depots, extension projects, etc. These were very successful as Mugabe showed great interest in all that he saw, and asked many searching and intelligent questions, which demonstrated his keenness. But, above all, he impressed everyone with his friendliness and the ability he had to communicate with all he met. On occasion, this caused great concern to those responsible for his safety, as he had the habit of breaking away from agreed routes, or programmes, in order to satisfy his curiosity on specific issues. In one dramatic instance, he actually accepted a lift in a small aircraft piloted by a prominent farmer Clive Nicol, in order to have an aerial view of what had been explained to him on the ground. As can be imagined, this caused his security personnel great consternation as they believed that he had been hijacked. All other onlookers felt it had been a good publicity exercise. The prime minister's genuine interest was quickly copied by other politicians, which obviously made my task of explaining and emphasising the importance and benefits of agriculture that much easier.

However, many difficulties remained in my quest for greater improvement in this sector across the whole country. One of those areas was in agricultural research. As mentioned previously, the tobacco sector was well funded and well served in this area through the services of the Tobacco Research Board. The other sector which enjoyed a certain amount of autonomy was hybrid seed production, particularly maize seed, which had its own breeding farm. The overall body catering for research was the Department of Research and Specialist Services (DRSS), which was within the Ministry of Agriculture. Again, we had an institute which was well served and run by able administrators and very capable and dedicated scientists under the overall control of a director. There was a place for private sector input, through liaison committees which consisted of representatives from both government and farming unions. In addition, the commodity associations of the CFU also made annual contributions towards funding research and, as with tobacco, these were collected at the point of sale. Despite the excellence of these arrangements, there was a growing feeling among commodity associations and their members that more needed to be done to improve the knowledge and advice available to them. Government funding was obviously a major constraint, but another area of concern to the farming bodies was the direction in which research should proceed, and in this regard, the farmers felt they needed more input and control. As a consequence, they purchased a farm, appointed a director, and opened their own research station. Again, it was funded by contributions from various commodities, which paid into a trust. The trust was managed by a Board of Trustees, which was appointed by the same commodity associations. The whole project went under the title of the Agriculture Research Trust (ART). It is worth recording that the private sector maintained their contributions to the DRSS, so what was paid to ART was additional money, not diverted funds. In this initiative, I again found myself in conflict with the official view.

Many believed that the overall research effort would suffer by diluting and duplicating the government programmes run by DRSS and the new programmes to be initiated by ART farm. I, on the other hand, believed that with additional monies, there was scope for an expansion of research, on a complementary basis, and not diminution on a competitive one. For this reason, I agreed to open the new station against the advice of my senior advisors, and a certain hostility from a few who felt their influence and positions were under threat. The following week, during the weekly cabinet meeting, Mugabe raised the issue by saying that he had been informed that I was undermining government's research programmes by supporting a rival organisation. His remarks gave rise to a few smirks by ministers who always seemed to enjoy watching a colleague being put down. After I had carefully explained ART's objectives, and my reason for supporting the project, Mugabe said it sounded like a good idea and he himself would be interested in seeing it for himself one day. To the best of my knowledge, he never did visit the research farm, but his endorsement of the scheme removed all opposition to it.

After accepting the agricultural portfolio, my first official visit outside Zimbabwe was to Britain and Romania. I was accompanied by my wife June and a number of officials, who quickly became involved in serious and productive discussions with experts within their own disciplines. This was particularly valuable to us, as we had suffered from fifteen years of isolation, and there were serious gaps in our knowledge pool. I was impressed and grateful for the friendliness and warmth with which my team was welcomed by all contacts, whether they were in the private or public sectors. My particular role was to establish contact at an official level, which often included permanent secretaries and/or ministers. I was given the use of a chauffeur-driven Jaguar, which caused June much amusement. At the beginning of our visit, she and I would travel in the rear of the car, while Ted Osborn, my PS, would be in the front, with the driver. However, I suffer badly from travel sickness and with all the stopping and starting in London traffic, I often felt very sick. To overcome my affliction, I swapped places with Ted, and he sat in the back with my wife and I moved to the front seat where I felt much better. Osborn was tall, slim, silver-haired, and always perfectly dressed, so whenever we arrived at a function, invariably the rear door would be opened by a welcoming official, with the words, 'Welcome Minister'. Ted would then unfold his long legs and glide out of the car, while I was still fiddling with the handle in the front, much to the amusement of my wife.

After five days in London, I left with a smaller team for Romania, while the remainder of the team concluded their business in England. We went to Romania at the invitation of their government following the support they had given in training and material to those engaged in the armed struggle against Rhodesia. Now they hoped to be able to capitalise on their investment and obtain a share in the largest industry in our country – agriculture. We were met at the airport by the Romanian Minister of Agriculture and his wife. He told me he had been minister for seventeen years. As this portfolio is often considered to be something of a poisoned chalice, I immediately warmed to him. He was a tall, broad-shouldered man with an easy smile and his wife was also very pleasant. Between the two of them, they made our visit memorable.

June and I were given a suite in the Grand Hotel, which was at a right angle to the former Royal Palace. Fearful of possibly saying the wrong thing, we would step onto our balcony to exchange views. I had not been in the hotel very long, when I had a telephone call from President Banana, who, unbeknown to me, was also in Bucharest. He was staying in a government guest house in the woods, just outside the capital, and he said he wished to see me urgently. I went to see him and found he was accompanied by Minister Sekeramayi. He told me he was leaving the next day, but before he left, he had a final audience with President Ceaușescu and would like me to accompany him, as his delegation was very small.

The following morning, I crossed the square and entered the Palace for the meeting. The interior was impressive, as were the many guards who stood completely immobile up two flights of stairs. They were all over six foot tall and wore uniforms which resembled guards from an Ivor Novello operetta. I joined the Banana delegation in an ante-room, but I still had no idea what I was supposed to do. We were ushered into a large room, with an extremely long table, with President Nicolai Ceaușescu, flanked by about thirty ministers and officials (many in uniforms). We were about eight strong and timidly took our seats, facing this battery of severe, unsmiling faces. Ceaușescu opened the meeting by welcoming Banana and hoping he had enjoyed his visit. Banana made the usual complimentary reply, accompanied by his habitual nervous giggle. After what I can only describe as a pregnant pause,

Ceauşescu asked Banana if he was ready to sign the agreement. Banana looking very uncomfortable asked which agreement. This brought an angry retort from Ceauşescu, who said the agreement they had been discussing all week. I was fast beginning to think I had been unwise to agree to join the delegation. However, Banana recovered some of his composure and explained that he was only a titular president and not an executive one, therefore, he did not possess signing powers, and could not help. This occasioned further vitriol from Ceauşescu who said a president was a president and had overall control of his country, and that he *would* sign. The atmosphere in the room was distinctly uncomfortable, and I imagined I could see hostility in all the Romanian eyes facing us. Banana made another feeble attempt to extract himself by claiming that he had not read the document, and he did not now have time as he had to drive to the airport. The short response to that remark was he was not going anywhere, and would certainly not catch an aeroplane until he had signed the agreement.

It was at this point that with a huge smile, he introduced me to the gathering, and said I had been sent out to study the agreement, with the full authority to sign on behalf of Zimbabwe if I was satisfied. That contribution did not seem to placate Ceauşescu, and it took me by complete surprise, as I had not previously heard about the proposal, and I felt ill-equipped to accept this new responsibility. Nonetheless, the suggestion was reluctantly accepted by the Romanians, and Banana, Sekeramayi, and the rest of our contingent left the room, the former still smiling broadly.

I was then confronted by three Romanians with a very official-looking document, beautifully bound, its sections separated by ribbons and seals. After a brief discussion, it was agreed that I would now be the Zimbabwean negotiator, and I would interface with my opposite number, the Romanian Minister of Agriculture. I left the Palace clutching the agreement and on reaching the hotel, sought out Osborn to relay my morning's experience. He said that he and other members of my staff would immediately read the proposed agreement and come back to me. This they did within an hour, saying that the whole agreement was totally unacceptable. However, as we thought it would be unwise to say so in as many words, we methodically went through every clause, making our own comments and suggestions, and then sent it round to the Romanian Ministry of Agriculture.

The essence of the agreement was that Romania would supply Zimbabwe with several hundred tractors of Italian design, which were being manufactured under licence at a factory in Brasov. There were many other clauses which guaranteed an adequate supply of spares, and included a large number of three- and five-ton trucks. The main difficulty with the proposals was we did not need the equipment, as our recognised assembly plants and franchise dealers had already established their own retail outlets and, more importantly, on a unit basis. In addition, the Romanian products were far more expensive.

As my team was in the country for a week, we continued with the programme which had been prepared for us, while different members of my staff took it in turns to redraft the agreement proposals. The wretched document went between the two parties, sometimes as often as three times a day. Realising that on visits such as ours you are always shown the best on offer, we were nevertheless suitably impressed with many aspects of their farming, in particular their fruit production and agricultural research. The tractor factor had formerly assembled aircraft and we were told with pride that aeroplanes had been made there as late as the 1930s. Unfortunately, it gave the impression that little had been done to improve the facilities since those days. The buildings were badly lit and poorly ventilated; perhaps, in consequence, production levels were extremely low, and quality control almost non-existent.

However, at the end of the week, we finally had a document I felt I could sign. It was proposed we would take three tractors of different horsepower and would locate them on one of the research farms on a trial basis. The tractors were to be accompanied by a Romanian engineer who would oversee the trials. My Romanian counterpart, whose name sounded like Michelangelo, signed it with a broad smile and a shrug which suggested to me that he did not hold strong views on the deal. (He looked like a survivor – I hope he was.)

The three tractors duly arrived accompanied by their overseer. One broke down almost immediately, so he was left with two to test on Zimbabwe's varying soil types, and differing weather patterns. The whole project quietly became forgotten, except for the poor Romanian engineer, who periodically sent reports home, mainly to inform his masters that he was modifying some component part, or replacing another, in an attempt to increase efficiency. After two years of this correspondence, one of the factory managers arrived unexpectedly, only to discover that his man had found a girl, and was living quite happily, hoping that one day, like the tractor, they would forget he was there. Unfortunately for him, that was the end of his romance, he was packed off home, and the tractors were parked in the shade, and may still be there.

I did, however, have one more meeting with President Ceaușescu, in July 1983, when he and his wife paid a visit to Zimbabwe. I do not recall it being a state visit as it was fairly low-key, although he was delighted to have been given the freedom of the City of Harare. Unexpectedly, Mugabe asked me if I could accompany Ceaușescu, his wife and his delegation to a commercial farm.

'Which one?' I asked, and was told, 'You pick, so long as it's a good one.'

The following day, I took them to a well-developed dairy farm, which was also producing high-yielding crops under irrigation. The farm manager was very obliging, showing his guests around the property, which also had extensive facilities for his workforce, including a well-run primary school and a very well-equipped and staffed medical clinic. After a few hours it was time to leave, and after handshakes all round, Ceauşescu turned to me and through an interpreter said, 'I like it; I will take it.'

I was flabbergasted and said it was not for sale, to which he replied that he didn't want to buy it, just take it. I reported back to Mugabe who asked me how I had left the situation. I told him about Ceauşescu's remarks and told him I'd been taken aback, but felt that a non-committal answer was the best response, as Ceauşescu was his guest, and I implied that the problem was now his. I do not know what passed between them, but I had the impression that the relationship cooled and the farm remained the property of its legitimate owner.

In November 1980, I went to Rome for the annual meeting of the Food and Agricultural Organization (FAO). The purpose of my visit was to make formal application for membership of the organisation on behalf of the Government of Zimbabwe. In reality it was a simple exercise: once the application form had been lodged, it was then voted on by every member nation, voting alphabetically, one by one. After this lengthy process had been completed, in which there were no negative votes, but three abstentions out of a total of 160 or so countries, we became full members. After making a few enquiries, I was told the reasons for the abstentions were that two delegations did not know where Zimbabwe was, and the third had never heard of it.

The following morning our small delegation trooped outside the building and, in bitterly cold weather, raised the Zimbabwe flag. It had been an interesting few days, which enabled me and my small delegation to meet other agriculturalists, plus many trade and aid agencies, and explain the position of Zimbabwe's agriculture, in particular, and Zimbabwe as an emergent country in general. Our cause was a little confused at times, because the computer had both my name and designation completely scrambled. Each delegate on arrival was asked to hand in his air ticket at the registration desk, where the clerks would check the details, and confirm onward flights. Unfortunately, they took my details off the ticket, but somehow misread the order. Most airlines produce a ticket which gives your surname, then your initials, and finally title. My ticket read Norman, D.R. Sen. (which was an abbreviation for Senator). This led to me being issued with a name badge called Dr Sen. Despite repeated attempts to point out the error, I was constantly told that computers don't make mistakes – a sentiment with which I agreed, for it is the human operator who makes the mistakes. From the day of my introduction to the FAO, I became one of its supporters, both for its analysis of food production problems, and its serious attempts to overcome them. The one major criticism I had was that the administration was overblown and top-heavy. However, that is a fault of many organisations, including governments at all levels. Regarding the FAO, however, this weakness could and should have been corrected by member nations, as over-staffing not only leads to inefficiency, but it has negative financial implications.

Another body with which I worked and became very familiar was the Southern Africa Development Co-ordinating Committee (SADCC), later renamed the Southern Africa Development Community (SADC). It was originally formed in 1980 to assist development in southern Africa, and counter the belligerent attitude of the then South African government. Despite the sometime natural suspicions that governments had of each other, I always considered real progress was made in developing and harmonising localised programmes, in such areas as telecommunications, power generation and distribution, regional transport, and above all else, food security. In fact, the latter became so well structured, that the assurance of adequate food for a whole region was virtually guaranteed.

It is a matter of great regret that this is no longer the case. Indeed, food security in Zimbabwe has been completely undermined by the ill-considered land reform measures which went hand in hand with the government's acquiescence to the illegal occupation of farms and ranches, without compensation to those who held legal title to those properties. Both these programmes, undertaken for political reasons, led to a rapid and disastrous fall in agricultural productivity. One of the big questions currently facing the country is, can the present unauthorised occupation of farmland be reversed leading again to a position of food self-sufficiency? In my honest opinion, the answer is yes, but I would not underestimate the difficulty of the task. It will need a massive change of heart and direction by political leaders, starting from the premise that it is not who owns the land but who can produce from the land, which is the critical factor in once again feeding the nation, and becoming a major contributor to regional surpluses.

I realise that it will be difficult for many people to accept that the measures and attitudes of recent years will have to be replaced by a new land policy embracing ownership, occupation and financing, in order to ensure that those working the land are knowledgeable, well-trained and motivated. I also strongly believe that measures will have to be quickly instigated to deal with thorny issues such as compensation and restitution, so that one chapter can close and another open without contentious issues being carried forward. Many views have been expressed on the question of ownership of title and many entrenched positions have been adopted. While I have no pretence at being an expert on the subject, I believe there is merit in examining the idea that all land should become the property of the state, which does not mean the government of the day, and all present title holders be recognised and fairly compensated. A properly constituted and financed land authority should be established, with one of its objectives being to enter into

Three Norman brothers (1942): Denis, John and Jim.

In 1954, Denis Norman with hands of tobacco: Bourton Vale
Farm, Matepatepa.

1953: Farm manager's house on Katumba section, Bourton Vale Farm, following a bush fire.

John and Denis Norman with Father Widlake. Bourton Vale Farm Matepatepa.

Denis and June Norman on their wedding day in 1955.

1955: Denis and June's first home, the restored manager's house on Katumba section and in 1956, the moment of departure from Matepatepa.

1959: Tobacco seed beds being sown by hand on Pelele Farm in Karoi.

1960: Pelele Farm House, Karoi.

(Below) 1968: The Norman family.

June and Denis Norman at their home in Norton.

Lord Soames with Denis Norman.

"FIVE hundred outstanding complaints—and they're all from me!"

1982: Denis Norman with Dr Anthony O'Reilly, CEO of H.J.Heinz when they bought Olivine industries in a joint partnership with the Zimbabwe government.

1982: Denis Norman with Princess Anne and the Director at the Hendersen Research Station in Mazowe.

1983, October: a rare photograph of President Mugabe laughing as Denis Norman invites him to open a new Dairy Marketing Board depot in the Eastern Highlands .

Row 1: Sydney Sekeremayi, Denis Norman, Daniel Ngwenya, Moven Mahachi, Oliver Munyaradzi, Fred Shava, Simba Makoni
Row 2: Richard Hove, Simbi Mubako, Ernest Kadungure, Witness Mangwende, Dzingai Mutumbuka, Nathan Shamuyarira, Edison Zvogbo, Herbert Ushewokunze, Simbarashe Mumbengegwi, Farai Masango, Emmerson Mnangagwa
Row 3: Maurice Nyagumbo, Joice Mujuru, Simon Muzenda, Robert Mugabe, Enos Nkala, Victoria Chitepo, Bernard Chidzero

PM ACKNOWLEDGES THE COURAGE OF THE COMMERCIAL FARMER

COMMERCIAL farmers in Zimbabwe received an accolade from Prime Minister Robert Mugabe during the celebrations marking the fourth anniversary of Independence.

In an address to the nation, Mr Mugabe said: "What Zimbabwe needs is the bold courage and zeal demonstrated by our commercial farmer, who, in spite of such hazards as successive droughts and crops diseases and such constraints as world recession, shortages of foreign currency and difficult markets, continues to take enormous risks year in and year out. I wish to commend him as well as the peasant farmer for his immense efforts, some of which have gone unrewarded because of the drought and the prevailing circumstances."

Meanwhile, an article on the situation of white farmers in Matabeleland published in New African magazine, praises Mr Mugabe and his ministers for doing everything within their power to keep the morale of whites high in that drought-stricken and dissident-torn province.

Says an article entitled Whites quit Matabeleland: "Since Independence Prime Minister Mugabe has done as much as any leader could do to help the white commercial farmers in their present difficulties. He has visited the farmers throughout Matabeleland. He has heard with considerable patience about their problems. He has toured the country with his Minister of Agriculture, Senator Denis

Norman, and held frequent meetings with the leader of the Commercial Farmers' Union, John Laurie.'

"The unpalatable decision to re-arm the white farmers, his erstwhile "enemies" was taken last year, and yet farmers in the Kezi area have quit the land of their birth."

The magazine comments that some people might argue that the removal of "privileged" whites from Matabeleland ranchlands could be a good thing, a move towards the creation of socialism. "Whatever the historic reason," it says, "whites continue to provide roughly 50% of the country's marketed foodstuffs, and government policy recognises this."

Keeping white morale as high as possible in Matabeleland... Senator Norman with the Prime Minister, Mr Mugabe, at a "meet the farmers" meeting during which local problems were discussed.

1982: Denis Norman with Pope John Paul ll and Robert Mugabe.

1982: Denis Norman with Prime Minister Robert Mugabe. Ceremony to lay the foundation stone at the new African Centre for Fertiliser Development (ACFD) in Harare.

MODERN □
farming

Summer '82

Angola: Kw 60   Malawi: K 1.50   Tanzania: Shs 15
Botswana: P 1.5   Mocambique: 60 MT   Zambia: K 1.50
Lesotho: R 1.5   Swaziland: L 1.50   Zimbabwe: Z$1

Into 1983 with a mood of cautious optimism

Norman interview
EXCLUSIVE!

President
State House
Harare

9th April, 1990.

Mr *D. Norman*

Ministry of *Transport and National Supplies*

Harare

Dear Mr *Norman*,

     I have pleasure in appointing you as Minister of *Transport and National Supplies* .... to carry out those duties and functions which go with this post, and any others that I, as President, may assign to you from time to time.

     I wish you well.

Yours sincerely,

R.G. MUGABE
PRESIDENT

ESTABLISHED 1894   BULAWAYO, TUESDAY, AUGUST 20, 1991

(Registered at the GPO as a Newspaper)   P.O. Box 585 Bulawayo. Telephone 65471, Telex 33481 ZMNews ZW

NRZ launches second phase of restructuring

Chronicle Reporter

THE Minister of Transport and National Supplies, Mr Denis Norman, yesterday launched the $700 million World Bank Railway II Project aimed at restructuring and strengthening the operations of the National Railways of Zimbabwe.

Speaking at the launching ceremony in Bulawayo yesterday, Mr Norman said the project would not only benefit Zimbabwe but the entire Southern Africa Development Co-ordination Conference regional grouping.

He said the NRZ moved an average of 14 million tonnes of traffic — both imports and exports — a year from Zaire, Zambia, Botswana and Mozambique and this clearly indicated that the project would not be of benefit to Zimbabwe only.

The World Bank Railways II Project was signed in January this year.

Important aspects of the project include the setting up of a performance contract for the NRZ's general manager.

Approximately 60 percent of the total costs would be in foreign exchange. The cost of the project is estimated on the basis of an implementation period of six years.

The project came into being after the signing of the loan agreement in January setting conditions covering a general cross-section of the NRZ's operations for the loan's effectiveness.

To Centrespread

Denis Norman climbing aboard a dredger in Rotterdam in the late 1980s
when he went to Holland to source a dredger for the Beira Corridor Group

To Minister Dennis Norman —
With warm best wishes, [signature] Ay Bush

Bush doubles US aid

WASHINGTON.

PRESIDENT Bush yesterday doubled the amount of American aid to Zimbabwe to support the current economic reform programme aimed at revamping the economy to create new jobs and stimulate growth.

At a joint Press conference with President Mugabe after a two-hour meeting at the White House, Mr Bush said Zimbabwe's economic reform had been strongly supported by the World Bank, International Monetary Fund and several American businessmen.

"American firms have expressed faith in your country because of the bold steps you have taken to allow market-led economic growth," he said.

Mr Bush said Zimbabwe and the United States shared the fundamental belief that governments must serve the people. It was against this background that Washington was happy with the political and economic changes that had taken place in Zimbabwe during the past year.

The positive changes, said Mr Bush, included the removal of the state of emergency, the adoption of the multi-party policy, the decision not to legislate for a one-party state, abandoning Marxism-Leninism as a guiding principle and the institution of the structural adjustment programme.

"As a result, we are going to double the amount of development aid originally earmarked for this year," said Mr Bush.

No figure was given.

By joining the American Overseas Private Investment Corporation, Zimbabwe will benefit from American investors through the financing of new projects for a period of between 10 to 12 years.

These projects would help Zimbabwe's private sector boost its expansion programme and generate more jobs. Mr Bush said the investment climate in Zimbabwe was now more relaxed so as to attract American business.

Zimbabwe would remain a leader in Southern Africa and its relationship with Washington was expected

to be warm and productive so as to serve as a basis for further progress.

"As you leave Washington, you are assured of the best wishes of the American people," said Mr Bush.

He said Zimbabwe's leadership of the Security Council during the Gulf crisis was critical and helped the United States and its allies to resolve the situation speedily.

The President said he hoped additional incentives to woo investors taken under the economic reform programme and Zimbabwe's stable political situation would attract more US private investment.

There were more than 40 private US companies doing business in the country.

President Mugabe said the total abolition of apartheid leading to the creation of a united non-racial democratic South Africa remains Africa's ultimate goal.

"That is why we in Southern Africa would urge that the remaining sanction pressures on the Pretoria regime be maintained until the goals of a

to Zimbabwe

25/7/91

reached an irreversible stage."

Zimbabwe would support steps to ensure the establishment of lasting peace in Angola. He hoped the two warring sides in Mozambique would quickly move towards a ceasefire and the establishment of a lasting solution to that country's 15-year-old conflict.

"We are mindful of our close co-operation and collaboration during the Gulf crisis as was evidenced during our presidency of the (UN) Security Council. We believe in the rule of law and hope that the momentum of bilateral co-operation will continue and lead to the establishment of a broader solution and peace in the Middle East, including the final, permanent, and satisfactory settlement of the Palestinian question," he said.

President Mugabe on Tuesday night called on African countries to implement the African Economic Community treaty through the strengthening of regional organisations such as SADCC and PTA.

In an hour-long address to African diplomats accredited to Washington at Africare House, where he

was a guest, Cde Mugabe said that if the AEC was established, African countries should eventually be able to trade freely.

"It's high time Africa moves away from petty squabbles based on ethnicity and concentrate on the development of the continent as a whole," said Cde Mugabe.

Cde Mugabe was scheduled to meet Acting Secretary of State Mr Lawrence Eagleburger, who will be deputising for Mr James Baker, currently on a Middle East peace mission.

The President was also due to meet the managing director of the International Monetary Fund, Mr Michel Camdessus, before visiting the new Zimbabwe embassy in Washington.

Today, the President is scheduled to meet Senator Paul Simon and Senator Nancy Kassebaum, before meeting other United States congressmen.

Before his departure for London en route to Abuja, Nigeria, Cde Mugabe will meet the World Bank president, Mr Barber Conable. — Ziana.

1994: President Nelson Mandela and Denis Norman.

1994: Denis Norman, Minister of Transport and Energy officially opening
the Insukamini Substation in Bulawayo, a joint initiative between the
Zimbabwe Electricity Supply Authority, the Zimbabwean and the Finnish
governments.

1986: June and Denis Norman

2011: June and Denis Norman on his eightieth birthday.

long-term leases with genuine, qualified farmers, in which the lease contracts could be used as collateral for raising both long- and short-term loans. This scheme with adequate safeguards should also be made available to those living within the present communal lands in order that they may have access to seasonal credit. If such suggestions were adopted, not only would production rapidly increase, but the protection of the land would be guaranteed, for in the event of farmer failure, the property would revert to the state for re-allocation, thus ensuring that land was always being managed by capable and qualified people.

My final thoughts on resettlement concern farm usage to suit ecological regions. Zimbabwe, with its wide diversity of climate, altitude and soil type, possesses a wide range of possibilities for a varied choice of both crop and livestock husbandry, and it should be possible, with careful planning, to select and encourage the main activities to be followed within those regions. If this is achieved, and with a sensible and judicious use of the plentiful natural resources, in particular land and water, the recovery programme can begin.

Another major asset in assisting the rehabilitation of agriculture, and hence the recovery of the country's economy, is that much of the necessary infrastructure is already in place, i.e. roads, railway tracks and power lines. No doubt it is in urgent need of upgrading and some replacement, but nevertheless, this could be achieved with international financial assistance. The support services required to allow agriculture to flourish are already in existence: there are research organisations, both public and private; the government has an extension service, as well as a veterinary department and agricultural colleges and training institutions. These services will all need to be reactivated and trained personnel recruited to fill the gaps left by resignations and redundancies, but nevertheless, the basic structures are in place. A national scheme along these lines would, I feel, satisfy most objectives and aspirations of both legislators and farmers, and ultimately restore agriculture to its pivotal and important position, in the nation's economic life. The wider aspects of growing an agricultural industry, such as storing, transporting and marketing, would naturally follow; many people and companies wish to be associated with a success story – it happened in the past and it could certainly happen in the future.

Again, I would see a co-ordinating role for SADC, particularly with its expanded membership which now includes both South Africa and Namibia. Some of the early decisions taken by the founding members were good, such as placing the headquarters in Botswana, and having a rotating chairman. However, the post of secretary general, although it has not yet caused a problem, could, I think, become divisive and should always be filled on merit. For example, the first person to hold this post was Arthur Blumeris from Zimbabwe. A consummate diplomat, he was a great success because he enabled people to understand each other. Unfortunately, he died towards the end of his first term in office, creating a vacancy for the post which was becoming increasingly influential within the region and beyond. Mugabe saw this as an opportunity for moving one of his cabinet members, who was causing embarrassment to him and his older colleagues. This was Simba Makoni, a man I knew well, and who had become a firm friend of mine. He possessed a fine intellect, had a great sense of humour and was always polite and correct. In our ministry, he was a great asset. He had the ability to quickly assess a problem, analyse the options, make a decision and have the courage to implement it. I knew from the beginning that he was too accomplished to remain a deputy minister, and it was not long before he was promoted to Minister of Industry. Around the cabinet table, he was more like a hurricane than a breath of fresh air. Not only did he quickly familiarise himself with the complexities of his own portfolio, but he also took a keen and lively interest in other areas. This inevitably led to clashes among cabinet members. Although he was usually correct in his pronouncements of others' weaknesses and failures, it did cause enormous resentment, particularly from older ministers. I tried to warn him that he was walking a reckless path, and urged him to modify his views, stating that he was still a young man, and his time would come. He would laugh and say he had nothing to fear as he was only guiding his older, less-educated colleagues in the right direction. However, the situation could not be sustained, and he was demoted to Minister of Youth, Sport and Recreation. Although he put on a brave face, I knew he did not enjoy his new posting. Mugabe, recognising his undoubted ability, felt a period at the helm of SADC would solve a number of difficulties. The only problem came from the SADC members who felt that Zimbabwe had had a turn in providing the secretary general, and that the post – like that of chairman – should be rotated. Another problem was Makoni himself, who during his period as Zimbabwe's Minister of Industry, had succeeded in upsetting some of the SADC ministers in exactly the same way as he had in Zimbabwe. Given this scenario, Mugabe asked Bernard Chidzero, who was Zimbabwe's Minister of Finance, and me, if we would visit the SADC countries to ascertain what support Makoni could expect if his name were put forward as a candidate for the post. Mugabe said that if it was not unanimous, then he would not want Makoni's name put forward, as he did not want to cause any disruption within SADC.

We set off on our travels and visited all member countries except Angola and Mozambique. Our findings were not encouraging and could only be described as cool at best and hostile at worst. In presenting our disappointing report to Mugabe, we put forward a suggestion which we thought stood a slim chance of working. Makoni's nomination would be prepared but not presented until the eleventh hour. During our discussions, we discovered that although no country favoured another Zimbabwean, there was also no consensus on any other person or country. This little ploy worked to the extent that when nominations closed there was only one candidate. Makoni was, therefore, elected, one might say by default, but in typical fashion he threw himself into his new job with great vigour, as he saw it as a challenge and one to which he eagerly rose. Through his dynamism and great organising abilities, he brought a sharp focus onto the region, which in turn led to substantial investments by both the international aid agencies and the private sector. So successful was he, that he was re-elected unopposed for a second term, and in total served for a period of ten years.

In the early 1980s, Mugabe put together a small team to visit the capitals of Europe, in order to introduce Zimbabwe to its growing number of trading partners. We began in London, where visits and discussions were arranged for the various ministers and officials in relation to their interests and responsibilities. For example, I visited an agricultural training college, a tractor assembly plant, and the Ministry of Agriculture. Mugabe himself was obviously having discussions at a political level. Once when I was present, he made three presentations to three different audiences.

The first was fair. He began by addressing a news conference. As so often on such occasions, he was nervous and fidgety, and experienced difficulty in explaining and presenting his views. However, the assembled journalists were sympathetic, and Mugabe was able to give a rational balanced account of his brief tenure as political head of an emergent country. Later that day he addressed parliamentarians in Westminster Hall. Here he was very strong and sure of himself. Politics was the stuff of life to Mugabe, and on this occasion, he revelled in the location and the company. His remarks were also well received and understood. However, his third and final performance that day took the place of a dinner at a London hotel, where fifty leading business people had been invited to listen to his address. Mugabe as a man did not much enjoy socialising. He lived by a fairly strict routine, which included daily exercise, no smoking, and apart from the small occasional sip of wine to honour a toast, he was a teetotaller; and he liked to retire early and rise early. This, therefore, was a misconceived occasion, particularly as he was not invited to speak until about 10.30 p.m., by which time the noise had increased and visibility diminished, under a haze of cigar smoke. If this was not bad enough, Mugabe was delivering an address on finance, not his strong suit. His speech had been prepared by an official from the Ministry of Finance, and I doubt whether Mugabe had read it before he rose to his feet. Having stumbled his way through a difficult half hour, he was not in the best of moods to take searching questions from an assortment of high-powered businessmen. Bernard Chidzero, his Minister of Finance, looked uncomfortable and embarrassed, which was a great pity, because it was an occasion at which the latter would have excelled. He was a very articulate man who knew his subject well, and delighted in participating in grand affairs. This event was a lesson in the importance of choosing horses for courses and what can go wrong when one does not play to an individual's strengths.

In late May 1982, I was invited to join Mugabe on a tour of Europe which included France, Italy, Germany and Belgium. On this occasion, Mugabe was accompanied by his wife, Sally, and five ministers. Meetings were held at a high level, with both heads of state and senior ministers. In Paris, I was invited by President Mitterand to join the Mugabes for lunch at the Elysée Palace, which was not a huge success, as our host seemed to have his mind elsewhere and also appeared to be in a great hurry. I did, however, have a meeting with Edith Cresson, his Minister of Agriculture, who seemed to be genuinely interested in our farming programmes. In Rome we met the Italian president and also the prime minister, but unfortunately, they were undergoing one of their regular political upheavals and I concluded that the senior civil servants were in charge of the country.

Our delegation was, however, granted an audience with Pope John Paul II. On the way to the Vatican we were accompanied by a police escort of both motor cars and motorbikes, all with their lights flashing and sirens blasting at full strength, none of which had any effect on fellow drivers or pedestrians, who totally ignored us and continued to overtake our cavalcade by the simple expedient of driving on the pavements either side of us. Halfway through our journey, the situation became more complicated when a fire engine approached us, also well illuminated and getting every possible decibel out of his siren. This then led to a confrontation between the police and the fire service, which was only resolved when the pavements were cleared of pedestrians, mopeds and baby Fiats, and both opposing parties were able to mount them and squeeze past without damaging any vehicle's paintwork or breaking any shop windows.

Mugabe and his wife Sally, who were Catholics, went into the audience chamber first, and after about ten minutes, the five accompanying ministers were ushered in to meet the Pontiff. Mugabe made the introductions, naming each minister and the portfolio he held, upon which the Pope would take his hand, and say, 'God bless you, my son'.

When it came to my turn, I was introduced as Senator Norman, Minister of Agriculture, upon which the Pope stood back and responded, 'Ah! Zimbabwe tobacco'.

I readily agreed and so he blessed me with the words, 'God bless agriculture, God bless tobacco and God bless you, my son'. When the audience finished we filed out past the Pope, who gave us each a medallion and a final blessing, urging me not to forget the tobacco industry!

The German leg of our journey was much more slick and

efficient, with high-powered meetings held to precise timetables, with what appeared to be the minimum of fuss. Again, we were lavishly entertained, culminating in a banquet hosted by the Chancellor Helmut Schmidt. He was a gregarious, fun-loving character who made us all feel welcome. During the dinner, I was seated opposite him and Mugabe sat next to him, but as previously intimated, Mugabe did not relish late night entertainment, and as a consequence was not a very animated guest. The Chancellor, therefore, engaged me in conversation and I enjoyed a fascinating evening discussing German culture and our mutual interests. Before we ended, I commented on the splendour of the palace in which we were dining. He heartily agreed with me and said they were very fortunate as the German state owned two such venues, both constructed some 200 years earlier. The one we occupied was built by the wife of the local prince for her lover; the other was situated in Cologne and was built by the bishop of that city for his mistress. He added that although it was a privilege to entertain in such magnificent surroundings, any suggestion that they should indulge in the practices for which they were built would be frowned upon today.

When our tour of Europe ended, we flew back to England, where the entire party left to return to Zimbabwe with the exception of myself, who stayed for further meetings. About half an hour into their flight, they were alerted to the fact that there was a bomb on board. The captain was instructed to fly to Paris where the plane was diverted to the outer edge of the airfield. This was done for two reasons: one was obviously to minimise the risk if there was an explosion; the other was that President Reagan had just arrived for a G7 summit meeting. Having taxied to a halt, the doors opened, the chutes were activated, and all on board unceremoniously slid to the tarmac, including the Mugabes. All passengers and crew were then taken to a remote building while bomb experts examined the aircraft for explosives. As in so many cases, nothing was found, and the alert turned out to be a hoax. While everyone waited anxiously for the result of the inspection, they began to speculate on what would have happened if the bomb had exploded in mid-air. The opinion offered by Simba Makoni was that it would have been a complete disaster as the only senior Minister not on board was me, and I would have become Prime Minister. I am told this remark caused great hilarity and broke the tension.

During the period of the first Parliament, a substantial number of Rhodesian Front MPs were either farmers or had farming knowledge. The spokesman for this group was Bill Irvine, a former Minister of Agriculture himself, and a very successful farmer. He was always uncompromising, entering every debate well-armed with facts and figures, and took great delight in questioning me on my annual expenditure vote, which he and others could keep alive for at least two days, and on occasion into a third, before he was satisfied with my answers – if, indeed, he was. To me, he was the best parliamentarian in the country; one who enjoyed the cut and thrust of parliamentary life. He was always firm, inscrutably fair, and I held him in high esteem. It always gave him and the other RF MPs great delight when questioning me in the chambers. I say chambers because as a senator, I sat in the senate, but under the constitution, ministers could speak in either house, but only vote in the one of which they were a member. I saw this as an excellent arrangement, because you were able to argue or present your case directly to the legislators and not rely on a deputy or alternate member to represent you. On the other hand, it did entail spending many hours in Parliament, leaving you to catch up on your office work whenever you could find the time. One rule I made for myself was never to take work home. I was prepared to stay at my desk until 10 p.m. or later, but once I closed my office door, that was it for the day; all unfinished business would have to wait.

The agriculture portfolio meant that most of your duties kept you in the country. But there were occasions when I was invited to represent Zimbabwe abroad. In 1981 I went to Bangladesh to attend a meeting of the Commonwealth agricultural ministers, which was an interesting experience, as it was a gathering of those representing the wealthy nations – the old commonwealth and those representing the poorer – the new commonwealth. Despite the disparity of our various countries, the general atmosphere and debate was extremely cordial. This I attributed to the single common factor, farming. I left the conference with the feeling that if agricultural ministers were in charge of governments, rather than people from other professions, the world would be a happier, healthier place, as it would be controlled by people with their feet on the ground and not their heads in the air; people with an understanding of simple problems, which needed simple, understandable solutions.

While in Bangladesh we had a group photograph with the country's president. We were ushered into a garden, where a row of chairs had been arranged, with each country's name on the seats. We were told they were for special delegates and the rest of us had to stand behind the chairs. Having taken up my position at the back, I noticed the chair placed next to the Bangladeshi president said Zimbabwe. I therefore strode to the front and sat down. This caused great consternation with the photographer and the security guards who began gesticulating and talking in high-pitched voices, saying the seat was reserved for the delegate from Zimbabwe, which as the newest member of the Commonwealth was, for the purposes of the photograph, the guest of honour. With much amusement from other delegates, we finally convinced them that I was indeed the said delegate, which was accepted with reluctance and surprise simply because I was not black. However, the resulting photograph was out of focus and not long afterwards President Ziaur Rahman was assassinated by members of the Bangladeshi Army, and I hope the little man with the camera did not suffer a similar fate.

One pleasant interlude on that trip was a river voyage on a ferry, organised by the Commonwealth Secretary General, 'Sonny' Ramphal. I had no idea how river people lived or existed until then. As we glided along we were given a very good commentary on local village life where citizens eked out a hard existence growing basic crops such as rice, fruit and vegetables; and if they were fortunate enough to ever produce a surplus, they had a little to sell. What fascinated me was the fact that the river, which is tidal, at certain phases of the moon could rise and fall by as much as ten metres. To counter this, the rice institute had produced varieties which had thirty-feet roots, so that the grain remained on the surface, and the crop was harvested by the farmer using a type of sickle from the safety of his boat.

I represented Zimbabwe as a delegate in the organisation known as the ACP, the African, Caribbean and Pacific group of states. This body meets with representatives of the EU to discuss quotas and tariffs of goods produced by former colonial territories. An agreement had been signed before Zimbabwe's independence which enabled the ACP states to trade with Europe in a vast array of goods, mainly agricultural, on favourable terms. This agreement was known as the Lomé Convention. Thanks to the efforts of David Smith, who was Zimbabwe's first Minister of Commerce and Industry in 1980, we were able to secure a beef quota into Europe, to be re-negotiated before the second convention in 1985. This concession was very important to us, as although there was insufficient beef to meet the country's demand, we did have a surplus of top quality hindquarter beef, which we could market at three times the price in Europe. Marketing was done through the government statutory board, the Cold Storage Commission (CSC). The profits generated through this trade were ploughed back into the Commission, which used them in two ways: first, and most importantly, by making finance available to support the small-scale farming sector rebuild their herds; and second, to upgrade and expand its slaughtering facilities, without drawing too heavily on the national fiscus.

Early in 1985, a conference was convened in Fiji, where ministers of both the EU and ACP would work out proposals for heads of government to consider in Europe later in the year. Richard Hove was now Zimbabwe's Minister of Trade and Commerce, but as the commodities affecting us were of an agricultural nature, mainly sugar and beef, he invited me to accompany him. Sugar was not a big problem; there were many sugar-cane producing nations present and we got what I thought was a generous quota by hanging on to their coat-tails, and receiving a benefit from their negotiating efforts. These quotas did not preclude us from selling non-quota sugar into our own previously established markets.

However, beef was an altogether more difficult product. The reasons were two-fold. First, the EU feared the importation of disease, particularly foot and mouth, from meat which may have come from contaminated herds or areas. This was something I understood and I fervently supported the rigid control and monitoring measures which were being insisted upon by the EU states. The second reason was more straightforward, the problem of over-supply in Europe; they did not need our beef. However, a precedent had been set five years earlier, and we were there to negotiate the level of tonnage to be allocated to the exporting countries over the next five years. The task was made simple as there were only five countries involved, and they were all African states. Zimbabwe was the sixth country concerned as we had been allocated a temporary quota which we were anxious to convert into a substantive one. The initial meeting went badly, and I quickly realised we were irritating many delegates by taking up too much of the conference debating time. I therefore put forward a suggestion that the question of beef quotas should be taken off the main agenda, and should be discussed at committee level by the parties concerned. This suggestion was accepted with alacrity by the conference, but as the venue was short of suitable committee rooms, we tended to meet in bedroom suites, which although short of seating space, which meant we had to take turns to sit on the floor, led to a more relaxed atmosphere in which to conduct our business. An Italian minister was the committee leader representing the EU, and I was chosen to lead the ACP team. I managed to secure the support of the Irish minister present by suggesting that as Zimbabwe was the second largest consumer of beef per capita in the world, after Argentina, we would be looking to import cheaper carcass cuts to fulfil the vacuum left by exporting our more expensive hindquarter beef into Europe. This arrangement would, I suggested, be of benefit to both countries as Ireland had a policy restricting all meat imports for fear of foot and mouth, but was always looking for export markets for its own beef. Time unfortunately overtook us before we could reach a recommendation to put before the planning body. The conference adjourned with the usual speeches and communiqués, and with a recommendation to reconvene in Brussels a few weeks later.

This we duly did, but by now the negotiations had adopted a far more serious and less relaxed tone. This meant that the compromise solution I had floated, and thought I had had accepted, now became more difficult to sell. The EU's stance was that the annual beef quota should remain at the same level as the previous one, 32,000 tonnes, but would have to be shared among six nations, and not five. On that basis, each exporting country could expect to suffer a weight reduction. Those particularly vulnerable were Botswana and Zimbabwe, who between them had a combined quota of just over 26,000 tonnes. My suggestion was that each country should maintain its quota but the overall sales in any one marketing year should not exceed 32,000 tonnes. This was unacceptable to our European counterparts, who pointed out that if each ACP state fulfilled its quota, the combined allocations would exceed the total by the size of the tonnage allocated to Zimbabwe. I argued that although this was a theoretical scenario, in practice it would never happen, as there would always be an aggravating factor that would prevent some countries from filling their whole quota. I considered it unfair that we should all be expected to take a cut, when the record showed that over the five previous years there had always been a shortfall, and insufficient beef had been supplied to fulfil the total allocation. I also put forward the undertaking that if each nation could meet both its beef allocation and satisfy the strict hygiene and sanitary requirements demanded by European veterinary and health regulations, we in turn would self-regulate our members. This argument did not find favour with the EU delegates, and again we ended in deadlock.

The venue was again moved, this time to Luxembourg. Fortunately, it followed immediately, so we were able to drive there, and continue our negotiations. A much larger problem was now emerging, in as much as the beef question was part and parcel of the whole agricultural protocol, and could not be considered in isolation. An agreement had been accepted on practically all other commodities, and thus there was great pressure on us to conclude the beef agreement. After two more days of intense discussions and lobbying, we still failed to agree. On our last evening, we continued to argue, until we were summoned to the full council meeting at approximately 3 a.m. We were told that if there was no agreement, they would have to impose one, as a draft communiqué had been prepared, and the negotiations were over for another five years. The French chairman, Monsieur Claude Cheysson, the Minister of External Relations, turned to the Italian minister and asked if there was agreement and he said, regretfully not. Asked why, he said he did not know, but Senator Norman was a very difficult man. At this point I became aware of a roomful of hostile eyes. However, the tension was broken by a French delegate, Edgar Pisani, the Commissioner for Development of the EEC, who said he knew me quite well, and always considered me to be polite and reasonable, so why would the chairman not ask me a straightforward question: 'Why do you not agree?' Cheysson, who was obviously tired and anxious to conclude this conference, barked across the table to me, 'Give me a straightforward answer; why do you not agree?'

Perhaps because I was also tired and definitely lacked negotiating skills and finesse at this level, I replied, 'Because I don't trust you.'

A shocked silence fell over the room. The chairman pushed back his chair and stormed round the table to where I was sitting, and said, 'Stand up!'

I duly obliged, and he said, 'I wish to shake your hand. After thirty-seven years in public office, I have often heard the expression, "Give me a straight answer", and you are the first person who has ever done so.'

He then moved quickly back to his chair and announced that my proposal was carried, and instructed the conference officials to draw up the agreement accordingly. My first action after we broke up was to seek out my Italian opponent, and we found a quiet corner where we could enjoy a drink together and to toast each other. The protocol was subsequently ratified, and we continued to enjoy a lucrative market for our high-quality beef, which was of enormous benefit to the cattle industry as a whole.

I returned to Zimbabwe a few days before the second general election in 1985. As expected, ZANU won the election, with ZAPU retaining its twenty seats in Matebeland, and Sithole's party winning three in the eastern part of the country. The Conservative Alliance of Zimbabwe (CAZ, Ian Smith's former Rhodesian Front party) won all the seats reserved for the white electorate, despite some spirited campaigning by a handful of independents. Bill Irvine phoned me the day after the results were announced and told me that he believed that Mugabe was about to drop me from the government, and that the twenty white CAZ members would be prepared to elect me as one of their nominees for a seat in the Senate. He assured me that I would retain my independent status, as in their view I could make valuable contributions to Senate debates. I responded by saying that I had not had any indication that I was about to be fired, and thanked him for his offer, which I took as a compliment. I said I had originally been appointed by Mugabe, and if he wanted to dispense of my services, that was his choice, but I was not prepared to become a political pawn to suit other people. Later that day, I received a hand-delivered letter from Mugabe, in which he stated his deep disappointment that the white electorate had yet again voted for Ian Smith and his candidates. He said that white Zimbabweans had obviously not appreciated what either he or I had done for them during the previous five years, so I was no longer required. I went home that evening, collected June, and then we went to an art exhibition which we had previously agreed to attend, but we both found it a little difficult to explain events. In a long interview with a press reporter a few days later, I told him I was appointed by invitation, and like all invitations, when the party is over, it is time to go home, which is exactly what I did.

A few weeks later, we flew to Australia, where I had been invited to present a paper at the bi-annual meeting of the Royal Agricultural Society of the Commonwealth. This was the second occasion on which I had been honoured. The first time was when the conference had been jointly hosted by Zambia and Zimbabwe. Having attended the opening in Lusaka, I had to return in advance of the other delegates in order to welcome the Society's President, the Duke of Edinburgh, to Zimbabwe. Mugabe had felt that as it was an agricultural conference, I should act as the government's host while they were in the country. I found the Duke a very easy and agreeable guest, one who had the knack of quickly putting at ease all those with whom he came into contact. He did not stick rigidly to protocol, which many black Zimbabweans did not seem to appreciate, and they may even have disapproved of his relaxed attitude. Motor escorts and close security were kept to a minimum, and often ignored altogether. Having greeted the Duke at the airport, the small cavalcade consisting of two motorcars in which the Duke and his staff travelled, accompanied by four police outriders on motorbikes, fell into line. I was invited to travel in the front car with the Duke. As we set off, the Duke said firmly that he wanted everyone to obey the rules of the road. As we left, the motorbikes switched on their flashing lights and put the sirens on full volume. All went well until we reached the first set of traffic lights, which turned red as we approached. Needless to say, the leading pair of motorbikes roared straight through. At this point I noticed a nervous tick in the cheek of our driver, which became more pronounced when the Duke barked 'Stop!'

This he duly did, but the two motorcyclists escorting us from the rear flashed past on either side of our car, following their colleagues in hot pursuit. Once the traffic lights turned green, we moved on, only to be met by four racing motorbikes coming from the opposite direction. By the time they had turned themselves around, and regained their positions in the cavalcade, we reached another set of lights showing red. On this occasion, two escorts went straight through and two remained with us, so in our next manoeuvre we now had one escort in front, one behind and two lost, by which time the Duke's instruction had given way to resigned amusement. We eventually arrived at Meikles Hotel, without causing damage to either ourselves or other bemused motorists who got entangled in that motoring charade. Following a short break which enabled the Duke to wash and brush up, we went down to the foyer of the hotel to join the escorts and drive to State House to meet President Banana. Although four gleaming motorbikes were parked outside the hotel entrance, there were no riders to be seen. The Duke turned to me and asked if I knew the way, to which I confirmed that I did, so he said, 'Let's go. Otherwise we'll be late.'

So off we set without the escort team. As we drew up in front of State House, they roared up on either side of our car and smartly dismounted; the sergeant in charge threw an impressive salute, and they gave a convincing performance of having escorted us the whole way. President Banana was extremely nervous throughout the meeting, and despite the Duke's efforts to put him at his ease, he seemed unable to relax.

The gathering of so many eminent farmers and agriculturalists coming so soon after Zimbabwe's independence was a large boost for our own industry. Not only did it provide the opportunity for our farmers and agriculturists to interact with farmers and professionals from a large number of countries, but it also provided us with a unique opportunity to show off our own industry. This we did by arranging visits to research stations, agricultural colleges, marketing depots, individual farms, both large and small, and more importantly, providing a venue through which our scientists, plant breeders, conservationists, and many other experts could explain their programmes, and give their assessment of the future of Zimbabwean farming. It certainly generated much interest, and, I believe, a much greater understanding and appreciation of not only the problems of Zimbabwe but also the enormous potential which existed.

The Australian conference was held in Melbourne, and was hosted by the Royal Agricultural Society of Victoria. As is the practice with these conferences, there are usually pre- and post-conference tours which enable the delegates to acquire a full appreciation of the agricultural base of the host society. These tours usually included research or experimental stations; often valued-adding industries, such as product processing and packaging; and always visits to successful farming enterprises. The state of Victoria excelled in their generosity and variety of visits organised; it was indeed a truly wonderful experience. At the end of the conference, June and I flew to Cairns, where I had made arrangements for a day of marlin fishing. Much to my surprise, and I am sure that of the skipper of the boat, I managed to hook one. As sizes go, it was not a big one, but 250lbs of fighting marlin on a 40lb breaking strain line, I found quite a battle. It took me two hours to boat the fish, but I had enormous encouragement from the young New Zealand deckhand who, in between pouring buckets of water over me to keep me cool in the humid heat, kept on calling out,

'Come on Grandad, you can do better than that!'

Near the end of this tussle, when it appeared that I rather than the fish was going to lose, he said, 'A little more effort! Think of all the after-dinner stories you'll be able to tell.'

To which I responded, 'I've been making them up for the last hour and a half.'

There were approximately forty boats which had left various harbours that day to try their luck with the big game fish. By tradition, if you landed one, the skipper hoisted a pennant to indicate that there was a fish on board. In our case, he did not have one for a marlin, so instead raised a sailfish flag. When we arrived back to the harbour, I was surprised to see a large crowd gathered on the quay to see what had been caught. As soon as we came alongside, the speculation and betting began: length, weight and any other combinations they could think of. The official who supervised the weighing was waiting for us, so the fish was duly hoisted up by block and tackle, and the weight recorded, along with the name of the fisherman, the boat, the date, etc., all of which was chalked on a blackboard and then placed next to the fish. I was then invited to hold my rod and stand in front of the fish for an official photograph. When this was completed, about thirty to forty Japanese tourists rushed forward and smiling broadly, all took turns at being photographed with my fish. I often wondered what they told their friends when they returned home. In talking to the official who did the weighing, I was surprised to learn that he came from Bulawayo, and by happy coincidence for his chosen career, his surname was Pike – a most delightful character.

The following day, our Cairns trip nearly ended in disaster. June and I went on a large boat to see the colourful fish on the Barrier Reef. Whilst my wife chose to go in a submarine with large glass windows, I opted for snorkel and flippers. On my return to the ship, I was standing on an iron-grated platform at the rear of the boat, when a large wave caused the ship to roll. I lost my balance and fell heavily on the platform, unfortunately damaging both feet, one quite severely, with a large underfoot cut, and the loss of two toenails. On returning to port, I went to the local casualty department to have my injuries attended to. It was a Saturday evening, and it took me back to my rugby playing days, when you'd go to hospital to have your cuts seen to, or in extreme cases, your fractures set, but you took your turn, along with all the drunks, drug addicts and motor accident victims who seemed to arrive in a never-ending stream. This occasion was no different, and even included an attempted suicide which occupied all available medical personnel for nearly an hour. But when I was eventually examined, the doctor and nurses could not have been more caring, for which I was very grateful. And when I left, to my surprise, they told me there was no fee. The foot caused me pain for a long time, and some two weeks later the threat of gangrene appeared and the horrific suggestion of amputation was mentioned. Fortunately, due to modern drugs, this proved to be unnecessary, but nevertheless it was nine weeks before I could wear a shoe again.

On returning to Zimbabwe, June and I went on an extended holiday to South Africa, after which we felt we could settle down to a life outside politics. I was fortunate enough to have been invited to join the board of a number of companies, and took a small executive post in a tobacco company. The most challenging, and certainly the most interesting position I accepted at this time, was chairman of an organisation called the Beira Corridor Group, or BCG. The idea behind this group was formulated by Eddie Cross, whom I had known for many years. He had previously been an economist, working within the Ministry of Agriculture, and because of his national expertise and broad vision for the future, he had served as general manager of both the Dairy Marketing Board, and the Cold Storage Commission. He was the ideal person to promote and attract international investors to such a large scheme.

The underlying concept behind the BCG was for the private sector to raise monies through debentures in order to be able to present rehabilitation schemes to potential investors or donors to restore the infrastructure of the corridor through Mozambique, linking Zimbabwe with the port of Beira. It was an audacious and ambitious project, as most of the communication links – road, rail pipeline and even the port itself – had long ceased to function, either as a direct result of armed conflict, or through neglect due to the lack of finance and maintenance. Beira, because of its close proximity to Zimbabwe, was the natural route for both our exports and our imports. Furthermore, it was of great benefit to both Zambia and Malawi, who could take advantage of Zimbabwe's rail and road network to reach the sea. After a series of promotional presentations, the BCG invited companies to subscribe $5,000 each in the form of debentures. Initially, some 250 companies came forward. These included a small number outside Zimbabwe, who supported the concept, and believed in its value. With this initial seed capital, the BCG could begin its operations. The approach to international investors was to convince them that if the essential facilities were restored, the commercial and industrial companies, both public and private, would indeed use them, thus ensuring them an economic return on the investment made. The BCG formulated a two-pronged programme, one international, and one regional. On the international front, Eddie Cross and I journeyed to Europe, Canada and the United States in 1987 to make presentations to interested parties. By and large we were well received. One notable exception was in Washington, where the Heritage Foundation condemned our efforts as being contrary to the aims of the Mozambique National Resistance Movement, who were waging a guerrilla style war against the Frelimo government in Mozambique.

On a separate occasion later that year when I was in New York pursuing BCG business, I suddenly received a message to go to Washington to meet the Secretary of State, George Schultz. This was the result of an embarrassing speech delivered by a Zimbabwean minister at a reception held in the grounds of the American Embassy in Harare to celebrate American Independence Day on 4 July 1987. The speech was supposed to be a toast to the good relationship between the two countries. Instead it was a vitriolic attack on America's foreign policy and its attitude towards Zimbabwe. To compound the embarrassment, the former US President Jimmy Carter was there. He left in disgust before the speech had been completed, quickly followed by all the delegations of the western world. I realised I was in for a tricky audience when I entered the room and the Secretary of State, who had already removed his jacket and had his shirt sleeves rolled up, was surrounded by about fourteen members of staff, some of whom I knew quite well. He began with no preliminaries: 'What the hell happened in Zimbabwe last week?'

Knowing my defence was weak, I replied I had not been present at the reception and I understood that Mugabe had apologised to President Carter. Schultz said that was not good enough and that an apology to America was what was sought. After a few more exchanges between us, during which his anger abated a little, the meeting came to a close. Immediately, on my return to Harare, I received a call from Mugabe's office, asking me to go and see him. The Prime Minister began the meeting by saying that he had heard that I had been to see Secretary of State Schultz and wanted to know how it had happened and what we discussed. I recounted the whole episode, at the end of which he smiled and said that I had broad shoulders and he was sure I had coped. I answered by saying my shoulders may be broad, but they were not designed to bear ministerial mistakes, especially as I was no longer in government.

The BCG regional effort was co-ordinated by David Zausmer and Chris Notley. The former arranged for a regular flow of local and international businessmen, plus an increasing number of journalists, to fly to Beira for one- or two-day visits. Slowly but surely, the potential was realised, and confidence in the scheme grew. Notley, who had previously been a member of the British army, and had served in Zimbabwe in the British Military Advisory Training Team concentrated on the security aspects of the operation. In this field, he became a real expert, and travelled throughout Mozambique, working with the Mozambican military authorities, and was able to assess the security and safety of the overall project, and present his findings in such a manner that they were clearly understood and appreciated by all who heard him.

Another interesting aspect of the BCG initiative was the build-up of confidence by officials on both sides of the border. Initially, although there was agreement and approval by both governments, there was a strong suspicion and even resentment by the Mozambican officials that Zimbabwe was interfering in their domestic affairs; indeed, some were inclined to the view that we could be trying to manage their country. There were also sceptics in Zimbabwe who felt the whole exercise was a waste of time and money, as they considered their counterparts would never be sufficiently motivated to make the project work. These fears and suspicions were slowly dispelled as people began to work together and understand each other. Such was the success of the whole project, that within the short space of ten years, we were able to record massive infrastructural improvements.

The reconstruction was taken in stages. The first two important areas were the railway line and the port itself. As the former had, through neglect and misuse, fallen into a state of disrepair, the decision was taken to lay a new one. This meant lifting the existing track, re-ballasting to get the correct levels, replacing the wooden sleepers with modern concrete ones, and finally relaying the rails, using a constant weight per length, which had not always been present in the existing line. A small problem arose as to how to dispose of the old wooden sleepers, all of which were hardwoods, some cut from the Mozambique forests, while a large percentage were made from Burmese teak. Burning proved to be ineffective; it did, however, provide the material for a new industry, that of making high quality track-wood furniture. Because the timber was so hard and heavy, and when polished had a beautiful sheen, it became extremely popular as dining room, office and verandah furniture. The industry still exists, but as the source of sleepers has become scarce, the furniture has become very expensive.

Other projects, allied to the railway system, such as station platforms and sidings, and modernising the signalling system were also undertaken as the major works were underway. Within four years, the entire railway system was capable of transporting goods to the port, to the capacity of approximately five million tonnes annually. Work was also proceeding in the port area, where extensive rebuilding was required. A decision was taken to change the handling facilities, from those of break bulk, to that of containers. Hence a new container park and quays had to be built. In order to facilitate this plan, a major dredging operation of the entrance channel had to be undertaken to cater for the larger ships. The channel, known as the Makuti Cut, is approximately twenty-two kilometres in length, with a sharp bend before entering the port area. The engineers calculated that it had to be deepened by at least two metres, and the sides bevelled on the bend site, in order to allow for the container ships to enter and leave. Although there was a dredger available, it was only used for maintenance and totally unsuitable for the task in hand. In addition, it had to be shared between the ports of Beira and Maputo. What we needed was a capital dredger to do the excavating work, while relying on the smaller dredger to keep the channel clean.

At the time these decisions were being made, I was in Europe on BCG promotional business, and I was invited by a Dutch dredging company to visit one of their operating dredgers in the North Sea. I had June with me at the time and we were taken in a small service vessel out to sea to board the dredger, which was employed cutting a channel for ore carriers to enter the port of Rotterdam. When we came alongside what to us looked like a huge ship, we wondered how we were going to be transferred. Rope ladders were then lowered from the deck above. They were held steady by the crewmen, and as the swell brought the ships together, we were instructed to grab the ropes and climb up. On reflection, it was an interesting, if slightly nervy experience, which had to be repeated when we left, but at least we had the comfort of knowing that if we slipped we would probably fall into the strong arms of one of the crew waiting below. The whole dredging operation was impressive and one which I thought would solve the problem of the entrance into Beira. On my return, I gave my report to the Beira Port Authorities who successfully negotiated a contract with the dredging company and the Netherlands government. A capital dredger duly arrived, and in no time at all, a deeper, wider channel was dug.

Another major port project was the re-siting of the oil terminal.

The existing terminal had been constructed many years before, to enable oil to be pumped through a pipeline to a refinery near Mutare. During the UDI period, due to the UN sanctions and the naval blockade in the Mozambique Channel, the terminals and the refinery were virtually in mothballs. With a deeper approach channel, larger tankers would be able to sail through the channel. However, deeper draught prevented them from drawing up beside the existing terminal. A new terminal was then built, approximately half a kilometre offshore. This was a real improvement on the old one as it was constructed with multiple pumps, which meant that different products such as diesel, petrol and paraffin could be dispatched at the same time. A decision had been made to cease refining at the Zimbabwe end of the pipeline, mainly because the plant bought during the sanctions period was now obsolete. The holding tanks in Mutare were modified to serve as a storage site to receive the refined products which were pumped into Zimbabwe from the port of Beira. The pipeline was later extended to a new underground storage site close to Ruwa, half an hour's drive east of Harare. The site chosen had a large depth of solid rock which was excavated into enormous chambers like a vast cathedral and, without any further lining, was deemed suitable for refined oil products. The removed rock was transported to an adjacent area where it was crushed and used for railway and road construction. The advantage of pumping fuel as opposed to transporting it by rail or road was enormous as it was substantially more cost-effective. The actual storage depot, for obvious reasons, was a high-security area, and was kept as much as possible a secret location. It was during my time as the Minister of Energy that I was invited to see the project before it was put into full operational use. It was so enormous and so impressive that I suggested that Mugabe should also pay a visit. This was arranged and I accompanied him there a few days later. He was not too happy – nor were his close security guards – when they were informed that they had to wear safety helmets and special boots, which were standard requirements on the site. To reach the storage areas, we had to walk down steep underground inclines which also caused a certain amount of trepidation. However, once in the working area, and having had the whole process explained to them, they were full of admiration, and much to the consternation of the site management team, Mugabe requested that the whole cabinet pay a visit the following week. His directive strengthened the view I had always held that if you could visibly demonstrate programmes and projects, and get experts to explain the intricacies of the operations, you could save yourself a great deal of time and effort in trying to advance your policies to those who had little or no knowledge of what you were endeavouring to achieve. In the overall scheme of things, it was proposed that the pipeline would later be extended into the Midlands province, and eventually through to Bulawayo. I do not know if this was ever done, and if not, it would have been a great pity.

The cold storage building in the port was also overhauled, modernised and made functional. This became essential for the exports of the growing horticulture industry in Zimbabwe, and was of particular value to the export of fresh citrus fruits. With certain products such as steel and sugar, it was felt prudent to continue to use the existing facilities in Maputo, which boosted the throughput of that port. This was of considerable advantage to South Africa, which was experiencing volume pressure on their own ports.

I have no hesitation in saying that in my opinion, the BCG project became one of the most significant major projects within the SADC region. It also illustrated that suspicious neighbours could work together in harmony, and, more importantly, it showed it was possible for the public and private sectors to develop a mutual trust and respect to the benefit of all contracting parties.

While I was actively engaged with the BCG a large political

change took place. Under the constitutional proposals signed at Lancaster House in 1979, it was agreed that no major changes could be made to the Zimbabwe constitution within the first seven years. The thinking behind this restraint is obvious: time was needed to give the new political structures the opportunity to work. In 1987, it was decided to amend the procedure of electing the ten white members of the Senate (Upper House) by appointing all 100 members of the assembly (Lower House) to sit as an electoral college and vote from a list of candidates who had submitted their names after having acquired the mandatory number of supporting signatures from registered voters. I happened to have a meeting with Mugabe while this change was underway. He mentioned that he would like me to stand as a candidate. To which I responded that I did not want another portfolio. His reply was to the effect that he was not offering me one, but nevertheless he would feel more comfortable if I was to return to politics, and take a seat in the Senate. With some misgivings, I agreed to stand. In order to be eligible, one had to submit a nomination form signed by fifty registered voters. I was a little diffident about approaching people and coercing them to support me in this way. However, I took the form to the Borrowdale Park racecourse the following Saturday, hoping I would meet one or two friends who would be prepared to sign. The first person I saw was Charles Rodgers, a friend of mine who had previously served with me on the CFU Council when he was chairman of the Cattle Producers Association, who gleefully put his signature to the piece of paper, and then noticed I needed another forty-nine signatures. At this point he rushed off to the Owners and Trainers Lounge, returning in about twenty minutes with all fifty signatures, which saved me the embarrassment of trying to sell myself.

In the end there were about forty-seven candidates who submitted themselves for the ten seats reserved for whites. I gained some satisfaction when I managed to garner the highest number of votes. Also selected was John Laurie, another farmer cum businessman. Laurie had previously been president of the Commercial Farmers Union where he rightfully earned the title of 'Gentleman John'. He was a very successful president, and owing to a small internal hiccup in the organisation, he served a three-year term of office as opposed to the usual two, which restored stability to the CFU and confidence to the farming community. He was later to take over the chairmanship of the Beira Corridor Group when I resigned in 1990, and again with his patience, perseverance and business acumen, he saw completed all the rehabilitation programmes.

Since 2002, Laurie has devoted his time and energies to trying to secure just compensation for the assets which farmers lost during the farm invasions and illegal takeovers, working extremely hard collecting and collating all the relevant information and producing accurate plans of each and every case.

However, my second stint in the Senate was to be short-lived – a mere three years. This was because again the government wished to make constitutional changes. This time they were more radical, and were to become disastrous to the future good governance of the country. Although the long-term effect was not easily discernible to me and many others, perhaps this was what the authors of the change intended.

The two major aspects of the new constitutional bill in 1989 with which I was unhappy concerned the position of the president and the abolition of the Senate. I felt at the time that Zimbabwe did not need an American style president as I had a nagging fear that with time the position could mutate into an Eastern bloc type of president; in other words, a dictator. I much preferred the British system of a titular head of state, and a parliamentary head of government. In order to be an effective leader, I felt the head of government should attend Parliament on a regular, if not daily, basis, allowing him or her to listen to and contribute to the debates. A country should be entitled to listen to the views of its leader, and to have the opportunity to endorse or reject those views through its elected representatives in Parliament. Regarding the abolition of the Senate, I considered the thinking completely flawed. A bicameral system of government surely is in the best interest of the country. How many pieces of legislation get passed at their first presentation on a wave of emotion? A second chance to review and question certain clauses and aspects of proposed government bills, I felt always strengthened and improved the bill, in order to achieve government's intention. However, the decision was taken in 1989, and the proposed constitutional amendments were passed by the assembly and sent for ratification or otherwise to the Senate. The bill needed 100 per cent support of both houses in order to become law, and much to my surprise it received that approval in the assembly, where I always thought the RF members would oppose such proposals. The day it was due to be debated in the Senate, the President of the Senate Nolan Makombe, asked me if I would speak in support of the bill, in order to give encouragement to the other white members. The bill was presented by the Minister of Constitutional Affairs, Minister Edison Zvobgo. He was a pretty good lawyer and a sound politician with an erudite manner and a pleasant personality. There is no doubt that at that time he held large political ambitions, and certainly had his sights set on the top job. He was the architect of this particular piece of legislation, but how he felt it would benefit him was unclear to me, and in the end it didn't. If the cards had fallen his way, I always felt he would have made a good president, particularly as by this stage he had quit his heavy drinking habit, which was of serious concern a few years earlier. He was very impressive in his presentation, and when it was opened for debate to the floor of the chamber, Senator after Senator rose to give it ringing endorsement. I remained firmly in my chair, watching the anxiety build on Nolan Makombe's face, as I made no effort to make a contribution. Eventually I felt I should put him out of his agony, and I rose to speak. Having made references to certain clauses, and having expressed some mild concerns, I told the chamber I would support the bill. I concluded my contribution by congratulating the minister on his presentation which he had done in his usual articulate manner, and finished with the words, 'As usual, the Minister came up trumps'. However, I have an accent which is not always easily understood by others, particularly Hansard writers. I was therefore a little horrified when I read the Hansard report the next day which stated I had said, 'As usual the Minister was in a trance!'.

On reflection, I felt no harm had been done, so I did not correct the copy and let it be printed as it was recorded.

Once the constitutional changes had been accepted and gazetted, Parliament was dissolved and new elections were held on 23 March 1990 to elect an enlarged, single chamber Parliament. This was to consist of 120 constituency members, elected on a first past the post basis; twelve members appointed by the president; eight provincial governors also appointed by the president; and ten chiefs elected by the Council of Chiefs.

Following the elections, which were won overwhelmingly by ZANU-PF, Mugabe invited me to go and see him, and I was told I was to be the new Minister of Transport and National Supplies. He had decided to combine these two ministries into one which I thought was an odd combination of responsibilities. This appointment was as surprising as the one I had received ten years earlier as the Minister of Agriculture. In 1980, I felt with my farming background and with a professional team of civil servants in place, I might be able to manage, but with very little knowledge of the transport systems and all their ramifications, I felt Mugabe had made a mistake, and I told him so. He, however, was adamant and said that with the experience I had gained from the Beira Corridor Group and my impartial attitudes to vested interests, I would be able to sort out the many shortfalls and mistakes which were beginning to appear throughout the national transport sector. I left his office with a feeling of, 'Help, here we go again.'

The first Minister of National Supplies had been Enos Nkala, who was referred to on one evening's news broadcast as the Minister of National Surprise. I don't think he was amused, but it was probably a fairly apt description of the portfolio. I quickly decided that no single ministry possessed the knowledge and expertise necessary to purchase and then distribute all government requirements, with such diverse items as school books, hospital equipment and veterinary drugs. After a brief period of trying to untangle the plethora of products and items for each and every ministry, I decided it was an unworkable task. I therefore returned to President Mugabe and suggested that the Department of National Supplies be disbanded and each ministry operate separately as did the Ministry of Defence, and purchase their own requirements within an approved annual budget. The president accepted this suggestion, which left me with the core part of the ministry, transport. I am convinced that this move not only improved efficiency, and made substantial savings within the different ministries, but it also saved a number of individuals from contracting a criminal record, as I suspected that there was a certain amount of over- or double-invoicing taking place. With the abolition of the supply department, the opportunity for fraud would be reduced.

The Ministry of Transport was a large and complex one, having responsibility for all air-related issues; rail and railway workings; road construction and maintenance and vehicle licensing, plus smaller but essential areas such as meteorology, lake navigation and safety. Again, I was fortunate in having a competent and dedicated deputy minister to assist me. Amina Hughes was born in Bulawayo and was familiar with the Zimbabwe railway system. When I arrived at my new office, she greeted me warmly but told me I was the third minister under whom she had served and wondered when she might be given the top job – a question I could not answer. She was later transferred to one of the Nordic states as the Zimbabwean Ambassador, a position I do not think she enjoyed, and I always felt her talents and experience could have been better utilised.

The two major airlines, Air Zimbabwe, the passenger carrier, and Affretair, the cargo carrier, were under pressure, with the main concern being with the latter. It was here that I quickly had my first clash with the officials. Xavier Kudani, a peppery little individual, was Chairman of Affretair, and one day he unilaterally sacked the General Manager, Ken Dodd, with immediate effect. I felt his action had been very high-handed, as Dodd's position had only been discussed with the airline board, and no approach had been made to me or my permanent secretary. The dispute concerned a contract awarded to a financial consultant who had been called in twelve months previously to assist with the airline's finances. After two months, the consultant asked for an increase in his fees which the board declined. It appeared, however, that he kept working for the airline at the enhanced fee without the board's knowledge. I felt it was strange that this was permitted to happen for so long without the board members being aware. When it came to light, the reaction was to summarily fire the general manager. A letter was written by Kudani to the PS in the Ministry of Transport informing him of their action and seeking my approval. I thought that if there was a case for dismissal, the proper procedures should have been followed, which would have enabled Dodd to state his position. I therefore promptly reinstated him, which led to a request from Kudani for a meeting the following morning. It was a frosty interview, in which he handed me a letter of resignation. I thanked him and asked him to wait five minutes in order that he could leave with my letter of acceptance. As I suspected, he went straight to the president and complained bitterly about my overbearing behaviour. This in turn led to President Mugabe asking me to go and see him. He asked for a full account of the incident, and when I had finished, he smiled and said, 'Amazing. I have been trying to get rid of him for three years, and you achieve it in three weeks.'

I then suggested that in the interests of efficiency and cost savings, we amalgamate the two boards – Affretair and Air Zimbabwe – under a single chairman, but because of the different nature of their business, retain separate management. This suggestion was accepted and after a little while the changes were effected, and Malcolm Thompson, an eminent retired civil servant, who had the support and respect of Mugabe, was appointed Chairman of the joint boards.

I did not consider it to be the proper role for government to manage a profitable airline. There are too many emotive issues which are weighted against profitability. These include employment, promotion, and even freeloading in the form of favoured individuals flying at no cost to themselves. Privately owned airlines do not suffer the same constraints, and can be more effective in their cost-cutting operations in a drive for efficiency and profitability. However, in 1990 we did not have the option of privatising the airlines, so we had to strive for improvements within the government machinery. Generally speaking we managed to improve our regional and international operations, but lost heavily on domestic routes. The reason for this was threefold: first, there was a lack of suitable aircraft for short-haul flights. Despite the presentation of many makes and models, the purchasing or leasing costs could never be agreed or successfully negotiated. Second, we possessed unsuitable airport facilities at our domestic terminals, particularly the runways at Kariba, Mutare and Buffalo Range which were too short for jet-powered aircraft. Again, the allocation of suitable funding for upgrading and lengthening never received high priority, and was never provided. The last constraint was the constant demand, usually by parochial MPs, for air services to remote areas, which would never be viable.

I also felt it prudent to invite other international carriers to fly to Harare. This policy was not always clearly understood by my parliamentary colleagues and others, who felt I was denying Air Zimbabwe the opportunity of expanding their destination base. The counter argument to these views was that we did not possess sufficient long-haul aircraft to service new routes; and, in addition, I was trying to attract more visitors and investors to Zimbabwe, and the provision of their own national airlines was a good inducement, while it also created additional revenues from landing and servicing fees. This policy worked extremely well for a few years, and we had a number of distinguished foreign airlines flying into Harare, mainly from Europe and African states, but Qantas also found it convenient to have a twice weekly service. All this increased activity inevitably placed strain on our limited airport facilities.

The three main international airports, Harare, Bulawayo and Victoria Falls were all operating in antiquated buildings that had not been designed for the increased number of passengers now flowing through their doors. Fortunately, the main runways were both long and strong, so no additional work was required in that area. In Harare we had an ancient radar tower, which had not functioned for many years, and we were warned by foreign carriers that if we did not install a modern and effective radar system, they would not continue to fly to Harare. Consequently, we went out to international tender, and a contract was awarded to a British company which moved speedily to supply and install the equipment we needed.

The question of improving the buildings was a much thornier problem to solve. It was quickly established that modifications and extensions to Bulawayo and Victoria Falls could satisfy the requirements in the short term. Harare, as the main entry point to the country, urgently required new and modern terminal buildings. Fortunately, there was much under-utilised space within the airport perimeter, so a new site was selected inside the existing boundary fence, and the process of finding a suitable designer, contractor and a donor with adequate funds was begun. Tenders for both the design and construction plus the funding were internationally advertised, and we received a large number of bids. After a due process of elimination, we finally narrowed the design construction bidders down to six. These companies were invited to Zimbabwe to make their presentations to the national tender board. Eventually it was recommended that the contract be awarded to Aeroports de Paris (ADP) from France who possessed an impressive track record on the international stage. We then launched our tender appeal for funding, based on the model produced by ADP. The successful bidder was the Japanese government, who offered 85 per cent of the cost, at an extremely low interest rate, with repayment over a forty-year period. All was in place – or so I thought.

However, a state in the Middle East suddenly produced an unsolicited bid of their own, which they vigorously peddled within the offices of government, beginning with the President's office, telling us we needed their design. They, uninvited, visited my house at approximately 10 p.m. one evening, and proceeded to roll out all their plans and sketches on my carpet. When I told them that not only had they failed to make a submission at the initial bidding stage, and they had not requested tender documents, but also that the Zimbabwe government had spent over a year assessing the various submitted bids, and had now awarded the contract, their reply was it could all be altered. I politely asked them who would fund their proposal, to which they replied that was not a problem as funding had already been sourced from Japan. They were not interested in my explanations that the Japanese had agreed to financially support the French design, and that I did not think they would willingly transfer that support to another unsolicited design. They told me that as the responsible minister, all I had to do was support their project and everything would be taken care of, including me, who would then be able to live in luxury for the rest of my life. At this point, I asked them not to insult me further and to leave my house immediately. Their final comments were to the effect that they would win the contract despite my opposition, and I was a bigger fool than they thought. I replied, maybe, but at least I slept well at night. At the following week's cabinet meeting, it was proposed that the country accept the rogue proposal. I vigorously objected to this suggestion, pointing out that the country had duly and assiduously followed all the correct channels in awarding the airport terminal contract, and I would not be party to a unilateral alteration from a correct award to an extremely dubious offer, which apart from anything else, would damage our reputation as a serious and honest country. After much debate, I conceded that we would re-tender on a limited basis, which meant that the final six tenders plus the new contestant should be invited to submit their proposals. This obviously meant further irritating delays, but I was concerned that as far as possible, correct procedures would be followed.

After due process, the tender board again recommended that the construction should be awarded to ADP. They had completed a thorough and detailed analysis of all the factors which included cost, design and local material content which enabled them to stand by their original recommendation. Armed with this report I went back to cabinet and submitted it as my final proposal. Again, it failed to find favour, and Mugabe, as I had seen him do in the past, suggested we put the issue aside for the time being. Despite my objections, he had total support of the others, and there the matter rested for a while.

It is interesting to note that within a week of my changing

portfolios in 1995, and when I was out of the country on agricultural business, the decision was made to award the contract to the Middle Eastern company who obviously had secured local political support, including that of my successor. I still think the wrong decision was made and I felt that ADP had been badly let down and our international reputation as a country with which to do business had been badly compromised.

During my five-year tenure in the Ministry of Transport, we were able to make modest improvements to the airport facilities in Bulawayo, Victoria Falls and Kariba, but unfortunately, the latter posed a real problem. Due to its location, it was almost impossible to lengthen the runway, as it was guarded by the lake at one end, and a range of hills at the other. Owing to these limitations, it was not possible to fly jet aircraft in and out. To counter this problem, we searched for suitable turbo-prop or piston-driven aircraft to replace our ageing fleet of Viscounts. Although many manufacturers presented their wares, none proved to be 100 per cent satisfactory and certainly did not match up to the reliable Viscount.

An interesting facet of my responsibilities was that of Zimbabwe's railways. The railway system was the second recognised system of transport in the country after the ox-wagon. The main trunk communication lines were laid at the end of the nineteenth and beginning of the twentieth century. They linked the major centres of Harare, Bulawayo, and Mutare to the ports both in South Africa and Mozambique, and provided a service for both the import and export of goods, as well as a vastly improved passenger service. The headquarters of the railways were situated in Bulawayo, and all their support services such as coach-building and workshops were established there. I made many visits to Bulawayo, to try and get a better understanding of their operations and to see if there were ways of improving their dismal financial position. Although the railways were operating at a huge loss, many of the difficulties were imposed upon them by their being forced to carry government products, particularly steel, for which payment was slow, or in many instances, failed to materialise at all. Moreover, it was pointless threatening to withdraw services until financial provisions had been made, as life in the country had to continue. The simple answer, as it appeared to me, would be to privatise the system. As a consequence, we took a lot of advice, and spent many hours trying to work out a viable system. The conclusion we came to was to sell off the entire railway interests, piecemeal, except the line of rail. A start was made by disposing of the road haulage business, which was known as the Road Motor Services (RMS). Other areas which could have been easily sold or franchised out, were the catering services, carriage cleaning services, and stations and platforms, where there were lucrative trading opportunities. We had an interesting enquiry for the purchase of the wagon repair shops and workshops. Sadly, none of these initiatives were followed through, and the momentum and interest quickly faded.

If the government had followed these suggestions, I am convinced that we could have had a viable and, more importantly, an expanding rail network. A new company could have taken over the entire rolling stock, and paid a fee for using the rail tracks. This would have opened the door for competing companies to also apply for operating licences. Service operations, such as signalling and security could also have been franchised out on a tendering basis. It became clear to me that, despite certain sympathies for the ideas, there was a general reluctance to allow the private sector to gain involvement in what was perceived to be an area of national and strategic importance.

One of the most rewarding aspects of the National Railways was the spirit and enthusiasm of the staff, from the general manager downwards. In many respects they were a close-knit community, who took pride in their company and worked hard to try and give satisfaction to their customers. But as can be imagined, they were terribly frustrated by the lack of development, and failure to modernise systems and equipment, due to financial restraints which were not of their making. There were also opportunities for improved catering facilities, both on passenger trains and at railway stations and sidings, but alas, the prospect did not find favour in official circles.

Despite the stalling on many of these suggestions and proposals, I still remain convinced that rail transport – both passenger and freight – has an important part to play in a large landlocked country such as Zimbabwe, which relies so heavily on its imports and exports that have to be transported through neighbouring countries. Once the rail infrastructure is in place, it makes sound economic sense to use it to transport heavy goods on railway tracks as opposed to tarmac roads, as the latter need constant repair and maintenance to cope with the damage caused by large road-haulage vehicles. The same argument also applies to the care and renovation of road bridges.

The one sector of the ministry in which we did make significant progress was the department of roads. There was an ongoing programme of road construction and maintenance, which was reasonably well funded by both government allocations and donor contributions. One of the reasons for this, I suspect, was because it was a visible programme and all could see and judge the results. Nevertheless, there were areas of conflict and concern, which led to much political infighting. The main one was the priority set by the ministry for the various projects, particularly road and bridge construction. The system adopted was that each of the seven provinces would annually submit their own priorities, then the ministry and their advisors would consider all the bids, and taking into account the capital sums available to them, would produce a rolling national plan. In order to fully understand the workings of this system, I undertook a nationwide tour to inspect the work in progress, and to try and make an assessment of the most urgent areas requiring attention. I was absolutely horrified to discover that there were only two projects currently being worked on in Manicaland, but even more inexcusable, none at all in either Matabeleland north or south, and in these two provinces, not a single capital project had been approved since independence in 1980; no new roads or bridges; no upgrades of existing roads; in essence zero, just small monetary allocations for routine maintenance of existing structures.

On my return to Harare, I held discussions with my officials, to try and get a logical answer as to why emphasis on construction favoured the three provinces in Mashonaland, little in others and none in Matabeleland. The only vague explanation I got was that decisions had been made to support the economic growth of the more productive provinces. The answer to those kinds of arguments is that you will never have economic growth if you ignore transport communications. But, unfortunately, as Matabeleland was a predominantly ZAPU supporting province, it was not favourably considered for capital development projects.[3] I put all future projects on hold, and invited the two governors of the Matabele provinces to arrange tours in their areas for myself and my senior officials, with the intention of including their most urgent requirements into all future allocations. In consequence, we quickly found funding for two new road bridges, and started a programme of major road construction. Before I left the ministry, we had drawn up plans to turn some of our main highways into dual carriageways. This programme actually began in the late 1990s after I had left the ministry and returned to the portfolio of agriculture, whereby

---

3 As we subsequently learned, Matabeleland had also been subjected to an onslaught by the Fifth Brigade, during which many thousands of people were killed. This, however, was a discreet operation, which took place in the mid-eighties, and one which was never brought to cabinet, at least in my hearing.

highway improvement projects began in all provinces when funding was available, and this proved to be very beneficial. The one mistake made was in awarding a key contract to a Chinese company, whose equipment was totally inadequate for the job, so they fell further and further behind schedule. This was a great pity, as this was an important step forward in the country's development programme, and there were a number of civil construction companies, both local and regional, who in this case could have built a superb new highway, within budget and on time.

One of the most exciting projects we embarked upon was to build a new road bridge across the Limpopo River. There was an existing bridge which connected Zimbabwe to South Africa which was constructed in the early part of the twentieth century as a rail bridge and was named after one of the South African diamond magnates, Alfred Beit. A small settlement developed on the Zimbabwe side and was called Beitbridge. The bridge itself was later modified and widened in order to accommodate road traffic. Many years later, with the ever-increasing quantity of road haulage traffic, combined with a substantial increase of the axle loading permitted for heavy-duty vehicles, the existing bridge began to show signs of fatigue. Structural surveys were undertaken and many discussions took place regarding the best option to be taken to ensure the eventual flow of two-way traffic between the two countries. Strengthening the existing bridge appeared to be the obvious solution, although it would entail very expensive improvements, which in time would have meant long and protracted delays to both rail and road traffic while the work was undertaken. Before any definitive decisions were taken, I was introduced to a Bulgarian, who I understood to be a general in their armed forces, who informed me that they had a few bridges for sale. I must confess that this piece of unsolicited news took me by surprise, but out of curiosity I decided to investigate his information more thoroughly. It turned out to be entirely true and the bridges he had on offer were of the Bailey bridge design. For reasons of which I never received the complete story, the Bulgarian government seemed to have obtained the design and specification of the Bailey bridge and built them for the Iron Curtain countries, the purpose of this being that in the event of another European conflict, they could throw them across the major continental rivers, thus being able to move their heavy armoured vehicles and troops swiftly across countries and borders. Fortunately, with the easing of tensions between the eastern and western European countries, this scenario never developed, hence the surplus of bridges. After many meetings and surveys which included the usual viability, finance and structural studies, a scheme began to emerge. The bridge would have to be adapted for civilian use, which meant that a road surface would have to be laid on top of the existing metal, in order to ensure a smooth transit over the river. Finance was made available to be secured by a proposed toll on all traffic using the bridge, which would be for road usage only, and the original bridge would be confined to rail traffic. To simplify the system it was agreed that Zimbabwe alone would borrow the money, and in return would collect all toll revenues. After the loans had been repaid and Zimbabwe adequately reimbursed for its contributions, the bridge would then become a joint asset between the two countries. The logistics of getting the bridge on site were considerable; it was dismantled in Hungary, shipped to the port of Durban in South Africa, and then transported by road to the site, which was adjacent to the existing bridge, and then re-assembled. It was similar to a giant Meccano operation.

Once the bridge was constructed, properly tested and pronounced ready for service, we had a joint opening ceremony. President Mandela and his delegation lined up on the South African side of the bridge and President Mugabe did likewise on the Zimbabwean side. Then both teams walked slowly to the centre, where there was the traditional ribbon. The two presidents were each handed a pair of scissors and on a 'ready, steady, go' scenario, cut the tape and the bridge was officially open. The opening party, plus the many invited dignitaries, then proceeded to the Zimbabwe side where a celebratory lunch had been organised, with the caterers coming from South Africa. It was a very jolly affair with President Mandela entering the merriment of the moment, which culminated in him inviting the waiters and waitresses who had come across the river, to join the top table for a group photograph. The rush was instant: some jumped over the table, chairs got knocked over, and close security guards were thrown into a complete panic. During it all, President Mandela laughed gleefully, while President Mugabe looked totally confused. The bridge was certainly a great asset and I would imagine that the outstanding loan has now been paid in full.

In the 1990s, owing to my connections with the BCG and my role in government, I travelled extensively in Southern Africa, which enabled me to meet many interesting people and observe different cultures and beliefs at first hand. One of the most fascinating trips was when I was included in the Zimbabwe delegation making an official visit to South Africa shortly after Nelson Mandela had been elected President. We began our tour in teeming rain and gale-force winds at Cape Town airport, which truncated the formal welcome somewhat, but the poor military band and saluting troops were still expected to be on parade and to honour our arrival. The highlight was attending and participating in a full cabinet meeting chaired by Mandela, in which both F.W. de Klerk and Pik Botha were in attendance as Deputy President and Minister of Mineral and Energy Affairs respectively. With many smokers present, the meeting was relaxed, informal and engulfed in a cloud of smoke, with Mandela addressing all members by their first names. Upon arriving in Johannesburg, we made a flying visit to Fort Hare University, from where Mugabe had graduated many years previously. Despite staying in Sandton City, the main objective here was to visit the vast township of Soweto. I was amazed by how large and diverse it was – deprived and overcrowded slums contrasting with substantial homes and manicured gardens. We visited an enormous, modern hospital, which would have been a credit to any city in the world, and the people turned out in their thousands to catch a glimpse of Mugabe. There was much chanting and cheering and he really was hailed as a liberator. At one stage the police were in danger of losing control as the crush barriers began to crumble and a section of the crowd got into the hospital itself and began jumping onto the beds of patients in order to get a better view and to take photographs of Mugabe. At this point, we were hastened out of the hospital and into a large student hall where we were all invited to address the students. This manoeuvre was eventually completed with the rapid deployment of additional police and overhead helicopters with loud-hailer sky shouts to control the ever-swelling crowds. The human pressure was great, but at no time did we feel frightened or threatened because the mood was one of jubilation, not hostility. The final mayhem of the day ensued when we left in numbered car order. Mugabe was obviously car number one and I was about four or five. We entered central Johannesburg at rush hour, and with a substantial police escort of flashing lights and wailing sirens, our cavalcade eased seamlessly into Sandton, until the lead vehicle wrongly turned into a residential cul-de-sac. This necessitated much reversing into bushes, driving over front lawns and complicated three-point turns, with the obvious result of a reversal of the hierarchy and Mugabe arriving back at our hotel bringing up the rear.

In 1992, while attending a SADC meeting in Swaziland, my PS July Moyo came into the conference hall in a very agitated state to tell me that he had heard rumours from Harare which said there had been a major cabinet reshuffle, in which many ministers had been removed, new ones appointed and some moved sideways; he had no details but thought I had been moved back to the Ministry of Agriculture. I decided to telephone the president's office and try and seek some clarification on the position. The staff member who answered the phone was in a highly excited state and kept telling me that seven ministers had been sacked, which seemed to amuse him; he was less sure as to who had been appointed or even reappointed. Eventually I calmed him down a little and asked if he knew what my position was, and he cheerfully responded, 'Oh, don't worry; you are still the Minister of Transport.'

The following day I flew back to Harare, and while I was collecting my suitcase from the baggage console, one of the handlers rushed up to me and said, 'Mr Norman, congratulations, you are the Minister of Energy', and I said, 'Oh no, I am not, I am the Minister for Transport.' His response was to grin broadly, saying, 'You are the minister of both!'

That is how I learned that a new responsibility had been added to my portfolio, which was then called the Ministry of Transport and Energy.

President Mugabe's decision to amalgamate two very large economic portfolios into one meant some very rapid and adroit movement of staff and reallocation of responsibilities, but fortunately the PS July Moyo was equal to all challenges, and the new combined measures were swiftly in place and qualified staff appointed to their responsibilities.

I did not know at the time, but quickly discovered, that the availability of power was in a very precarious position, to the extent that it all but collapsed six weeks later; in other words, the lights went out. Again I adopted my usual approach and went on a familiarisation tour of the power stations to try and assess the magnitude of the problem. It was generally believed that because of the low water level in Lake Kariba, we were unable to generate sufficient power for our requirements. Lake Kariba had been constructed in the 1950s to provide water for hydro-electric power turbines on both the north and south banks of the Zambezi River, in order to generate affordable energy to what were then the states of Northern and Southern Rhodesia. At that time, it was an enormous undertaking, which created the largest man-made lake in the world – though its stature has subsequently been overtaken by other dam projects. While it was true that the water level in the dam was low, and generation had to be reduced in order to conserve water, the major problem lay with the four thermal stations, which to all intents and purposes had ceased to function, through neglect and lack of maintenance. The three small stations situated in Harare, Bulawayo and Manyati were admittedly old, but they were still capable of functioning properly, if they had been correctly maintained. The fourth one at Hwange was the monster in the system, with greater generating capacity than the hydro-power station at Kariba and the three smaller thermal stations put together. Regrettably of the six installed generators, only one was working; the other five being in various states of collapse through overuse and under maintenance.

It was while I was looking over this sickening sight at the Hwange station, that I had a very lucky break. An unknown African worker sidled up to me, and told me that he knew the name of a man who could reconnect the power within the station. When I asked him for his name, he replied: 'Later'.

I noticed he had a very fugitive manner, so I did not press him for further information. However, later that day, when my tour was coming to an end, I again noticed this worker who appeared to be edging closer to me. Then suddenly he pressed a piece of paper into my hand, and melted back into the crowd. When I had a moment, I looked at the note I had been given, and it contained a single name. Making enquiries among my staff, they told me that the person named had previously been the station manager, but had been removed by one of my predecessors, Herbert Ushewokunze, because he was white. Further enquiries revealed that he was living in England, was unemployed, perhaps because he was too old to get a gainful job, was having marital problems and was generally miserable. I managed to get a message to him, offering him back his old position as manager in charge of Hwange power station. He replied immediately accepting the offer, and said he would be arriving in the country within the next 48 hours. He also mentioned he would not be staying over in Harare, but would be travelling straight to Hwange, as he was anxious to get started.

Following his arrival, he quickly began to restore the situation, and within a couple of weeks or so, he had managed to coax a second generator into action, and had two more stripped down and under a reconstruction. As I have no engineering knowledge whatsoever, I allowed him to go ahead with his resuscitating programme, but kept track of progress, both mechanical and financial, through my senior officials. After approximately six weeks, he requested a meeting with me in my Harare office, which I willingly granted. I was enormously impressed with him when we met. He had the ability to explain the problems in layman's terms, but more than that, he was able to assure me that we would be back to full capacity within six to nine months. This news was a great relief, as many people were predicting that the whole plant was obsolete, and what was needed was a new power station, which would take several years to build. He then surprised me by requesting two weeks leave, and when I responded by pointing out that he had only been in Zimbabwe for a few weeks, he said he needed to return to England to get his clothes and other essentials. This I conceded was a fair request and off he went. In the meantime, I went through the process of securing a work permit for him. Initially, he was granted one for twelve months, which I managed to get renewed twice, each time for a further year. Unfortunately, I later learned that at the end of three years, by which time I had moved back to the Ministry of Agriculture, the government declined to grant any more extensions. This was a great shame, because this man was a very able, dedicated and competent generating engineer. The legacy he left behind was a completely refurbished power station, with the ability to function to its correct design capacity. Sadly, following his departure, once again outage failures were experienced due to the lack of supervision and maintenance, and the inability of government to provide adequate funds for the essential work which was necessary to keep an ageing plant and equipment working.

Whilst the major effort was to resuscitate the Hwange power station, we were able to increase output from the three smaller stations situated in Harare, Bulawayo and Manyati. Another small but helpful scheme was to increase the power coming in from South Africa to Beitbridge. This increase was small, but it did enable us to remove a section of the lowveld from the national grid, and rely on Eskom, the South Africa power corporation, to service that area. On the demand side, I realised that I would need maximum co-operation from all major consumers. Feelings were already running high, with many sectors of the economy beginning to blame government for allowing the situation to manifest itself in the beginning. Threats of power shedding and / or rationing, to be enforced by financial fines, were inflaming an already volatile position. I therefore contacted all major user organisations and invited them to send representatives to meet with me and my officials, to try and work out a common and sensible strategy to see us through the crisis period. From the outset, I was extremely encouraged by the positive attitudes adopted by the delegates who came to the initial meeting. We formed a task force, comprising members from all organisations, and we agreed to meet every Monday for as long as it took to solve the short-term problems. I described to them the severity of the situation, and went on to outline some of the plans and proposals I had for the improvements, both in the short term and on a more permanent basis. In return I invited them to give us their ideas on how we could lower consumer use until the day came when we would have a larger supply available. All sections of the community came forward with sound, workable solutions, with the greatest contribution coming from the mining section, led by the Chamber of Mines. Massive support was also given by the Consumer Council which did surprise me, but on reflection I felt that they were pleased that as an organised body they had been recognised, and as a result were anxious to play a positive role. However, I was disappointed in the farming sector, particularly the CFU, who declined to participate, even on an exchange of knowledge basis. They may have had valid reasons for not wishing to do so, but to me it was regrettable that they kept to themselves.

This small but effective task force continued to meet on a weekly basis for six months, by which time the dangers of a complete black-out had receded, and more reliable sources of power were slowly becoming available. On the broader front, additional supplies needed to be urgently secured. Opportunities existed in three neighbouring countries. First, there was the hydro-electric power station in Zambia, situated on the Kafue River, which at this time had excess capacity which could be fed into the Zimbabwean grid through Kariba. Second, there was the large hydro-electric scheme on the lower Zambezi, which had the turbines located at Cahora Bassa in Mozambique. The capacity here was totally underused, because the power interconnectors to distribute the electricity to South Africa had, for political reasons, not been constructed. Finally, there was South Africa itself, which had surplus thermal capacity at Matimba in the Transvaal. This could be connected to the Zimbabwe system by building power lines to a new transformer terminal at Insukamini sub-station near Bulawayo. The construction of the new interconnectors from Mozambique and South Africa, plus a small upgrade at the Kariba power station, would supply the country with an additional 1,100 megawatts, thus increasing our secure availability by 50 per cent.

On paper, this all looked relatively easy, but because of the political climate in the region, and the deep mistrust among the governments, it almost felt like a mission impossible. The easier scheme to start with was obviously the one which would provide us with more power from Zambia. But even here, there was an element of inherited mistrust, which went back to the time of the break-up of the Federation of Rhodesia and Nyasaland in 1963, as Zambia did not believe they received their fair share of the assets; and the fact that the first power station built at Kariba was sited on the south bank of the river, i.e. on the Zimbabwe side, still rankled. The power station on the north bank was constructed at a later date. However, after many meetings, we finally persuaded the Zambians to agree to sell us additional power from the Kafue plant, the effect of which was felt immediately as the infrastructure required was already in place.

The other two schemes would require many government agreements and major construction works, both in the form of power lines and transformers. I believe the whole area was fortunate in that Eskom in South Africa had Ian McRae as its chief executive, a dynamic man of vision and charm. No obstacle seemed to stop him, as he believed that every problem had a solution. Indeed, it was largely due to him that a distribution network of power lines were built in central and southern Africa. So, it was agreed that a line would be built from Cahora Bassa, entering Zimbabwe through Mount Darwin in the north-east with a sub-station placed at Bindura, to connect the entire internal network. The interconnection from Matimba to Bulawayo had an additional difficulty, in that the line had to pass through Botswana, which in effect meant yet one more agreement. The Botswana government initially were not too keen on this proposal. However, after several meetings, an agreement was reached, in which the selling point was that they could have access to the power flowing through their country at any time in the future. Considering they had not incurred any capital costs, I believe they got a bargain agreement. The contract to construct the 400-kilometre line was signed in Harare in May 1993, which effectively gave Zimbabwe access to an additional 500 megawatts which would go a long way to meeting its required need of an estimated 3,000 megawatts. It is interesting to note that despite there being no official recognition between South Africa and Zimbabwe, special dispensation was made for the South African Minister of Public Enterprises, Dr Dawie de Villiers, a former Springbok rugby player, to visit Harare for the signing ceremony. Botswana was represented by Mr Archie Mogwe, the Minister of Mineral Resources and Water Development, who had held many portfolios in that country. He was a man of charismatic character, who seemed perpetually jovial, though he could be a tough and unbending negotiator who always put his country's interests first. After three years, we had not only replaced and enhanced our own generating and distributing capacity, but through regional agreements, had ensured the availability of sufficient power to meet anticipated off-take for the next seventy-five years. Although this was an extremely satisfying position, I felt we should continue our search for additional power sources, which I considered would guarantee cheap energy, and also give the country additional revenue, through the sale of surplus power to neighbouring states, particularly South Africa. The most natural source was hydro, and the obvious site would have to be on the Zambezi River. Hydro is not only a clean and non-polluting source of power, but, capital costs aside, it is relatively easy to produce. The Zambezi had already provided two major schemes, with dam walls having been constructed and turbines installed at Kariba and Cahora Bassa.

Other suitable sites however, still remained, and prominent among them was one in the Batoka Gorge, situated downstream from the Victoria Falls. The gorge itself is extremely deep and would require a wall two and a half to three times the height of the Kariba wall, but as the gorge at this point is quite narrow, the length would be much less. We went ahead and commissioned a number of surveys, physical, economic, environmental, etc., and all came up with positive reports. As the river is the international boundary between Zambia and Zimbabwe, the ideal arrangement would have been a joint venture. In addition, we needed the assent of downstream countries, which meant Mozambique and Malawi. Both these countries gave their consent, once we had proved that there would be no interruption in the river flow through their territories.

However, Zambia was more difficult. They argued that they had no present need for additional power, and if further supplies were needed in the future, they could increase their source at the Kafue site, which was already operating. After many meetings, we could not break their resolve on this issue, our main negotiating point being the revenue-generating income we could both enjoy from the sale of power, plus the erection of another major tourist attraction, as had been developed on Lake Kariba and its adjoining shoreline. They were adamant they did not want to go to the international finance markets to borrow large amounts of money for capital projects. Eventually, they conceded that Zimbabwe could go it alone, providing they had the right to participate at any time in the future. Although this arrangement was not ideal, in order to make progress we decided to press ahead with the project.

However, another major obstacle was raised by many so-called conservationists and do-gooders, who showed concern that many species of wildlife, both large and small, would be destroyed, along with their habitat. I personally received a number of threatening letters, usually anonymous, from as far afield as Japan, India and California. I seriously doubt if any of them had troubled to read the intense, comprehensive report on the environmental impact, which had been produced by international consultants. If they had, they would have noticed that the identified area was both remote and barren, supporting no wildlife except a few small troops of baboons, who would have made their own evacuation plans, and a few Taita falcons who built their nests in the cliff faces of the gorge. However, we were assured they would move their nests higher up the cliffs as the water rose. In addition, the objectors chose to ignore the very real advantage of creating another clean, safe and cheap source of energy for a part of the world with a deficiency of energy fuels and a heavy reliance on wood as the only source of domestic heating. In other words, they seemed perfectly happy that trees be cut down with no thought of the serious detrimental effect that would have on the environment.

Another advantage that was overlooked was the potential for another tourist resort around the shores of the lake that would have provided a boost to local employment and the economy as a whole. Despite the setbacks, my enthusiasm for this scheme remained high. I was convinced, following the example of Kariba, that the scheme was viable, given that its generating capacity would be two and a half times greater than Kariba; and that we would be able to service the interests on the capital loans, and repay the loans themselves from the sale of power. The total cost in 1993 was estimated to be $4.1 billion. On that basis, we began talking to potential investors. Here, unfortunately, the story ends, because I failed to persuade my fellow ministers to commit themselves to the scheme. As was so often the way, they did not reject the plans, they just procrastinated until we ran out of time. In addition, given the Zambian opposition, my leaving the energy portfolio, and my successor having no interest in pursuing the project, it seemed to go on permanent deferment. Hopefully one day the Batoka Gorge project will be revisited, as it is probably the best potential local power resource available to the region. Inevitably, the cost will have increased, as surely it is always the case that the first price is the best price. Another example of a deferred capital expenditure project is the proposal to divert water from the Zambezi River to Bulawayo. I believe the first survey on this project was done in about 1905 and since then at least another four feasibility studies have been undertaken and basically they have all come to the same conclusion: namely, that the scheme is sound and viable, but expensive. Unfortunately it will remain that way and it will mean that if it is not constructed, the best opportunity to develop and vitalise Matabeleland will never materialise.

Another project which greatly interested me was the Inga scheme on the Congo River at a point where there are a number of falls and cataracts. Not only could a series of power stations be built, but no large retaining wall would be required, thus avoiding the objections which would inevitably be raised when another artificial lake is created. The turbines would be driven by the flow of the river, which would be diverted through narrow ducts, to create the force required to operate the turbines and then the water be returned to the river, and repeated through the next bank of turbines situated lower downstream. The total capacity of this scheme, depending on which survey is favoured, would generate enough power for most of Africa, with a surplus being available for Europe. Such a scheme must eventually be the answer to most of Africa's energy problems, and the real catalyst for all economic growth on the continent. Unfortunately, due to the turbulent politics in the Democratic Republic of the Congo, investment for this project has been very slow, though I understand that a start has now been made and limited supplies of power are now being generated. I remain convinced that the future energy source for Africa remains hydro, but it does need a great deal of regional co-operation, and more evidence of political stability before worthwhile investment can be attracted to the continent. In May 1994, Mugabe was invited to pay a state visit to Great Britain. Most of his official delegation flew to London on 14 May, but Mugabe left with a much smaller team the following day for an overnight flight to Frankfurt. Cabinet member and Planning Commissioner, Richard Hove and I were chosen to accompany him on this part of the journey. The reason for spending a night in Germany was that it was easier to meet the scheduled arrival time at Heathrow Airport by flying in from Europe than if we had journeyed the longer distance from Harare. However, despite exceptionally heavy rain, our aircraft landed, taxied to the arrivals spot and opened its doors within ten seconds of the scheduled time, which as Minister of Transport, made me feel extremely proud of Air Zimbabwe and their crew.

President Mugabe was met at the airport by Princess Margaret on behalf of her sister, Queen Elizabeth, but due to the torrential rain, formalities were kept to a minimum and they were ushered into the waiting motor cavalcade and driven to Horse Guards Parade in central London to be officially welcomed by the Queen and the Duke of Edinburgh. In the meantime, Richard Hove and I were met by our drivers who were waiting to take us into the city. As usual when I was on a visit to London, I chose to stay in a different hotel to the majority of the delegation, not because I did not like them or did not get on with them, but because I found over the years that I appreciated time and space to be by myself, especially at the end of the day, when I wanted to unwind without feeling obliged to participate in general conversation.

On this occasion, on arriving at my hotel, my driver enquired as to what I would be doing that evening, to which I responded that I had no definite plans and looked forward to a quiet night. He said he did not think that would be the case and he would wait for me until 7 p.m. to see if he was needed. I thanked him for his concern and said I'd let him know, but I doubted it would be necessary. In the middle of the afternoon, the telephone in my bedroom rang and a man introduced himself by saying he was calling from Buckingham Palace, and the Queen would graciously like to invite me to the State Banquet that evening in honour of the visit of President Mugabe. Having obtained the necessary details from him, I went in search of my patient driver who I found listening to his car radio, and told him what the revised plans were for the evening, to which he grinned and said, 'I knew you'd be doing something special Guv.'

The banquet was a truly magnificent and glittering event with 170 guests present including many members of the Royal Family. I was seated next to a splendid Vice-Admiral, Sir James Weatherall, who knew all the protocol and procedures for state functions, and he kept me well entertained with his knowledge and British humour. At the end of the meal, no less than fourteen bagpipers from one of the Scottish regiments paraded around the room in their swirling kilts playing stirring Scottish melodies, which was impressive, if deafening when they marched directly behind us. After dinner, it was the form to retire to a large chamber adjacent to the banqueting hall for after-dinner drinks, a cigarette, if that was your predilection and a general informal mingle with the other guests. The royal guests circulated with aplomb and I enjoyed a pleasant conversation with Princess Margaret complete with her long elegant cigarette holder as was the fashion of the day. No one can leave before the Queen, and on this occasion she was obviously enjoying herself, so stayed until well after 11 p.m. Once she had retired there was an ordered scramble to exit, and I suddenly realised I had no idea which way to go. Fortunately for me, the Prime Minister John Major noticed my dilemma, and being more au fait with the palace than most, said, 'Follow me; I know a quick way out of here.' So Norma, his wife, he and I scuttled down some back stairs and arrived at the courtyard collection zones well ahead of the main body of guests.

Shortly after my phone call that afternoon from the palace, I had received a second call from the prime minister's office, inviting me to lunch with him the next day. So, the following day after discussions with officials at the Ministry of Agriculture – cross-portfolio discussions were not unusual – I went to No. 10 Downing Street for the luncheon engagement. It was a relatively small gathering, with much light-hearted banter and laughter, and given the well-known cricketing interest of our host, much lively discussion about the game. Again, I was extremely lucky as I was sitting between Baroness Lynda Chalker, who I had got to know very well through her position as Minister of Overseas Development, and the Bishop of Leicester. I remember discussing with him the merits of fox-hunting, the desirability of women priests and the moral case for Sunday horse-racing. All those issues were very contentious at the time, and I am pleased to recall that we concluded in positive agreement on all three topics.

As I was leaving No 10, the Lord Mayor of London said he was looking forward to meeting me that evening. I confidently reciprocated and said so was I, but I was unsure to what he was referring. Upon climbing into my waiting car, my same cheerful driver turned to me and said, 'Oi, so it's off to the Guildhall for the Lord Mayor's banquet tonight then Guv?'

I told him definitely not, as I had not had an invitation. He responded by saying that he had an instruction to drive me there and that was what he was going to do – once I was changed into my dinner suit.

We duly arrived at the Guildhall and I felt very apprehensive. I followed the stream of guests up the stairs between the ranks of helmeted pikemen, but noticed that they were dividing into two columns, left and right. I decided to take my chances on the left, as there seemed to be greater numbers in that queue and I thought I stood more chance of slipping in anonymously than in the thinner right-hand queue. On reaching the front, I was asked for my invitation, and red-faced I had to say I had not received it. At that point I was politely asked to step aside and someone would come and see me. My worst fears had now been realised and I imagined being escorted back down the stairs, between the uniformed pikemen, who would probably be smirking in silent amusement. Shortly, someone did arrive, full of apologies, and said there had been a bureaucratic blunder and the invitation had gone astray, and would I follow him and join the right-hand queue. On reaching the front, I was confronted by a tall, smart, broad-shouldered individual with impressive military braid, who was taking the invitations and after glancing at them, was announcing in a loud, precise voice the title and name of the guest who would then walk forward between the rows of already seated dignitaries to be greeted by the Lord Mayor and Lady Mayoress. Near panic now gripped me, and rather desperately I put my hand in my pocket, where fortunately I found one of my ministerial business cards, which emboldened me somewhat. I formally handed it over to the impressive gentleman making the announcements, who took one look and said, 'Oh, it's you is it?' I looked perplexed, but he smiled and said, 'We always get one person who tries to gatecrash these functions.' With that, he duly boomed out my post and name, returned my card to me and gave me a large wink. The banquet was another splendid and memorable occasion, and Mugabe gave a speech which was well received by the distinguished company who had been invited to hear him.

The following evening it was the turn of our president to reciprocate the warm hospitality shown to him by holding a banquet in honour of the Queen at Claridge's Hotel. Again, there was a large gathering of the good and the great, with, on this occasion, a larger number of Zimbabwean citizens. I felt very honoured to be included in the processional party which was led by President Mugabe and Queen Elizabeth, and I was invited to escort the Duchess of Kent to her seat. During dinner she was charming and showed great interest in the current situation in Zimbabwe. The evening provided me with a second privilege, as seated on my other side was Princess Michael of Kent, who was well versed on Zimbabwe as she had visited the country a few times whilst staying with her father who had lived in Mozambique. She was also familiar with Cape Town, and when she discovered we knew places and people in common, conversation became very easy and I was able to relax and enjoy the evening. The whole three days offered me memorable experiences, and my admiration for the Royal Family was greatly enhanced by seeing first-hand the amount of work and effort they put into their public service, all of which they conduct with grace, poise and seeming ease.

In 1995, President Mugabe dissolved Parliament and called for a general election. Having been involved at cabinet level for many years, I felt the time had arrived to bid politics goodbye and return to the private sector. I therefore sought a meeting with Mugabe and clearly stated my views, while thanking him for the confidence he had shown in me, particularly as a non-party politician and also as a white man. He was very courteous, but said that he still had work he wanted me to do. I thought he was thinking of the power projects under construction and discussion, and also the new Harare airport terminal building. I responded by saying I would be happy to advise in whatever capacity he thought appropriate, but I did not wish to remain in mainstream politics. The day following the election, he invited me to go and see him, and said he wanted me back as the Minister of Agriculture. This came as a complete surprise to me, and I told him that having already served for five years in that capacity, I felt it was wrong to return. However, he remained adamant that that was what he wanted, so I agreed to accept this post for one year, which he considered ridiculous, and said I must stay for at least three years. I told him that I would like to reserve the right to leave when I felt like it. I privately considered a two-year stint would be enough.

Then, in 1996, there was change. It had been rumoured for some time that Mugabe had taken a mistress much younger than himself and that she had given birth to their daughter. These reports were either vigorously denied or dismissed as media gossip. Bar the fact that the lady in question was already married, and that Mugabe was still married to his first wife Sally, none of this would have caused great concern to the country, except they were accompanied by unconfirmed reports of excessive expenditure within State House. It is perhaps well worth noting that Harare, and before that Salisbury during Ian Smith's premiership, had always been a citadel of rumour. However, the lavish lifestyle of this premiership was dramatically exposed when, after Sally's death, Mugabe married Grace, with whom he by now had two children. It was a wedding on a grand scale with no thought given to the cost, and to which many companies and individuals were 'invited' to contribute. To me personally, it was suggested that a suitable gift would be a pedigree beef bull which would enhance the blood line of Mugabe's own herd. After consultation with our son, Howard, we duly transported a young Brahman bull, accompanied by its pedigree certificate, to the bride and groom, with a note wishing them a long and happy life as a couple, together with a footnote saying how we looked forward to visiting them the following year to view the progeny resulting from our gift. A week after the wedding, we received the news that our bull had been slaughtered to help feed the wedding guests.

June and I attended the wedding ceremony and the reception which followed. The service itself was held at the Kutama Mission chapel, the same Mission in which Mugabe had lived as a boy.

It was an extremely lengthy performance as it was held in two parts. First, there was the Catholic marriage in English and Latin on the right-hand side of the chapel, complete with candles, incense, hymns and a personal papal blessing from the Vatican read aloud; then the whole wedding party shifted over to the left for another ceremony conducted in Shona by local traditionalists involving animal skins, bones and dancing. Having repeated this process several times, I estimated we were in the chapel for nearly four hours. We then proceeded to the reception which was held in the grounds of the Mission, in what appeared to be acres of marquees. I have no idea how many people were there; some estimates put the number at 10,000. It could have been half that number or twice that number, but for a wedding, it was a lot. The main guests were invited into the principle marquee, which had a raised dais with a draped curtain behind it, through which, at the appropriate moment, the wedding party emerged, accompanied by a fanfare of trumpets. It was obvious that Grace was enjoying her moment of arrival. Mugabe looked less sure about proceedings. He and his best man, President Joaquim Chissano of Mozambique, plus a few close family members, were wearing dinner suits with white gloves, causing a guest to inadvertently but accurately remark that they looked like members of a black and white minstrel show. Perhaps another reason for Mugabe's unenthusiastic countenance was the rapturous applause given to President Nelson Mandela who appeared just prior to the groom.

The feasting and celebrating went on throughout the night and most of the following day. The difficulty June and I had was how to make an exit from such a jamboree without appearing rude or ungrateful, and how to extract our car from what looked like a gridlocked parking area. Fortunately, help was at hand in the form of President Mandela, who sent a message to say he would like to greet me. I duly went to his table, where we exchanged pleasantries, and he then told me he had to fly back to South Africa. I told him I also needed to leave, and would it be in order if I followed his car when he departed? He readily agreed, so while he made his farewells to the Mugabes, we slipped away to our car, and when Mandela left, we tagged onto his motorcade, complete with wailing sirens and flashing lights.

It was only after the dust had settled that serious questions began to be openly raised about excessive, unbudgeted expenditure emanating from the helm of government. The wedding was a showcase of this profligate spending but the instances of this – the president's annual birthday parties for example – became more common.

On returning to my old office in the Ministry of Agriculture, I found much was the same, but other elements had altered, and in some instances were changing fast. Most of the changes concerned individuals and personnel. There was a new Permanent Secretary, Boniface Ndimande, whose interest lay more in land than agriculture. On both occasions when I was appointed to the portfolio, agriculture stood alone. When I was no longer in office, it was changed to Lands and Agriculture. Fortunately, the deputy secretary, Tobias Takavarasha, was a long-serving member of staff, and was wedded to both the ministry and the industry. Another area causing concern was the Grain Marketing Board (GMB), where the chief executive, Renson Gasela, was under suspension on suspicion of fraud. As the GMB was still the agency for purchasing, storing, selling and exporting most of the grain and cereal crops, this was a disturbing situation to say the least. Having studied the available evidence, which appeared very grey and blurred, I was convinced some corrupt practices had taken place, but at what level and by whom and to what extent, was unclear. Many names were being banded around, including my predecessor, Kumbirai Kangai. A commission had been set up to investigate the allegations and report to me. A year later they produced a report, which like the allegations themselves, remained inconclusive. There was, therefore, no case for keeping Gasela in suspension. I felt, however, it would be unfair to him, and his life would be intolerable, if he were to return to his former position. After negotiations between government lawyers and his own, a financial deal was struck, which enabled him to terminate his position on fair and favourable conditions. I still believe he was innocent, and my view was enhanced when another scandal broke, again involving financial irregularities within the GMB, long after he had left, but curiously the name of Kangai re-appeared, and by coincidence, once again, he had been the responsible minister. Ndimande stayed for several months after I had been reappointed, but his heart was never really in his job. Added to which, he had a huge dislike of disagreements, often, unfortunately, a recurring motif in an industry with many hard-headed individuals, who also hold strong, even severe, views on what is required for the benefit of the industry. So, he eventually resigned and left to go back to his farm in Matabeleland the following day. Takavarasha was appointed acting secretary, but was not promoted to PS for several months, an inordinate delay, and an irritating situation for both him and me. It was particularly annoying as it could have damaged our effectiveness in certain crucial conflicts which were developing within the tobacco industry.

Serious discord was being fomented by a businessman named Roger Boka, who unashamedly set out to take control of the marketing and research side of the industry. Both these aspects were controlled by fairly stringent government legislation, which had been on the statute book for many years, but was subject to frequent periodic reviews in order to ensure that first, it remained relevant; and second, that it continued to serve the best interests of the industry, which was still the country's largest single exporter. The administration of these two acts was by separate boards, appointed by the Minister of Agriculture, in consultation with both the tobacco growers, represented by the Zimbabwe Tobacco Association (ZTA), and the buyers represented by the Tobacco Trade Association. This arrangement had operated very successfully for a great many years, and had, through a self-regulating system of levies and contributions, been largely financed by these two organisations, with government's role being that of watchdog and guardian, to ensure that all sectors, including the public, received maximum benefit. However, this well tried and trusted system suddenly came under severe pressure, which threatened to seriously damage and demoralise the production of tobacco within the country, and also destroy the confidence of the major buyers in many parts of the world.

Roger Boka had managed to get himself nominated as a board member of the Tobacco Marketing Board (TMB), and systematically began to take it over for his own personal gain. He was a very clever and astute man, who declined to take the chairmanship of the board, preferring to work behind someone else, whom he could secretly manipulate. He had a very bullying, aggressive manner, which intimidated many people; the most notable one being Ndimande who could not cope with the insults and threats that were hurled in his direction. When I replaced him with the deputy secretary, Boka found himself facing a man who was very brave and refused to be browbeaten by a bully. Another of Boka's tactics was to distribute memoranda, letters, selected passages from minutes, etc. to cabinet ministers, members of parliament and most importantly to President Mugabe himself, many of them taken out of context. Yet another approach was to feed loaded questions to selected members of Parliament, for them to put to ministers in the House, with the intention of causing embarrassment and discomfort. Unsurprisingly, most of these questions were aimed at me, but occasionally they were asked of other ministers, such as finance. He had three particular MPs who were only too willing to serve his interests in this campaign, but as they became more confident in their destructive roles, so they became more careless with their falsified material.

They finally overstepped the mark when they accused me of being in the pay of an external company, which had been awarded a government contract to market our beef exports into Europe. They stated that they had irrefutable evidence that their information was correct. However, my staff managed to identify the typewriter that had typed the accusation, but not the person who had used it. I eventually had the satisfaction of hearing them, on the instructions of the Speaker, apologise to the House for having misled it with a false statement and they were forced to withdraw the accusations. If they had made those statements outside Parliament, I believe I would have been able to bring a case of defamation against them, but they claimed parliamentary immunity as they had spoken within the chamber. However, from that moment onwards, questions relating to the administration of the tobacco industry ceased. I also had no trouble from the president's office, as he and his advisors largely ignored most of the unsubstantiated material they were receiving, and advised me to deal with Boka as I saw fit. The latter was using his considerable influence to seek appointments for both board members and staff, but even more insidious, he started to campaign to take over the control of the activities and finances of the Tobacco Research Board. In many ways this organisation was key to the whole of the industry. Over the years, it had been directed and serviced by many brilliant and dedicated scientists of various disciplines, which had given it an international reputation that was second to none. Unfortunately, in my endeavours to protect the research programmes from Boka's underhand methods, I came under attack from the ZTA, who misguidedly felt I was directly interfering in the running of the internal affairs of the research board, which they felt was tantamount to government interference. Despite many meetings with the hierarchy of the ZTA, I failed to convince them that my aims were to protect and not to control this vital cog in the whole of the tobacco economy. I felt my approach was correct, and continued with my efforts, buoyed up by the large amount of support I was receiving from the research organisation itself, and also the Tobacco Trade Association, who both shared my views and concerns. I decided a public debate on the issues would serve no purpose, so quietly pursued a quest to undermine the power of Roger Boka.

He had at this time applied for a licence to open and operate his own tobacco auction floor. There were already two operating floors, which provided enough selling space, with a comfortable surplus for future expansion. A third floor was therefore unnecessary, and would only add to the overall cost of selling tobacco, as it in turn would have to be staffed and serviced, which basically would have to be funded by producers and buyers. However, to deny Boka a licence would only have strengthened his vitriolic campaign that the industry was being controlled by the whites to the detriment of the blacks. In the meantime, the atmosphere around the TMB table was becoming intolerable. I therefore decided to call a meeting of the full board, in my ministry boardroom, with myself in attendance. The meeting began with hostility and mistrust on all sides, which I chose to ignore, and insisted we stuck to the agenda items. After some three hours of discussion, general agreement was reached on several issues. When the meeting ended, I asked Roger to join me for a discussion in my office. Once inside, he immediately went on the attack. I quickly told him I had not asked him to my office to listen to him talking to me, but I had a message I wanted him to understand from me. I proceeded to tell him in no uncertain terms that I was fed up with his aggressive and unnecessary approach to the whole tobacco issue, and if he thought that his continuing assault would persuade me to resign, he was mistaken. I then invited him to report our conversation to President Mugabe if he felt it would enhance his case, but also assured him I would be reporting it in any event. I then informed him that his fixed period as a board member was about to expire, and I would not be reappointing him as I felt he was too disruptive a person to make any meaningful contribution in that forum. I went on to tell him that I thought, with his undoubted energy and talents, he could make huge strides in providing opportunities within the tobacco industry for emerging black participants, which would strengthen and not destroy the industry. I also assured him I would do everything within my power to assist his endeavours, but I would not be dictated to on how to run my ministry.

During this meeting, he had gone unusually quiet, but concluded by thanking me for the discussion, and also saying how much he appreciated my offer of assistance. He then made the most outrageous proposal I had ever heard. He began by asking me if I knew how much liquid gold you could get in a 12-volt car battery. I responded by saying I had no idea, and had never even considered the thought. He told me the weight, and said with such a battery you could drive a motorcar from Harare to Beitbridge, the border post between Zimbabwe and South Africa and a distance of approximately 600 kilometres, providing you did not stop more than once. He then said he could supply me with such a battery, from which the distilled water had been drained and the cavity replaced with liquid gold. Once I had passed through customs on the South African side of the border, his agents would remove the battery and substitute it with a normal battery for my return journey, having paid me for the value of the gold. I told him it sounded a fascinating idea, but I was not interested. Then to my great surprise, he said that many of my cabinet colleagues were already participating in such a scheme. It was at this point that I realised he was being serious, so I told him I would not undertake such an activity, to which he responded by saying his scheme was foolproof, and between us, we could become good business partners. On reflection, I am convinced he was trying to set me up. Others may or may not have smuggled gold out of the country on such a scheme, but I am certain that had I agreed to this ridiculous proposal, on arrival at the border post my battery would have been removed and inspected, and I would have spent a lengthy time in prison as a result of my naivety.

In 1997 Roger Boka built his own tobacco selling floor amid much controversy, mainly because it appeared that he had either flouted or ignored most of the local government by-laws pertaining to erecting and operating a commercial enterprise in a proposed residential area. However, with his usual strong-arm tactics, he went ahead regardless. On the scheduled day for the opening of the tobacco sales, I was invited by both the established tobacco selling floors to officiate at their opening. This was a fairly traditional ritual for the minister, who was expected to say a few appropriate words about the industry and then call a starting price for the first bale on offer, and thus set the selling season in motion. Boka, however, had grander schemes in mind. He had invited the president to officiate on his floor, and to ensure success, he had sent out numerous invitations, about 5,000 I was told, to invited people to witness his achievement of breaking into the country's major export industry. He certainly tried to make it a gala occasion, as he had hired marquees for the important guests, and for the others he had arranged food outlets, and traditional bands and dancers. The only setback was the non-arrival of the president. After about a three-hour delay, I was summoned to a telephone to speak to President Mugabe, who enquired as to what was happening. When I explained to him that everyone was waiting for him to come and officially open the new tobacco floor, he astounded me by saying he knew nothing about the invitation, so would I perform the honours instead. I was very surprised, especially as there were a considerable number of cabinet ministers there, who normally only attended public functions when the president was officiating, so that they had a chance to be photographed by the press, or better still appear on the ZTV's evening news broadcast. Secondly, I had noticed on my way to the selling floors that there were policemen at every intersection. This was standard practice when the presidential cavalcade was moving through the city. Police would control the entire route, to ensure that the high-speed cars could fly down the roads uninterrupted. That morning, the duty police must have wondered what they were doing, and probably concluded that there had been another bureaucratic bungle.

My second big surprise came when I told Boka that the president was not coming and had asked me to deputise for him. Boka just smiled, and said he knew this would happen, because the president was his personal friend, and he would not want to upstage him, as this was his great day, and the president wanted him to enjoy it and receive the praise and accolades he deserved. I was dumbfounded, but I still had to make a short speech, acknowledging Boka's entrepreneurial skills, and the president's unfortunate non-appearance. However, none of that seemed to matter, as my ministerial colleagues, along with a large section of the press, had already melted away and as everyone else had by this time consumed copious quantities of the free beer on offer, they did not worry if there were speeches or not.

It was not long after this farcical occasion that I resigned from government and politics, so my association with Roger Boka faded away. But his death a short while later was almost as dramatic as the dysfunctional life he lived. He apparently died aboard a private aircraft bound for Harare airport. On arrival the plane was ordered to park well away from the terminal buildings. An ambulance went out to the plane, and his death was announced shortly afterwards. However, there was no public viewing of the body, which is traditional with prominent persons, and a funeral was hastily arranged. I felt that somehow there were still unanswered questions, but no one seemed to ask them.

I had felt for a long time that it was time to move on from a political life. I wanted to spend more time at home and with my wife, having realised that there was always life after politics. Previous attempts to leave the political arena had failed because I thought it prudent to quit at times of elections. In April 1997, the country had completed two years of a five-year parliamentary term, and I thought it would be a good time to leave, causing no problems or consternation to either me or the government. I therefore wrote a letter to Mugabe requesting a meeting to discuss my pending resignation. I met him the following day, and he expressed surprise and disappointment at my decision to quit politics. After a long amicable discussion, he reluctantly conceded that he couldn't make me change my mind. I left him on the understanding that I would formally submit my resignation in writing, and that I would make a public announcement at the appropriate time. The only other person, apart from Mugabe, who was aware of my decision, was my wife June. In order to formalise my departure I had to utilise the services of my private secretary, Dora. I explained to her what I was about to do, and said she would have to prepare the letter of resignation for my signature. As I did not want this knowledge to be leaked in any form, I had to ask her to keep the information secret until I had officially made it known myself. Not I would imagine an easy task for her, in a country which thrived on a diet of rumours and counter rumours, but to her great credit, she kept her silence.

I chose to leave on the evening of Tuesday 30 April, and decided to inform the news media the afternoon before. I therefore asked my PS, Tobias Takavarasha to arrange a news conference in the ministry's boardroom. He naturally showed surprise, and politely enquired why I needed a press conference. I replied that we had not spoken to the news media for some time, and I felt they needed an update on our activities. He did not look very convinced, and a few minutes later I heard him asking Dora if she knew anything, and she said not. In the meantime she had prepared about twenty copies of a statement for me to hand out to journalists that afternoon. Half an hour before the conference was due I had a visitation from my deputy minister, Olivia Muchena, accompanied by Tobias, who said they were extremely worried as to what I wanted to tell the press. The time had now come to declare my hand, so I told them what I intended to do, and said I would appreciate their presence when I told the media. Having made my announcement, there were the usual questions, as to why and why now. A number of journalists had difficulty in accepting my reason for leaving, and suggested alternative motives, such as I had lost confidence in the government; had had a major fall-out with Mugabe; had lost the support of the farming community; was suffering from serious health problems; or had been offered an international position. All these suggestions I dismissed and the announcement was made more or less as I had written it. The radio carried the story on their 4 p.m. newscast, and when I arrived home at about 6 o'clock, all four of my children plus their spouses were there with celebratory bottles of champagne to welcome my return to private life. I still had one duty to perform and that was to write to the Speaker of Parliament informing him of my action, and that after that day I would cease to be a member of his honourable house. I attended my last cabinet meeting the following morning, at which Mugabe made complimentary comments and thanked me for my long service to the nation. In the afternoon, I went to Parliament and made my farewells to the Speaker and MPs, and when I got home that evening, the feeling was similar to leaving school, and a whole chapter had closed. I had no regret at having made the choice to resign, and I felt I had been honoured to have been invited to serve in the government for such a long period.

5

Outside Politics

Prior to and post-1997

Besides having more time to spend on my farm, I also occupied a number of non-executive board positions in a few companies and retained my post as President of the Zimbabwe Agricultural Society, all of which gave me great pleasure. Zimbabwe, being a provincially populated country heavily dependent on agriculture, developed a rural tradition of celebrating the end of the farming season before beginning the hard task of preparing for the year ahead. These rites in the seasonal calendar still continue.

The most common form was an agricultural show, in which farmers and their wives could compete amongst themselves, by presenting their produce to be judged against each other. It also provided a venue for the major suppliers of farming inputs to show off their wares and persuade farmers of the need to purchase them. These shows were held throughout the country; the only difference being one of scale. During my time in government, I attended many of these events and they were always enjoyable. It was almost standard procedure that I would make a speech and June would present the awards, which usually meant that we would return home with a magnificent bouquet of flowers. On one occasion, however, because June had shown interest in an iron foundry stand, she got presented with a three-legged cast iron cooking pot, which to this day in the winter months is still in use as a coal scuttle and often attracts admiring comments.

In the remote rural areas, I found the enthusiasm for these annual events just as enjoyable and rewarding as the larger ones in the provincial capitals, and I was always heartened by the gifts of eggs and pumpkins which were generously presented to me, but was a little alarmed on one occasion to find two live chickens on the back seat of my car with their legs tied together!

The first show at which we officiated was the Kadoma and Chegutu District Show in September 1982 and my first duty was to inspect the guard of honour. This was made up of members of the youth league who were wearing khaki overalls and 'tackies' and carrying wooden rifles. Although being called the youth brigade, few, if any of them looked under the age of thirty-five. However, nothing daunted, I walked between the ranks, holding my trilby hat, whilst the police band politely played 'March of the Grenadiers'. Having done my duty, I retired to the front row of the VIP stand. Hardly had I done so, when someone tapped me on my shoulder, and said, 'Your hat drill was appalling!' It was the local MP, P. K. van der Byl, who went on to tell me that if I insisted on having a hat, I must 'wear the bloody thing' and not trail it by my side. When we adjourned for a mid-morning coffee break, he asked me if I was taking the salute at the end of the day, and I replied that I had not been told so, but had presumed that I might. He then asked if I knew how to take a salute, and shaking my head, I invited him to instruct me. He said, 'At the end of the proceedings, the parade commander will advance towards you on his charger. He will give the order, "general salute". Then, drums will roll and he will draw his sword and slowly raise it in front of his face. You will be wearing your hat, and you will lift it off your head and slowly lower it to your right side. *Never* do that damn silly thing of placing it on your left tit! After the national anthem, the parade commander will slowly reverse the procedure and you will replace your hat – got it?'

I replied, 'Got it.' I then enquired if he would still be there at the end of the day, and he said he had another appointment. The moment duly arrived with the sun beginning to set and the mounted police had completed their musical ride. The commanding officer came forward, saluted me and then ordered the general salute. After he and I had duly completed all respective motions with sword and hat, he requested permission to ride off, and a voice behind me said, 'Well done!' PK had indeed stayed to the end.

Another very enjoyable show was the annual Bulawayo Show. Being at the centre of the cattle-ranching area, it had a slightly different emphasis to shows held in Mashonaland, as it was orientated towards the livestock industry. I remember a prize-giving ceremony when the guest of honour, and fine rancher, Ian de la Rue, suddenly lost his voice in the middle of his address. Unfortunately, no one had thought to place a glass of water on the podium. He was rescued by an enterprising female steward who rushed forward with a bucket of water; between them, they decanted some of the contents into one of the splendid silver trophies waiting to be presented, from which he took a long and comforting swig, to the cheers of the show spectators.

All the smaller country shows, despite being venues where farmers could exhibit their finest animals, produce and crafts, also had ring events, mainly for equestrian competitors, but also for entertainers such as drum majorettes, marching bands, musical rides, etc., which greatly enhanced the atmosphere. Once, when

I was farming in the Karoi district, the event coincided with the twenty-fifth anniversary of the area being settled for commercial farming. It was therefore decided to have a festival at the end of a week of district celebrations. There were no cattle lines or sheep pens; the focus was on entertainment. Displays such as dog handling, Scottish dancing, float parades, a vintage car rally, sky divers, etc. provided magnificent performances to entertain everyone who had gathered for the day.

However, one of the planned spectacles was a demonstration of aerial crop spraying by a local flying company. This entailed a number of treetop height passes by three aircraft flying in close formation, and at the critical moment releasing their spray over the area. Instead of using insecticide, the tanks were filled with dyed water in the colours of the Rhodesian flag – green, white, green. Despite detailed briefings with the pilots and strategic oil drums filled with diesel-oil-soaked straw which we lit to give off plumes of black smoke to indicate the wind direction, the planes flew in from the opposite direction and dumped the dyed water on the crowd.

Mrs Wrathall, wife of the then President of Rhodesia, John Wrathall, who was later to present the awards and prizes, was wearing a large white, big-brimmed hat, which suddenly looked as if it had developed a bad case of verdant measles. She sportingly laughed the incident off, but the master of the Corps of Signals band took a much more belligerent view and threatened to leave immediately and take his band back to barracks. As their snow-white tunic tops now resembled badly designed battle fatigues, I suppose he had a point. However, the band had been engaged to play at the Show Ball, which was to be held in the local hotel that evening, so the threat of withdrawal caused great consternation. Finally, the day was saved by the quick-thinking chairman, Stuart Maclaren, who persuaded the outlet selling barbequed chickens to feed the bandsmen as much as they wanted. This, plus a conciliatory talk with the bandmaster calmed him down, and they agreed to fulfil their engagements. Some time later, the flight commander and his two assistants turned up, and with big grins on their faces: 'Sorry about that!' said the former. No doubt they thoroughly enjoyed the chaos they had created – Oh to be young and mischievous!

The major show in the country was obviously the Harare Show, which lasted a full week, and had a long pedigree of excellence. After 1980, it became a tradition that the guest of honour should, if at all possible, be a head of state or government. It therefore followed that the invitation was issued by President Mugabe and not the Show President. Over the years, we had the presidents of most neighbouring countries coming to open the show. All appeared to have enjoyed their role, obviously some more than others, and some left more of an impression than others. I well remember the visit of President Julius Nyerere of Tanzania, who was very relaxed as he toured the showgrounds and was anxious to talk to the many stand-holders regarding their products and wares. A prominent Zimbabwean farmer, Hamish Smith, who was one of the leading pedigree cattle breeders in the country – both beef and dairy – was so impressed with Nyerere's interest in the cattle industry, that he gave him a pedigree heifer to commemorate his visit. Later Hamish's brother David, who was also a very successful farmer with a distinguished career in politics, having held top portfolios in both Ian Smith's and Robert Mugabe's governments, approached Nyerere and said a heifer on its own was not much use, so he would like to donate a bull to go with it. The Tanzanian president thanked him profusely and I thought the giving of gifts was now over, but not quite, because David Smith returned and said, 'I forgot to ask you, which would you prefer, a dairy bull or a beef bull?' To which Nyerere promptly replied, 'I will take one of each!'

This largesse on behalf of two generous Zimbabwean farmers did cause the veterinary department some serious headaches due to the necessity of hygiene certificates, suitable quarantine centres, and all that goes with exporting live animals from one country to another. Eventually two animals left – not three – but what happened thereafter I never heard.

Another notable visitor who left a lasting impression of his visit was President Nelson Mandela. His visit caused so much excitement among the crowds that the tour of the show grounds was a nightmare for the security personnel. It seemed everyone was anxious to catch a glimpse of him and he for his part was very happy to shake hands and engage with as many people as possible. This naturally slowed down our progress and we had to make the unpalatable decision to leave out some of the stands which had been identified for a visit, because of time constraints. I did feel extremely sorry for those companies who had agreed to host him for a few minutes, only to be told that he would not be coming, as not only were they looking forward to meeting him, but they had also put in special efforts for what would have been a once in a lifetime experience. This was also understood by Mandela and he particularly asked us to pass on his regrets and apologies for not being able to meet and greet them. This we did and they fully understood but nevertheless remained disappointed.

The year, 1993, was the centenary of the first agricultural show held in Salisbury, so we thought it would be suitable if we invited a member of the Royal family to be our guest of honour. In consultation with the Show Patron Robert Mugabe, he expressed a wish to invite Prince Edward. An invitation was duly sent and graciously accepted, and it turned out to be an inspired choice. Not only did he make a clear and appropriate opening speech, but he showed real interest in the exhibits, and many who met him were impressed by his knowledge of many very different subjects. During his brief stay in the country he also made time to visit Prince Edward School, which was named in honour of his great uncle the Prince of Wales during his visit to Rhodesia in 1925.

Robert Mugabe always took a keen interest in the annual Harare Show, and on a Friday, which was always the day of the official opening, he would spend the best part of it at the showgrounds. His routine never varied. He liked to start with a visit to the cattle lines, where a few animals of each breed, along with their breeders, would be lined up for his inspection. He would then move from breed to breed chatting to owners and remarking on the quality of the beasts. After a time, he came to know most of the breeders and would comment on their past successes or enquire about their future programmes, which always seemed to bemuse casual observers. After the visit to the cattle breeders, he would go on a tour of the exhibitors' trade stands, which always included one government or government parastatal stand. On one occasion the prison service stand was selected for such a visit. When we arrived, we were greeted by a very large uniformed man, with highly polished shoes, very short shorts, and impressive epaulettes on his shoulders and with much braid on his cap who threw one of the smartest salutes I had ever seen. The President acknowledged this with a wave of his hand and continued walking for one or more steps, then suddenly stopped and turned, and said, 'Dupe, is that you?' To which the officer replied, 'Yes Sir.' Mugabe shook his hand and said, 'Come with me.'

They toured the stand talking and laughing much to the surprise of the small entourage following them. It turned out that the officer, whose surname was Du Plessis, had been Mugabe's gaoler when he had been in prison, and was now the deputy commissioner of the prison service. On leaving the stand, warm handshakes were again exchanged, and the President told the former gaoler that he always thought he would make it to the top, to which Du Plessis replied, 'I always thought you had a good chance too, Sir.'

Surprisingly, in November 1997, I was invited by the Minister of Finance, Herbert Murerwa, to join the board of the Reserve Bank of Zimbabwe (RBZ). I held that position until the end of March 2003. I found this position interesting and at times stimulating, but also extremely frustrating. As the nation's bankers, I always felt we were guardians for the country's finances. On the upside, following independence in 1980, Zimbabwe had made steady, if not spectacular, progress as a nation. Many of its social services such as health and education had expanded, bringing enhanced benefits to the people. Tourism had shown enormous growth, which was extremely visible in new and modern hotels, the establishment of luxury safari camps and through the construction of many small but efficient holiday resorts within the country's varied beauty spots, which attracted many regional and overseas visitors. The manufacturing sector also showed significant growth, particularly as more local raw materials were being utilised for the production of high-quality products. Of particular note in this area was the availability and increased choice of top-class food and beverages. The textile industries also grew rapidly, which in turn led to the formation of many small companies producing products which were uniquely Zimbabwean, and which soon became much sought-after items on the export markets. The manufacture of silver and gold for the jewellery and decorative market also quickly became established, and even today high-valued items are still popular throughout the world.

But despite this, the country was slowly and surely slipping further and deeper into debt. The basic reason was the ever-increasing demands the government was making for money to meet its expenditure programmes. Taxation in all its forms was failing to meet its expectations. Likewise, earnings, mainly through exports, were proving insufficient, which led to the government increasingly relying on borrowings.

They needed the money to fund an ever-expanding civil service which was far too big for the economy and the size of population; indeed, it had become a safe haven for many who might not have been able to hold down a job in a more demanding environment. This had been a prime concern of mine for a long while. The whole decision-making process within the country began to slow down, as those who should have been responsible for keeping the wheels of government turning, were incapable of doing so, either through idleness or incompetence. I realise it is easy to criticise, and even easier to generalise, but I still hold to the view that if numbers in the public sector had been strictly controlled and salaries made more attractive, it would have led to greater efficiencies and a more professional corps of civil servants who would have had to live up to certain standards. I do recall a half-hearted attempt was made in the early 1980s, when the Finance Minister, Bernard Chidzero, raised the alarm about the burgeoning size of the civil service, and persuaded cabinet to instruct all ministries to reduce the number of people they employed. We were given two weeks to present our proposals but unfortunately they all came to naught, because most ministries failed to respond to the request and, when they did, their only suggestion was a reduction of the lowest paid workers, such as cleaners, etc. who were certainly not the cause of escalating costs. If implemented, such changes would have resulted in negligible savings, and thus the fundamental problem of having too many paper shufflers was not addressed. Likewise, the growth in the size of Parliament itself was both unnecessary and hugely expensive. For a country with the population of plus /minus twelve million people and a relatively small economy, we could have been governed by approximately 80 parliamentarians, from which number no more than fifteen would be needed at ministerial level. This would have led to large savings not only in salaries, but also in special allowances, such as housing, secretarial services, chauffeur-driven vehicles and many other benefits allocated to those in positions of authority.

Another area which was beginning to weaken the service and credibility of government was the increase of corruption within the ranks. I know this is an unsavoury topic, but once it becomes an established practice, it is very difficult to eradicate and again weakens government's cause and profile. Also, in August 1998, the government had entered into a costly military operation in the Democratic Republic of the Congo (DRC), the justification for which was never fully explained. Of course, rumours of vast sums of money being secured by service personnel and mining entrepreneurs and salted away in various tax havens circulated at the time, but as is usually the case in such a scenario, no one was charged hence no one was prosecuted and nothing was ever proved.

Closer to home, minor incidents of misappropriation of funds and goods, allied to reports of corruption within government services, had begun to manifest themselves. These problems were constantly discussed within the RBZ boardroom, and the solutions were generally agreed. They amounted to three basic measures. First, to drastically reduce the size of the public service, including the number of ministers, deputy ministers, permanent secretaries, etc. But the many attempts to downsize over the years, after Chidzero's first look at the problem, had the same results. They always focused on a head count, which meant that employees at the lower end of the wage scale were made redundant, but as they were not the high earners, the overall effect on cost reduction was at best minimal. It is always a mistake to try and reform a system from the bottom up, when the highly rewarded culprits occupy the most senior positions. The second area in which to make enormous savings was to reduce the size of the armed forces. It was difficult to see the necessity of maintaining and equipping a regular and reserve defence force of approximately 50,000 personnel which we had at that time. Again, half-hearted attempts were made, by reducing the number of other ranks, but this was always offset by promotional increases among senior officers, thus continuing to escalate the defence budgets, with no measurable savings at all.

The third area in which the overall economy could have been improved – one which I strongly supported – was the privatisation of the loss-making parastatals. Much of Zimbabwe's business was run by state-owned and operated companies, and to be fair to the country, they were inherited at the time of independence in 1980. However, times change, and trading patterns alter, and to survive, one has to adapt to the new order of operations. This was being resisted by the government, mainly on the premise that with privatisation, they would lose control of these enterprises, and would in effect hand them over to the private sector. This was, of course, correct, for within the private sector, both nationally and internationally, there normally exists the ability to raise the capital to purchase and fund such operations, and also to attract the right skills and level of management required. In addition, large publicly owned companies are ultimately responsible to their shareholders, who are usually more discerning on correct procedures being adhered to, and strong performance levels being attained, thus ensuring those investments are properly protected, and serve the purpose for which they were intended. From 1995 onwards, huge losses were being experienced in the state-run enterprises, particularly Air Zimbabwe, the National Railways of Zimbabwe, and Affretair which eventually was liquidated in 2000 with debts to the tune of $500 million. In all three of these companies, there were potential buyers and investors, of which I was aware from my time spent as Minister of Transport. If the correct policies had been pursued, the government could have realised large injections of capital by breaking up and selling off these assets. This would have given the country the opportunity to develop new, modern and efficient transport systems, at minimum cost to the exchequer, but unfortunately the mindset of some ministers was such that they viewed the sale and disposal of government assets as losing both management and financial control and passing this across to the private sector, or in some instances external investors, who they feared might have different agendas and aspirations.

I never felt comfortable with the manner in which the government ran its own road transport facilities. It was housed in a department within the Ministry of Transport, the Central Mechanical and Engineering Department (CMED) which operated from depots in each of the nine provinces. It may have worked efficiently in the past, which I doubt, but certainly by the time I arrived it was a non-functioning organisation. Due to severe financial constraints and a large degree of incompetence, they were rapidly becoming junk yards for broken-down machinery and parking bays for crashed vehicles. Much of the heavy equipment used in the construction sector was parked, as it was broken beyond repair, or alternatively, it was too costly to repair. My solution to the problem was to sell it off as scrap and salvageable spares, and in future hire all equipment required from the private sector, and let them carry the costs of maintenance and replacement. Again, I bumped up against the arguments of selling off assets, and the result of the rejection of this approach led to all programmes getting further behind schedule and in many instances being abandoned altogether.

The other area which caused concern was the allocation and use of ministerial motorcars. On obtaining power in 1980, the new government lost no time in equipping itself with a fleet of new Mercedes-Benzes. This was quickly followed by a second fleet of four-wheel-drive vehicles on the basis that parliamentarians lived in rural areas and ministerial duties often took them to remote parts of the country. I thought that both these arguments were very unconvincing. When I took over the portfolio in 1990, the problem had really escalated, for two reasons. First, the number of ministers plus deputy ministers had significantly increased from thirty-six to forty-seven; and, second, many of the originally allocated vehicles had been badly misused, and although they were relatively new models, were redundant wrecks in the CMED repair yards. I put forward a number of proposals to try and rectify the situation such as limiting the number of vehicles allocated to each ministry; insisting on no replacements until the vehicles had been used for five years; acquiring less expensive but still well-performing vehicles; and finally scrapping the allocation scheme altogether and replacing it with one of vehicle hire. This would mean renting cars from private sector companies who would supply both vehicles and drivers; they, in return, would maintain and service the said vehicles. The contract for such a scheme could run for say five years and then go out to tender again. Needless to say, none of these suggestions found favour in the corridors of power. Instead, parliamentarians felt that I was trying to restrict their ability to move freely and easily around the country and to deny them the pleasure of a privilege that was regarded by them as a right. But had such measures been implemented, I am sure massive savings could have been made in this area.

Another huge drain on the financial resources was the iron and steel giant, the Zimbabwe Iron and Steel Company (ZISCO). This plant required significant capital injections to completely modernise its production methods in order to meet the requirements of the steel users. A large market for steel exports, especially in Japan, India and China, could not be exploited because of the company's inability to raise sufficient money to recapitalise its ageing and antiquated plant. Many countries showed keen interest in buying the company, but again the government were reluctant to lose control over what once had been a profitable enterprise.

In the agricultural sector, having successfully privatised the Dairy Marketing Board and the Cotton Marketing Board, it would have appeared logical to have followed those successes and sold off the Cold Storage Commission, a state-owned beef and cattle company which enjoyed a virtual monopoly on beef exports. This company, in addition to slaughtering cattle and processing the various cuts and products, also owned extensive cattle ranches, ran large feedlots where animals were fattened on high protein rations, and managed cattle sales within the communal areas, where they also acted as residual buyers. It would therefore be true to say that the highly sophisticated, well monitored beef industry in the country revolved largely around this company. But sadly, it was losing vast sums of money, and like all other parastatals, was operating within government-imposed price controls, and relying on government-funded subsidies in order to survive. Again, by divesting and selling off the component parts, it could have regained its former profitability, and thus avoided the government having to support it with large injections of cash every year.

I always viewed slightly differently the remaining parastatal under the Ministry of Agriculture, the Grain Marketing Board (GMB). This was the company responsible for purchasing grains from the farmers, storing the product, supplying the domestic market, and after ascertaining that sufficient stocks were being held until the next harvest, selling the surplus on either the regional or the international market. As grain – particularly maize – forms the staple diet of the local population, it is plain common sense that a sufficient stock at an affordable price be available at all times. If that means subsidisation then so be it, but the subsidies should be at the consumer-end of the scale, and not deducted from a realistic price paid to the farmer.

During my years in public office, I often heard the expression, a 'cheap food policy'. This view was usually expressed by those attending conferences dealing with world poverty and related matters. My thoughts on the subject were always that they were approaching the problem from the wrong end. A 'cheap food' policy inevitably led to a 'no food' result. Simply stated, if you cannot afford to pay the farmer, he cannot afford to grow food. Having said that, I have always had the greatest sympathy for the poor and undernourished peoples of the world, and I feel not enough attention has been given to long-term solutions to their desperate needs. In the short term, yes, it has to be food aid; but, unfortunately, this can be poorly managed and in some instances the food is misappropriated. Therefore, stricter control and monitoring of those programmes is urgently required. However, in the longer term, greater emphasis should be placed on assisting existing poor farmers to increase their own production. These people are already *in situ*, and with the right assistance and encouragement, could make a major contribution in reducing the world food deficits, which as the population continues to grow, are sadly increasing. To place my thoughts in proper context, what the world needs is not food aid but aid to grow food.

Having stated my views on the GMB, I nevertheless felt there was some scope in reducing government financial support by commercialising the operations of the grain silos and depots for example. These financial burdens and difficulties were often discussed around the boardroom table of the Reserve Bank of Zimbabwe and the board members made repeated requests to the Bank Governor, Dr Leonard Tsumba, to set up a joint meeting between members of the board and the government, to be represented by the Minister of Finance and his senior treasury officials. Regrettably, no such meeting ever took place, for the very good reason that the minister was reluctant to participate in such discussions. I tried on numerous occasions to persuade him to meet with us, and despite his assurances that he would do so, he never did. I even tried to convince Mugabe that such a discussion would be beneficial in trying to map out a programme to halt the country's deteriorating financial situation. He also agreed with such an approach, but countered by pointing out that we should deal directly with the Minister of Finance. The latter, Herbert Murerwa, was one of the nicest of all the cabinet ministers, and always polite and well spoken. However, I always felt that he would never make a mistake, because he would never make a decision. His overall philosophy seemed to be that if you ignore a problem for long enough, it will eventually disappear (maybe that is why he managed to last for so long). I also felt there was reluctance on the part of the Bank Governor to press for a joint meeting, in case it became confrontational. Leonard Tsumba, like Herbert Murerwa, was also a decent man, but he strongly believed there was life after his fixed term of office; hence he was very careful not to upset anyone whilst he was the governor, in case it jeopardised his chances of landing a lucrative position once he had retired from his governorship. To add to the general malaise affecting the whole economy was the fact that despite his self-belief, President Mugabe did not possess a strong knowledge of economic and financial affairs; because of the firm grip he had on the political life of the country, few, if any, dare challenge his views when expressed. This fear was instrumental in allowing the fiasco of the land takeovers to develop in the early 2000s.

In 2001, I was approached by Timothy Stamps, the Minister of Health and Child Welfare, with an invitation to accept the position as the inaugural chairman of a company which was to be formed and would assume total responsibility for the purchase and distribution of government medical drugs. At the time, the invitation had little appeal to me for a number of reasons. First, despite having served alongside him for a number of years, I always regarded Stamps as a slight oddball. He took great pride in describing himself as being a communist (which I do not believe he was). In cabinet discussions, he delighted in making inane and stupid contributions

providing co-operation and support, would ensure growth in both services for the benefit of all citizens.

For a long time, crime had been a worrying problem and was escalating, particularly, but not exclusively, in Harare. Burglaries, bag-snatching and car-jacking became everyday occurrences in which the perpetrators were assisted by the inability of the police to react to the incidents. Sometimes this was the result of a lack of roadworthy vehicles, and sometimes the failure of the telephone system, but whatever the reason, it often resulted in the victim having to fetch the police to investigate the crime, by which time the scent had often gone cold. To counter this dilemma, many individuals and companies began to employ private security firms to guard their premises, which I suppose could have been favourably argued as creating more employment, but in reality, one finished up paying twice – once for itemised protection and once through taxes – for a hamstrung police force. Such setbacks, although irritating, were in themselves not disastrous, and the majority of the population learnt to roll with the blows and continue with their daily lives.

What was of major concern, and quickly led to a dramatic degeneration of the country, was the land grab which began in 2000. The situation rapidly deteriorated into brutality and chaos, resulting in much bloodshed, vandalism and a swift decline in all forms of farm production, forcing the country to become a net importer of food, and the national coffers to quickly become depleted, as inflows from agricultural exports were hugely reduced. The question often asked is how did this tragic situation come about, and why was it allowed to continue, apparently unchecked? Many opinions have been advanced, some suggesting that it was always Mugabe's intention to take over all the land, and he always had held the view that land rightfully belonged to the original people of Zimbabwe and had been stolen from them after the arrival of the white man in the country in the late-nineteenth century. Others argue that owing to Mugabe's advancing years, he was losing control of the country, which was increasingly being taken over by the military leaders. There was some validity in this school of thought, as most of them – it not all of them – owed their positions to the patronage they had enjoyed from Mugabe since independence, which was further strengthened by the formation of the Government of National Unity and the incursion into the DRC. Therefore, if he were no longer in office, their positions could be terminated by an incoming president, thus losing them the considerable financial incomes they had been able to generate, plus the political power they were able to exercise. It, therefore, appeared to suit both sides to maintain the status quo, which has served their combined interests for so long.

There was another factor which I believe had a much greater bearing on the deteriorating situation, and that was the insidious and malicious role played by the Zimbabwe National Liberation War Veterans Association, normally referred to as the War Vets. This group was formed after independence by those who had fought in the liberation struggle, in order to have a collective voice with which to promote their cause, or to air their grievances. In that respect it was similar to other ex-servicemen's organisations around the world. For years, they were fairly dormant, and to many people, unknown. This situation rapidly changed after their leader, Chenjerai 'Hitler' Hunzvi, had a meeting with Mugabe in 1997 which effectively enhanced their organisation, and brought them great publicity. To this meeting, Hunzvi took two other members of his organisation, but Mugabe was on his own as the War Vets wanted to talk to him alone. Having stated their case and stressed that they were the ones who had done the fighting which, they argued, eventually led to the Lancaster House conference and finally the independent state of Zimbabwe, they had received little recognition or reward for their efforts. The meeting finally ended with Mugabe promising to pay each registered member of their association $50,000, plus a pension of $2,000 a month for life, with the Zimbabwe dollar trading at eleven to one US dollar. Needless to say, no provision for such payments had ever been made, and the Ministry of Finance received instructions to find the money. The war veterans went away well satisfied with the success of their meeting. The recognition given to the War Vets led to many disaffected people claiming membership, ignoring the fact that the majority of them were too young to have participated in the armed struggle. In reality, the organisation became a haven for those who were harbouring grievances against society, availing them of an opportunity to vent their fury without fear of arrest or prosecution.

Of course, the $50,000 bonus was quickly spent – or in many cases misspent – and the $2,000 was soon considered insufficient, so after approximately two years the War Vets requested another meeting, pointing out what they thought was an inadequate payment. This meeting led to a doubling of the pension to $4,000, but they were told there could not be another *ad hoc* bonus. Again, they appeared to be reasonably satisfied with this position. However, their contentment did not remain for long, because yet again they requested a meeting with Mugabe, and this time they stated very strongly that it was because of their efforts he was President of the country, and that they had fought to gain the land and not been given any of it. Now the problem facing Mugabe was similar to anyone who does a deal with blackmailers; you pay once and they will return and ask for more and continue to pressurise you until there is nothing more to give. On this occasion, I think that Mugabe, in desperation, more or less told them to take it, and from then on it was downhill all the way. The government tried to take back control of the problem by passing legislation which in essence said all land belonged to the state. But this only worsened the situation as many other worthies, such as judges, generals and politicians now started invading and occupying land to claim as much as they could before it was all taken.

The farm invasions which followed were on land owned by white farmers, and in some instances, black farmers who were considered to be sell-outs; in other words, soft targets. The mayhem and destruction caused by marauding gangs of thugs, in many instances encouraged by either local warlords or local officials who were anxious to acquire land for their own benefit, was outrageous and has been well documented. One of the saddest episodes of this whole sordid exercise was the reluctance of the police to protect those under attack and regrettably, in some instances, to actually encourage the attackers. The other cause for great concern was the inability of the many courts to uphold the law, which led to further escalations of breaches of law and order. Unfortunately, in most cases, the new occupiers of the farms showed little inclination or desire to produce on their illegally acquired property. This may have been because of a lack of farming knowledge, or as I suspect, a complete disinterest, having completed their objective of depriving the previous owners of their property and selling whatever assets they had managed to purloin.

From the year 2000, June and I began to consider our future. Our eldest daughter, Kathryn, and her husband Tim, who had had his job indigenised, decided to leave the country and relocate to Australia. Along with many others in a similar situation, they felt the time was right to move on, whilst they were still just young enough to begin a new life in another country and finish their two teenage children's education in Australia, thus giving them the opportunity to qualify and seek employment in a wider market. Our son Howard was also experiencing constant invasions by marauding gangs, each claiming they had been sent to occupy his farm on behalf of one influential protagonist or another; in many cases they were highly placed representatives of the ruling ZANU-PF party. All this was extremely unsettling to him and his wife, Fenella, and their two young children. Occasionally it had its moments of unusual humour. In one instance, he was perched on the top of a high-sided grain lorry, watching his wheat as it was being augured in from the farm silos to be transported to the GMB depot. Suddenly there was much shouting and a group of youths, armed with sticks, fan belts and various cudgels, arrived and ordered him to stop loading, as they were taking over the farm. Within ten minutes a rival gang similarly armed also arrived on the scene and loudly proclaimed that they had been sent to occupy the farm and ordered the first arrivals to depart immediately. This led to the most enormous fracas, with both 'teams' entering the fray with great gusto. However, before the casualty rate became too high, a third party arrived in the form of a detachment of riot police who had been summoned by one of the participants on his mobile phone, and without asking any questions, also joined in the baton-wielding melée. In the meantime, my son was still perched about fifteen feet above the ground, having literally a bird's eye view of the proceedings. Suddenly the fighting faded and then ceased and heated discussions commenced. These quickly gave way to smiles and laughter and the police inspector called up to my son and invited him to come down. After reaching the ground, he was told that everyone was very sorry, but they had come to the wrong farm!

What was not so amusing was an incident which occurred later, which could have had a very different ending. One day, a neighbouring farmer and his wife, who had been repeatedly harassed, had their homestead surrounded by a large hostile crowd, who were claiming ownership and demanding that the current owners vacate the property forthwith. They used their farm security radio to call for assistance. Howard, along with a number of others, all went to see what they could do. They drove through the gates of the security fence and parked their vehicles in the driveway, as darkness fell. The intruders promptly locked the gates and took them all hostage. Many of the invaders were armed with rifles and some had been drinking heavily, and consequently the ensuing stand-off became increasingly belligerent. I was alerted to their position about two hours after the incident had happened and was able to contact one of the hostage farmers, who gave me a whispered overview as to what was happening. He also said the battery in his mobile phone was low, so he could not stay on air. I told him to switch off and I would contact him every second hour, to get an update on the situation, and in the meantime, I would see what I could do on the outside. In the end I was able to do very little. I tried to get through to the Minister of Home Affairs, only to be told he was out the country. I tried to speak to the Commissioner of Police but was told that he was unavailable. I tried the home of the Provincial Governor, who, although sympathetic, said it was not his problem. In all hostage-taking situations, you have to be careful you do not inflame the captors, for as time goes on, they also start to become apprehensive and more likely to resort to aggressive action. I spent a great deal of time with the president and staff of the Commercial Farmer's Union who were trying to deal with the local leader, Joseph Chinotimba, vice-chairman of the Zimbabwe National War Veterans Association. He told them he would be visiting the farm the following morning. So, we decided we would also go and see if we could hold a discussion with him on the access road before he reached the homestead. When we arrived the following morning, we were informed that a senior police officer had been called to the scene and we were advised to stay well back. After a short while, we were told that he had negotiated their release and they were coming out in their own vehicles. Shortly after this, they arrived in a convoy of farm trucks, no worse for their ordeal, except being hungry and cold. As we all drove away from the farm, we met Chinotimba and his delegation coming at high speed from the opposite direction. Neither group stopped but I later learnt that Chinotimba was beside himself with rage, as he felt that owing to the relatively large number of farmers who had been held on the farm, he would have had strong bargaining counters with which to pursue his policy of forced takeovers of white-held farms.

Our second daughter, Diana, had married Mike Skea, a young farmer, who with his father and two brothers, ran a large and successful enterprise very close to where June and I farmed in the Norton area. Their main crop was tobacco, but they also produced substantial tons of maize, and ran a large beef cattle operation. They began to get 'visitors' calling to claim the farm as their own; some even established squatter camps on the perimeter of the property, in order to validate their claim ahead of competing rivals. Eventually, in 2002, as happened to so many other farmers, an eviction order was issued, giving them a short period of time in which to vacate their property. Fortunately, as we lived only a few miles away, they moved onto our farm with us. Sadly, as in so many similar incidents, vandalism was the first action the new owners took, delighting in destroying what existed in preference to using what they had obtained. Howard and his family were, by this time, already off his farm and living in Harare, so in effect both families had lost their farms and now had to consider their futures. After much agonising and many weeks of discussion, they finally decided to make applications to emigrate to Australia and make a new start for themselves and their children. This was a large blow for June and myself, as we now faced the bleak prospect of having no children left in Zimbabwe, and we had now to make serious assessments as to what we wanted to do and where we wanted to live.

At this stage, apart from a couple of low-key visits from individuals purporting to be war veterans, we had not been threatened in any form. One day I did receive a telephone call from June to say a delegation of war vets were at the entrance to the farm waiting for my return. When I arrived shortly afterwards I was met by four individuals. On asking them if I could help them, they responded by saying they had come to view their farm. I asked them what they intended to grow and they said maize. I then asked them further questions, such as what varieties, what level of fertilisation, plant population per acre and so forth. Each question resulted in them having a discussion and then asking me for my opinion. Eventually they said they thought my farm sounded too difficult to manage and they would go and seek another. On leaving, they thanked me for all my information and asked if and when they found a suitable farm, could they return and glean further advice. To this I readily agreed and, as expected, I never saw them again. We only had this one mild attempt of a farm takeover, although we were constantly being robbed of valuables and goods. Most of the thefts were of an outside nature, items such as electric motors, borehole pumps, paddock fencing, power lines etc., but we did also have three burglaries in the house, where items of great sentimental value were stolen. These incidents, along with the impending emigration of our children, decided us that the time had come to pack up and leave. The big question we now faced was, where would we go to retire? Despite much persuasion for us to go and join the three families already in Australia, we did not fancy the idea at our stage in life of trying to establish ourselves in a country with which we had no connection, although we always had great admiration and respect for the Australian people. Cape Town in South Africa was also another possibility, but we decided against that choice on the basis that with three children living in Australia and one in England, it would not be the right location. In the end, we finally decided to try and sell the farm at the best price we could get in a very unfavourable sellers' market and move to England.

Despite the fact that many people and families were leaving Zimbabwe at that time, I presumed my departure was likely to attract a certain amount of criticism and be viewed as deserting my post and leaving others to face the consequences of an uncertain future. However, I felt that after a very long time spent in public life, and that I was now in my seventies, I was entitled to choose where I wished to end my days. But, to the contrary, with one notable exception, I never heard of any public condemnation. In fact, I was heartened by the many wishes of good luck and messages of appreciation we received from a large cross-section of the community, many of whom were complete strangers to us.

At the end of 2002, our family gathered for Christmas and New Year in Cape Town, for a final African gathering, before we all began our departures to start a new life. For June and me it was traumatic to bid goodbye to Diana and Howard and their respective families, who left in early January to return to Zimbabwe and then fly out to Australia. We had already suffered this experience with Kathryn and Tim when they left in 2000. We did glean some comfort from the fact they were all travelling together, and at the other end, Kathryn and Tim would be there to welcome them, and from their earlier experience, help them settle into a new country. On our return to Zimbabwe, I began my search for a buyer for my farm, and as I indicated earlier, this was not an easy exercise. After a few bad starts and false dawns, I eventually came to an agreement with a man named Anthony Mandiwanza, who was a very prominent businessman in Harare, his main position being CEO of the Dairy Marketing Board. Although the negotiations between us were always amicable, I know that within a stable economic situation, I could have achieved a far higher price. I just hope that today he is still enjoying the farm that June and I developed and loved.

My pending departure from the country I kept a secret and continued serving the boards to which I had been appointed. The reason for my reluctance to make my intentions public was twofold. I did not wish to have any farewell functions dedicated in my honour, and also, I regarded our move as a very private affair, which we did not wish to share in a larger arena. Inevitably, I had to inform the companies and organisations to which I was associated or attached, that I was leaving. I did this three days before my departure, and judging by their reactions, this news came as a great surprise. The Governor of the Reserve Bank, Leonard Tsumba, insisted on giving a board dinner for June and me, which was extremely kind of him, and in addition to making many warm and complimentary remarks, also presented us with farewell gifts.

The one remaining person I wanted to inform personally was President Mugabe. After the many years of knowing him and working with him, I felt it was only good manners and common courtesy to notify him of my movements. As usual, he received me in the most affable manner, and after a short while spent conversing on small subjects, he enquired as to why I wished to see him. When I told him of my intention to leave the country, he looked very surprised, and his first comment was I should not leave Zimbabwe. I enquired why this was so, and he replied that he did not want me to, and he felt comfortable knowing I was there. Flattering as that may have been, I told him my plans were made and I was going. He responded by suggesting that I went for a short while – he suggested no more than three years – and then return. At this point, I diverted the conversation by asking him where the country had all gone wrong. Again, he looked surprised, and said, 'Has it all gone wrong?'

I countered by saying I knew it had, and he knew it, but the question was, why this was so? He then conceded that the situation was not good, but claimed it was not his fault – a common excuse for many leaders – and said it was all because of Tony Blair, who had reneged on previous British guarantees, and had let Zimbabwe down. At this point, Mugabe became very vocal and expressed his utter contempt for Tony Blair and the entire Labour government, which he considered to be completely untrustworthy.

I had heard him express these sentiments on previous occasions, and they were views to which he was completely committed, and as an observer of the political scene in Zimbabwe, both pre- and post-independence, I think I can understand some of Mugabe's frustration. He felt the Labour party leader not only failed to understand him or his policies but did very little to try to understand. I remain convinced that if there had been a change in their parsimonious and hostile attitude to Mugabe, he in return would have acted differently; and even if their positions were not wholly reconciled, at least a more harmonious atmosphere would have been created.

Since the 1997 election in Britain, which brought in the Labour government, Mugabe increasingly began to associate white Zimbabweans with Blair and his Labour government. I am not at this point suggesting that the demise of Zimbabwe can be attributed to the latter, but I do feel if his government had had a more open approach and tried to understand the difficulties of creating a viable multicultural country, and had been prepared to listen rather than dictate, events may well have been different. It also reinforced my belief that the Conservatives in Britain were more understanding of the changing conditions in Zimbabwe, and as such, were able to be more proactive and supportive.

In the meantime, June and I had begun the distressing task of dismantling and disposing of many of our precious possessions which we had accumulated over nearly fifty years of marriage. Not only was this a difficult exercise in many regards, but it was also heartbreaking. Eventually, most of the work was completed: some items were sold, some were given to friends, many were donated to charities, and all that remained were the items which we wished to send to England. The freight-forwarding company duly sent their packers, and the following day the container arrived and we watched as all our packing boxes were carefully loaded and then driven safely away. Our last meal in our home was a dinner which we ate sitting on two old rickety canvas chairs, around an upturned wooden box, on which was spread an old towel for a table cloth, with a sputtering candle in a bottle. The ironic similarity of this meal to our early farming days in Rhodesia was not lost on us – life had indeed come a full circle.

We experienced a very emotional moment when we finally bid farewell to our staff, especially as one shook with uncontrollable sobs, and was completely incapable of speaking. As we drove away from the homestead and farm, it was with great difficulty that we kept our eyes focused firmly ahead and avoided looking back. When we arrived in Harare, we checked in to Meikles Hotel, where we were going to spend our last night before we left Zimbabwe. Again, it was history repeating itself, it was the same hotel – although rebuilt and modernised – in which I had spent my first night in the country fifty years earlier. June suffered one more enormous disappointment that evening, when we went to the cathedral cloisters, to bid goodbye to the inscribed stone under which her Mother's ashes had been laid, only to be informed that the entrance gates to the cloisters were locked on orders of Bishop Kunonga, the new self-appointed Bishop of Mashonaland, who was just beginning to exert his own political agenda. We had to leave just after five the following morning to go to Harare airport to catch our flight to South Africa. Much to our surprise, the hotel provided us with two motorcars instead of one to transport us, and we were told this was standard practice because of the high incidence of carjacking on the road leading to the airport. On leaving the hotel, I had one pleasant and very moving experience, because when I went to settle my account, I was told by a smiling desk attendant that our stay was a complimentary gift from the hotel in recognition of the service I had given to the country. It was made even more generous as they had provided us with the Presidential suite.

When we arrived at the airport, it was dark and gloomy, as they were experiencing a power cut. This in turn meant the computers on the check-in desks were not working, so we had to be checked in manually. I placed the luggage which was going into the hold on the scale and waited while the check-in clerk stared, calculated, and then recalculated, and finally looked at me and said, 'Mr Norman, your luggage weighs more than twice your combined allowance.' I showed great surprise, and gently suggested that his scales may not be properly calibrated. His face eventually broke into a broad smile and he said, 'Oh, what the hell', shook my hand and wished us a safe journey.

We flew out of Zimbabwe with very heavy hearts and many misgivings about all we were leaving behind and questioning our decision after experiencing the warmth and understanding of its ordinary, decent citizens, typified by the sobbing servant, the friendly hotel staff and the cheeriness of the airport employee. Having changed planes in Johannesburg, we arrived in Cape Town, where we were going to wait before we began the final leg of our journey to London. We had booked a passage on a container ship, the SA Winterberg, but were informed that they could not accurately tell us the time of departure, as we would be travelling on a working vessel and freight took priority, so when loading was complete, the ship sailed on the next tide.

On the fourth day we received a telephone call to say a car would be collecting us to take us to the docks. The ship was enormous (85,000 tons), we had a very comfortable cabin, and there were only eight other passengers. We were told we could go anywhere on the ship but it was made very clear that it was a working ship and the sailors would be attending to both the ship and the containers, and as such would have priority of movement. We took our meals with the officers and had the use of a small lounge off the dining saloon. The menus and food were excellent, our fellow passengers were interesting and the ship's company was pleasant and helpful. The biggest joy for June and I was the quiet and peace that the voyage provided; for the first twelve days we silently cruised (more like glided) on a calm sea, in beautiful warm temperatures, with practically nothing to do, which gave us ample time to pause, reflect and prepare ourselves for a completely different life without being interrupted by outside influences. We did a lot of talking, much reminiscing and gently unwound and adjusted our thoughts. June also took the opportunity to revise and complete the book on Zimbabwe gardens which she had spent many years writing, and finally had it published in 2010. This book not only told the story of the creation of some of the most beautiful gardens in the country – both private and public – but chronicled the events and people who through sheer hard work, great vision and a love of beauty were able to create such wonderful gardens, often using local materials such as rocks and indigenous trees and grasses. She was assisted in her endeavours by two great friends, Jilly Byatt, who originally conceived the idea of such a book and painted the illustrations for it, and Diana Fraser-MacKenzie, who took all the photographs. Between them, they produced a beautiful record of what was achieved, but now sadly many of those creations have been lost, either through neglect or wilful destruction and are gone forever.

After eighteen days at sea, in which time we had called at Las Palmas, Le Havre and Rotterdam, and learnt an enormous amount about the large and integrated industry of containerisation, we finally sailed up the Thames estuary, and docked at Tilbury. It was a fantastic experience, and one which fitted our needs at the time to perfection. We were met dockside by Deborah, Simon and their three children, who greeted us with a very loving reception, which was particularly pleasing for June who had never lived anywhere outside Zimbabwe, and also made me feel good after being away from England for so many years. After a few weeks, we settled into a house in West Sussex, and started to learn how to adapt to an English way of life, at the same time not too sure how long we would be living in Britain, because if there was a political change in Zimbabwe leading to a more stable society, we would seriously consider returning there.

6

Reflections

When I first arrived in the country in 1953, I was relatively young and very naive. As far as I was concerned, I was simply coming to join my brother in Africa in gainful employment. Living and working in remote rural areas, without access to either a radio or newspapers, I was isolated from the stirrings of black nationalism which began to manifest themselves in the townships and urban areas from the late 1940s. My interest was probably not awakened until my second job with Jack Quinton, who was not only a dynamic, voluble character, but was also a Member of Parliament, representing the largest rural constituency in Mashonaland and who later became a minister in Edgar Whitehead's government with the responsibility for native agriculture. It was due to him that I really became interested in what was taking place in the country, and also the region, because at this time Rhodesia had become a member of the Central African Federation.

The nationalist movements were beginning to generate momentum and attract local support with the formation of the

Southern Rhodesian African National Congress in 1957. Initially, this was in the form of civil disobedience, but moved on to vocal demonstrations, and eventually grew into violent urban disruptions. In 1955 the Salisbury City Youth League was formed and they organised an important bus strike to protest against fare rises in the capital. The following year the league merged with the Bulawayo branch of the African National Congress to form the Southern Rhodesian National Congress (SRNC). These protests were dealt with by the police, using batons, tear-gas and dogs. In the rural areas we were aware of what was taking place, but because it did not directly affect our daily lives, we tended to ignore the disturbances in the urban areas, and hoped the problems would either solve themselves or would miraculously disappear. This careless attitude dramatically changed when the first armed attacks on civilians began in the 1960s. In 1964 in Chipinge, an armed element of ZANU carried out the first terrorist act in the country in which a farmer was murdered. This was followed in April 1966 when seven insurgents crossed the Zambezi, committed an attack and double murder in Hartley, and were subsequently all killed in an engagement with the police in Sinoia.

Unfortunately, the collision course was set by then, and fourteen years of armed conflict began and steadily escalated until finally coming to an end with the signing of the Lancaster House agreement. I have tried to relate the events that followed that agreement, as I observed them, and in some cases, participated in them.

Since retiring from public life, I have often wondered if my participation in politics made any significant difference to the development of Zimbabwe following its independence in 1980. Obviously, I am not the right person to pass judgement on my successes or failures. However, I can try and analyse what may have been the outcome of certain scenarios owing to my presence and input at the time decisions were made and policies adopted. From a distance, it is probably easier to try and assess if events might have turned out differently, and whether timely decisions were made by both me and those who shaped the country's future on the larger canvas.

As far as my own contributions were concerned, I always felt I was a middle-of-the-road operator, one who was always prepared to listen to both supporting and opposing views. Having made a judgement on an issue, I was prepared to promote or defend my position. I know that can be interpreted as being inflexible, but having listened to arguments and given due consideration to all the facts, I never saw the need to vacillate further, and I usually found others would respect my position, even if they did not agree with me – and I did not win all my arguments by any means.

On being offered a cabinet post in the first Mugabe government, my initial reaction was to reject the offer for two reasons. First, I did not want to become a politician; and, second, I did not feel I was competent to take charge of one of the most important portfolios in the government. But the Governor, Sir Christopher Soames and his immediate staff, assured me of their full support and tried to convince me that I would be able to manage. I also received assurances from David Smith, who actually went further when he told me that if I did not accept the offer, then he would also refuse to join the new government. Had this happened, I understand, with hindsight, that it would likely have been catastrophic for the country, because what I subsequently discovered of Mugabe's character was that he always reacted wildly, and sometimes violently, at being rebuffed or ignored. And if Smith and I had refused to serve, I believe it would have jeopardised any thought of reconciliation, and significant positions such as Chief Justice, Commander of the Army, Commissioner of Police, the Head of the CIO, and many other posts would not have been offered to the then white incumbents. This, in turn, would have led to a massive loss of confidence within the white community and possibly some serious racial disturbances.

Whereas the situation remained calm, if with certain trepidation on all sides, and this allowed the new regime the time and space to quietly and quickly begin to run the country.

I soon felt comfortable in my position as the Minister of Agriculture for a number of reasons: first among them was the sound advice and strong support I received from all members of staff in that very large technical and scientific ministry. I was also greatly encouraged by the positive support I received from all sections of the farming community whether they were commercial farmers, the African Farmers' Union or the Master Farmer's Association. All gave me the impression that despite predictable difficulties, they appreciated what was being done on their behalf. In addition, the farm supply industries such as the fertiliser and chemical companies, seed houses, mechanical franchise holders, banks and finance houses, also gave me great encouragement and support. The government statutory boards that held a dominant position in fixing farm producer prices were also helpful and co-operative. In order to achieve a broader understanding of the value of a strong, vibrant agricultural sector, I deliberately tried to convince my fellow ministers of its importance, by adopting a friendly and co-operative approach, and avoiding any interference in their portfolios in the belief that they would reciprocate with regard to mine, which by and large proved successful. Another advantage of the closer relationships established with my political colleagues was the development of a greater trust and co-operation on an unofficial basis and I managed to get a number of people released from detention. This included farmers who had hidden their weapons and failed to disclose them, of which there were many. Most of them were identified by dissatisfied members of their workforce or by other workers who felt that by informing the authorities they were playing a patriotic role. As many of those detained are still living, I feel it would be inappropriate to mention names. One disconcerting incident included an informer who reported that his employer had disposed of a cache of arms and ammunition in his farm dam. The security forces duly arrived with large pumps and drained his dam dry, only to discover they were on the wrong farm, which resulted in one relieved farmer and one extremely annoyed one. On numerous occasions, I was also able to hasten the bureaucratic system and speed the approval of visas, permits, licences etc. if I felt the delay was unnecessarily impeding progress. It often entailed the assistance of a minister, who would then instruct the responsible officials of the necessity and urgency of granting approval. Having developed this trust, in return, I was able to arrange meetings and introduce many of my ministerial colleagues to some of the influential people I had met through my association with SADC, the Beira Corridor Group, the Food and Agricultural Organization and other similar organisations, for which they were always grateful. I always saw myself as a team player and if I could legally assist the government in a situation, I was happy to help.

In addition, I always attempted to take President Mugabe and other ministers to visit particular programmes, be they in agriculture, transport or energy and whether they were technical, scientific or developmental. I did so because I believed this would achieve a better appreciation of the many complex activities taking place within the relevant ministry. My colleagues always seemed to enjoy these visits, and they were much appreciated by the staff and workers on the projects, who enjoyed the opportunity to interact with senior politicians. I was also occasionally asked to assist with difficulties which arose in the cultural and sporting world when all that was really needed was a certain amount of calmness and common sense for sanity to prevail. Following independence in 1980, the new government was keen to develop Harare in a way which represented its own ideas, values and culture, which was understandable. One example was the erection of Heroes Acre, in which those who had contributed to the independence struggle could be laid to rest in a respectable site and be suitably remembered for their ideals and their achievements. Another development was the construction of a large new stadium which could be used as a sports venue but could also be a focal point for political rallies and national celebrations. Both these developments were situated on unused municipal land on the outskirts of Harare, adjacent to the Bulawayo road. In consequence, there was little objection or concern raised to their construction. However, there were other areas closer to State House and the Prime Minister's residence which were considered desirable sites on which to build government housing and offices in order to concentrate and contain the business of governing in one specific area. Again, it was an understandable concept. The major difficulty, however, was that the places identified were already being used for different purposes. The first one sought was the Royal Harare Golf Club, which was an immaculate eighteen-hole championship course established in 1898. Between 1980 and 1985 two attempts were made by the Ministry of Local Government to obtain this land, and on each occasion I was prevailed upon by the golf committee to intercede on its behalf. Consequently, I made representation to Mugabe, pointing out the advantages of having such an outstanding sporting facility which had grown and been developed over the past eighty years, and also the value of having such a large, green open space in the centre of the city. On each occasion, he listened to my case, and then directed that another site be found. This decision then led me to defend a section of my own ministry, namely the National Botanic Garden, which was established in 1949 and the first director, Dr Thomas Müller, appointed in 1962. Owing to his enthusiasm and botanic knowledge, a magnificent garden had been created, reflecting all the ecological regions of Zimbabwe through all the major species of indigenous trees and shrubs in the country. In addition, there was a research and educational centre, but suddenly all this was under the threat of development. Again, I was called upon, and following my discussions with Dr Müller, we felt the best way to illustrate this botanical resource would be to demonstrate its value to the entire cabinet, and so I arranged for them all to have a guided walking tour of the garden led by the director himself. It turned out to be a real success with the latter revelling in having such a high-powered group to whom he could explain his passion and programmes, show off his results and express his aspirations. It was all conducted in a friendly, good-humoured manner and fortunately everyone agreed that the Botanic Garden was too valuable an asset to discard. So apart from placing one anti-aircraft gun on a small kopje, the garden, the director and his staff were left alone to continue.

One other area that was never really under threat but was never fully understood was the Borrowdale Race Course. So, I thought it would be prudent to acquaint the government with the complexities of horse-racing, and at my instigation, the chairman of the Mashonaland Turf Club issued an invitation to Mugabe, Nkomo and cabinet ministers to a day at the races. This provided the club with the opportunity to explain the intricate business of racing to government by introducing them to breeders, trainers, owners, jockeys, veterinarians, farriers, etc. They also had the methods of betting explained, which some tried but with varying degrees of success. Following that visit, a few maintained a modicum of interest for a little while, though I suspect many of their staff caught the racing bug. It is interesting to note that when Pope John Paul II visited Harare in 1988 the only venue large enough for him to hold an open-air mass was the Borrowdale Race Course.

One thing that did surprise me about Mugabe was his interest in sport, which I first became aware of just after the 1980 election. On the eve of the Easter weekend break, I was leaving his office and expressed the hope that he would have some time to relax over the forthcoming holiday. He responded by saying he would be going to Harare Sports Club to see the national cricket team play a visiting side. Somewhat astonished, I asked him if he knew much about cricket. Laughing, he replied, 'I was educated at Fort Hare, you know.'

I said that did not quite answer my question but I took his point. For many years he was a regular visitor to the international cricket matches where he would discuss with the cricket administrators the varying abilities of the individual players and tactics such as field settings and declaration timings.

Even more surprising to me was the interest he took in rugby. I discovered this quite by chance when I was asked if I could help the Zimbabwe Rugby Football Union who were hosting the Surrey county team from England. A week before the team was due to leave the UK, they were told that the tour had been cancelled, because one of their players had at some time played a game in South Africa. This, our Minister of Sport deemed infringed the Gleneagles Agreement, which boycotted sports teams that had played in the Republic. Having agreed to see if I could assist, I arranged to see Mugabe early on the Monday morning before the first match on Saturday at the police grounds. I explained the position to him and tried to present as positive a case as I could, then I waited with a certain amount of apprehension for the outcome. Mugabe calmly began by asking if he had understood my request correctly. Was I seeking permission for fifteen to twenty fit young British men to come to Harare to drink a lot of beer and then run onto a playing field and physically compete with an equal number of local young men; and then, afterwards, join up with them to drink more beer, all in the name of fun? When I told him that he had more or less summed the situation up correctly, he said, 'Tell them to come, and tell them they will be very welcome in our country.'

I never saw him at a rugby match, but during the World Cup

in South Africa in 1995, we discussed the teams and the results on a regular basis, as he had one of his staff tape the matches for him to watch in the evenings.

Of course, it is pleasant to recall one's perceived successes, but life is also made up of disappointments, of which I have also had my share. It would be true to say that most of them occurred in the transport and energy sectors rather than the agricultural field. I believe this was because it was easier for vested interests to influence or block proposed schemes or projects. One of my greatest frustrations was the reversal of the contract for the new Harare airport building as soon as I had left the Ministry of Transport, when it was awarded to an inferior design presented by a company which failed to bid in the initial stages and only arrived on the scene when an Arab financier interfered and made lucrative offers to individual people, one of whom was closely related to Mugabe.

But my greatest sadness and deepest disappointment was in the land grab which led to a rapid decline in agricultural production and had serious consequences on the health of the economy. Could more have been done to have averted this catastrophe? As mentioned in Chapter 3, during my time in government I never held the portfolio for land, so in effect I did not have that responsibility. But on both occasions after I had left the Ministry of Agriculture, my successor was made the Minister of Lands and Agriculture. Up until my resignation at the end of April 1997, the question of land takeover without purchase or compensation had never been discussed at cabinet level. Of course, there had been rumours and speculation, but none seem to have been treated very seriously. It was only some six months after I had resigned that the whole land question became a major political issue. It was a key bone of contention during the referendum campaign in early 2000 in which the government sought support for constitutional changes that, among other proposals, would have ensured Mugabe remained president beyond the two-term limit already in place. The campaign became bitter and confrontational with the opposition MDC, led by Morgan Tsvangirai, leading a spirited attack on the government. The result was an emphatic 'no' vote which although initially accepted by the government, led to bitter recriminations, particularly against white farmers who were accused of encouraging their work force to support the opposition. It was during this period that the most violent of the farm invasions took place. And once the invasion momentum had started, the government took practically no measures to halt it, in the belief that it would result in popular grassroots support and sustain them in power. The consequences of these policies and actions have been well documented and analysed, so I will not comment further except to reiterate what a tragedy the whole land issue turned out to be, where with cooler heads and enlightened thinking, it could have all been so different.

I have frequently expressed my view that the country could still recover from its present demise and again become a prosperous and progressive nation with sensible land usage and sound agricultural programmes as the key mechanism for this revival. To return Zimbabwe to its former status as the major agricultural producer in the region will be a formidable task, but because of the magnificent natural resources which exist, I feel with sound, unemotional planning, much could be achieved. The measures to be taken would need to be bold and imaginative, and would take much courage and determination to implement. I would suggest the starting point would have to be to establish who is the legal title holder of the property. This should not be too difficult as the records could be checked through the deeds office. In addition, most of the information needed has already been painstakingly acquired by an organisation known as Valcom, which was established with the specific objective of identifying the rightful owners of the properties, and to establish the value of the fixed and moveable assets at the time they were taken over. Thus, the starting point for fair compensation for illegal acquisition already exists.

The next step would be the more difficult and contentious: establishing the value of the properties, and how the dispossessed would be fairly compensated. In this regard, much work has already been done too. A great deal of the credit for this detailed information must be given to John Laurie, who has worked tirelessly during the past few years, collecting and collating the information and data necessary with which to formulate a plan to ensure that this controversial problem can be quickly resolved. So, I would suggest with sufficient goodwill by all participants, a reasonable solution could be reached. This could lead to the next stage which would be the exciting one, of reconstructing the industry, regaining productivity, and fulfilling the traditional markets, nationally, regionally and internationally.

However, while none of this will be easy, I still maintain that it is possible. It will obviously take considerable amounts of capital and an extended period of time, but I think much could be achieved over a ten-year recovery period. Agriculture was, and could become once again, the pivotal industry in the country. But for any restoration to be fully effective, there has to be political will and resolve for it to happen. With the demise of the Mugabe regime, there will be many individuals and groups who are seriously considering and planning the future for themselves but also, we hope, for the nation as a whole.

Epilogue

In this book, I have endeavoured to share my memories and to record some of the events I have witnessed or experienced during a varied and generally enjoyable life spent in both the public and private sectors in Rhodesia and Zimbabwe.

It is inevitable that some will disagree with my views, and others will contest the validity of my memory. I willingly concede the right of disagreement, only noting that I also have the right to record events, accompanied by observations, as I perceived and understood them.

I lived a full and interesting life in Zimbabwe, and I have been given the opportunity to participate in the wonderful and varied textures of a vibrant country, populated by some of the warmest, nicest people you could ever wish to meet. In addition, I have had the opportunity to travel both in Africa and to other parts of the world. Contacts made and people met – from the most humble to the most influential of their day – will always stay with me. Even if not mentioned in this book, they will remain woven into the fabric of the life that I was privileged to share with my forever supportive wife, June, without whose encouragement and love none of this would have been possible.

Changes have finally come to Zimbabwe, most notably with the resignation of Robert Mugabe as President in November 2017 and the election of Emmerson Mnangagwa as leader of ZANU-PF and his subsequent appointment as president. Although it is too soon for an assessment of these changes, I believe, like most people, the country now has reason to hope. I say this for three reasons. First, a change of leader was always going to be well received by the majority, as Mugabe had long exceeded his tenure. There is, thus, a bedrock of goodwill and a desire to make things work again. Second, the changes were instigated with virtually no force, which delighted and surprised the country, and made the transition smoother than it might otherwise have been. And, third, Mnangagwa's initial rhetoric offered conciliation to those who may question his past, his future direction, and his desire to eliminate the pervasive corruption gripping the country. Notwithstanding his history, his advantages are that he is a strong, positive, articulate and well-educated man, who is also a good communicator with a warm sense of humour. He, and successive governments, have an enormous task ahead of them to unify the nation; to convince the outside world of their genuine intentions and to rebuild the broken economy. In conclusion, I wish Zimbabwe well and remain confident that the country will not only regain its political and economic stability, but will develop and exploit its abundant natural resources, whether they be mineral, agricultural or human, to the benefit of all its citizens, and the central African region as a whole.

9 781779 223357